T0373138

THE I TATTI
RENAISSANCE LIBRARY

James Hankins, General Editor

ARIOSTO

LATIN POETRY

ITRL 84

LUDOVICO ARIOSTO
• • •
LATIN POETRY

EDITED AND TRANSLATED BY

DENNIS LOONEY

AND

D. MARK POSSANZA

THE I TATTI RENAISSANCE LIBRARY
HARVARD UNIVERSITY PRESS
CAMBRIDGE, MASSACHUSETTS
LONDON, ENGLAND
2018

Series design by Dean Bornstein

Library of Congress Cataloging-in-Publication Data

Names: Ariosto, Lodovico, 1474–1533, author. | Looney, Dennis, editor,
translator. | Possanza, D. Mark, editor, translator.
Title: Latin poetry / Ludovico Ariosto ; edited and translated by Dennis
Looney and D. Mark Possanza.
Other titles: I Tatti Renaissance Library ; 84.
Description: Cambridge, Massachusetts : Harvard University Press, 2018. |
Series: I Tatti Renaissance Library ; 84 | Texts in Latin with English
translations on facing pages ; introduction and notes in English. |
Includes bibliographical references and index.
Identifiers: LCCN 2017018926 | ISBN 9780674977174 (alk. paper)
Subjects: LCSH: Latin poetry, Medieval and modern—Italy.
Classification: LCC PA8125.I6 A75 2018 | DDC 871/.04—dc23
LC record available at https://lccn.loc.gov/2017018926

Contents

ॐ?॰?

Introduction

꿇§ᛁ§꿇

The Life of Ludovico Ariosto

Born in Reggio Emilia on September 8, 1474, Ariosto grew up in Ferrara, where his father, Nicolò, was a captain in the service of the ruling Este family. His mother, Daria, was the daughter of a scholar and poet, Gabriele Malaguzzi. Ludovico was probably given grammar lessons in Italian and Latin by Luca Ripa, a humanist who attended the famous local school run by the descendants of Guarino Veronese. This elementary instruction prepared him well for the study of Latin literature and philosophy at the University of Ferrara. Gregorio da Spoleto, a private teacher who instructed Ariosto in the humanities during the 1490s, is the individual most responsible for transforming him into a Neo-Latin poet who would later become one of the great vernacular humanists of the Renaissance. Envisioning for him the career of a civil servant, his father forced him to study law, which he did with reluctance in the early 1490s. In 1495, Ariosto delivered the inaugural oration in verse for the academic year at the university, choosing as his theme the praise of learning (*De laudibus sophiae*).[1] His earliest surviving letter (January 9, 1498), written in Latin, documents his participation in a broader humanistic culture beyond the university. He requests from the Venetian printer and humanist Aldus Manutius books of Platonic and Neoplatonic philosophy: "There is significant interest among scholars to have the books of Marsilio Ficino and others who translated into Latin anything written by the Greeks about this school."[2] In these same years he was actively involved in the Ferrarese revival of classical studies, collaborating on important theatrical productions of Terence and Plautus.

Ariosto's studies were cut short by his father's death in 1500, which obliged him to assume the responsibility of head of his extended family. To earn a living he began to serve Cardinal Ippolito d'Este in various capacities, mainly diplomatic and administrative. He represented Ferrarese interests during the papacies of Julius II and Leo X, undertaking numerous missions to Rome in the first two decades of the 1500s. After a break with his patron Ippolito for refusing to follow him to Hungary in 1517, Ariosto was welcomed as a courtier by the cardinal's older brother, Alfonso, who had assumed the leadership of Ferrara at the death of Duke Ercole in 1505. Ariosto published *Orlando Furioso* in 1516, revising it in 1521, to bring it into line with the linguistic strictures of his friend and fellow humanist Pietro Bembo. Shortly thereafter Alfonso appointed him the local Estense official in the mountainous province of the Garfagnana, on the border between Tuscany and Romagna, from 1522 to 1525. Despite his dissatisfaction with the position, made difficult by the complicated political relations between Ferrara and Florence, Ariosto was an effective commissioner. When he returned from the Garfagnana, he supervised the ducal theater, enabling him to collaborate with artists such as Dosso Dossi, who designed sets for several of his plays. In 1528 he produced his comedy *La Lena* (The Procuress), perhaps his best theatrical work, for the festivities surrounding the wedding of Ercole II and Renée de France. Ariosto dedicated his final years to literary projects in the company of Alessandra Benucci, whom he wed in 1528, but secretly, so as not to lose his ecclesiastical benefices. In 1528 he accompanied Duke Alfonso in a ceremonial encounter with the Holy Roman Emperor Charles V as he passed through Ferrarese territory near Modena. In 1531, Alfonso d'Avalos, a high-ranking soldier in Charles's imperial army, granted the poet an annual pension of one hundred golden ducats. Both the emperor and Alfonso d'Avalos rewarded Ariosto for his talents more handsomely than his Este patrons had ever done. The definitive third edition of the

Furioso came out in 1532 with four new episodes, which increased the poem's length by 5,600 lines and expanded it from forty to forty-six cantos. At some point in his final years, the aging poet may have had inscribed over the door of his home the elegant Latin couplet still visible: "It's small, but just right for me, at no one's beck and call, not shabby, yet purchased with my own money, my house."[3] Ariosto died in Ferrara on July 6, 1533.

Ariosto the Humanist

Arguably the most important Italian poet of the Renaissance and perhaps the most important European writer before Shakespeare, Ariosto's fame deservedly rests on his narrative poem, *Orlando Furioso*. In it Charlemagne's war against the Saracens serves as a backdrop to explore typical Renaissance themes, such as love, madness, and fidelity, with an elaborate subplot that dramatizes how these themes affect the dynastic fortunes of Ariosto's patrons in the House of Este. The poem was published in over one hundred editions by 1600, so great was its popularity. The additional works that Ariosto composed have inevitably come to be viewed as minor in comparison to the magnitude and renown of his big poem. They include 214 letters, five plays, seven satires in verse, and dozens of lyric poems in Italian and Latin.

In an autobiographical satire composed in Italian around 1523, Ariosto recalls having written poems during his earlier years "in more than one language."[4] Between around 1494 and the middle of the first decade of the sixteenth century, Ariosto composed a significant body of poems in Latin, sixty-seven of which we can attribute to him with certainty, with an additional eight of a more dubious provenance (five uncertain and three apocryphal), totaling approximately one thousand lines of verse.[5] Ariosto's *carmina* include love lyrics, poems on politics and war, and poems to and about Ariosto's friends, relatives, patrons, and famous contemporaries. These poems have not been translated into English, they are not read in the original, and consequently what they might reveal of Ariosto's foundational encounter with humanism, of his formation as a poet before he began writing the *Furioso*, has been almost completely ignored in the substantial body of Anglo-American criticism devoted to Ariosto. Italian critics have paid more attention to them, but hardly enough.[6] In particular, critics have not appreciated the depth of Ariosto's learned engagement with classical models, a prejudice that may date back to Virginio Ariosto's comments on his father's scant interest in reading Latin: "He wasn't very studious, and he sought out few books to read. He liked Vergil, Tibullus for his diction. But he enthusiastically recommended Horace and Catullus. Not so much Propertius."[7] In fact, his Latin poetry reveals a poet in dialogue with Horace's *Odes*, Statius's *Silvae*, Martial's *Epigrams*, and Catullus's *libellus*, as well as Vergilian poetry, Ovidian elegiacs, and in more than one place, Plautine comedy. Whatever its shortcomings, Virginio's list gives us a glimpse into the poet's workshop, where Horace and Catullus take pride of place. From Horace, Ariosto learned many of the metrical patterns for his more ambitious poems, and he saw a literary model of how to project a certain detachment from patrons and the court.[8] From Catullus, Ariosto learned early on about metrical variation, and later in his life he perhaps saw in the *libellus* a literary model for constructing a book out of his own poems with their engaging variety of meters and subjects.

In a letter of October 15, 1519, Ariosto's comments point to the problematic status of the corpus of his Latin verse. Responding to a request from Mario Equicola for a copy of an unspecified Latin poem, he wrote, "Concerning the ode you asked me about, I will look for it among my scattered drafts and I will polish it up as best I can and send it to you."[9] It may be that later, near the end of his life, Ariosto wanted to bring those scattered compositions together into one volume. On January 15, 1532, he formally requested permission to have paper shipped across the boundaries of Gonzaga territory near Mantua for the massive project of producing the third edition of the *Furioso,* and he adds this note: "I also have in mind to print some other little things of mine," perhaps a reference to publishing his Latin verse.[10] Immediately upon his death in 1533, his brother Galasso wrote to Bembo seeking help "in getting his book [*Orlando Furioso*] and all his other compositions, Latin and vernacular, printed."[11] In the history of the transmission of Ariosto's *carmina,* the most significant fact is that they were first published posthumously in 1553, twenty years after the poet's death. Moreover, the printed first edition was based on a manuscript that, as far as we can tell, does not survive intact. As a result, there are textual *cruces,* which editors have been unable to solve on the basis of the evidence provided by the autograph manuscript and the *editio princeps;* for those passages one must resort to emendation.

Unlike other cities in the central and northern areas of the Italian peninsula (Florence and Padua come to mind), Ferrara did not have a distinct literary tradition to speak of in the Trecento. Dante called attention to this deficit in his review of dialects in *De vulgari eloquentia* 1.15.3–4. The various currents of French and Franco-Venetian narrative poems and prose works on Carolingian and Arthurian themes circulating among the cities and courts of the north found an audience in Ferrara. But when Guarino Veronese arrived in 1429 at the behest of Nicolò III to set up his school at the court of the ruling Este family, tastes began to change rapidly. Before Guarino died in 1460, his successful promotion of humanism over the next three decades prepared the ground for an extraordinary flowering of classically-inspired writing in Latin and in the vernacular. One of the main exponents of this new literature in the second half of the Quattrocento was Matteo Maria Boiardo, remembered today mainly for his vernacular narrative, *Orlando Innamorato.* Boiardo combined the different strands of Carolingian and Arthurian stories into a new storyline: Charlemagne's fiercest knight, Orlando, of all people, in love! But Boiardo is as important, arguably, for his translations into Italian of Apuleius, Cornelius Nepos, Herodotus, and Xenophon, as well as for his pastoral poems in Latin that celebrate the achievements of Duke Ercole I d'Este, and his classicizing lyric poems in the vernacular, *Amorum libri*. Guarino's teaching bore fruit in humanist poets such as Boiardo, and it prepared the way for the even more stunning later seasons of Ferrarese letters in the Cinquecento, with the works of Ariosto and Torquato Tasso.

Guarino's son Battista took over the school after his father's death in 1460, and in subsequent decades it remained an important focal point for an impressive group of humanists and courtiers. These humanists included Michael Marullus Tarchaniotes, Tito Vespasiano Strozzi, his son Ercole, Alberto Pio, Pietro Bembo, and Celio Calcagnini, among many others. All of these men, it turns out, figure in Ariosto's Latin poetry in various ways. He either addresses poems to them, or alludes to their Neo-Latin works, or writes about them, directly or indirectly, in his Latin verse. Guarino's legacy guaranteed a writer like Ariosto the linguistic and material means to read Latin works in the original (and Greek works in Latin translation); in addition, the school, and the local university with which it had a symbiotic relationship, nurtured a vital interpretive community of kindred spirits essential to Ariosto's development as a Latinist.

A fascinating glimpse into this world of Ferrarese humanism as it had developed at the beginning of the Cinquecento is provided in a dialogue in Latin written around 1507 by the Estense court historian and erudite man of letters Celio Calcagnini, the *Equitatio* (A Dialogue on Horseback). The roster of participants in the dialogue, while differing slightly from the list of Ariosto's direct addressees in his Latin verse, is an honor roll of Ferrarese and Mantuan humanism at the turn of the century, including Calcagnini,

Lilio Gregorio Giraldi, Demetrio Mosco, Daniele Fini, Mario Equicola, and Ariosto. The interlocutors engage in a wide-ranging discussion of philosophical, literary, and philological questions reflecting the growing interest in Neo-Platonism among these leading intellectual figures in the Ferrarese orbit, under the influence of the revival of interest in Plato in Florentine humanism associated with Ficino.

We can date Calcagnini's dialogue to around 1507, a crucial juncture in the creative life of Ariosto. Up to then his career had been essentially that of a literary Neo-Latin humanist, a classically-inspired court poet of this circle of similarly inclined men. Although his training in law was incomplete, he shared the knowledge of jurisprudence with many of them. Something was about to happen in the trajectory of his work as a poet that would change everything. In Calcagnini's dialogue, Giraldi urges Ariosto to reveal what he has been writing recently. The exchange is as follows:

> Ariosto, since you've been thinking for a while and seem ready to talk, be my helper in the conversation and give us your thoughts on the feats of giants and heroes and, one might say, unworthy feats (a work which I know is fermenting in your mind), or give us your opinion on what we've just been talking about. You know that bit of wisdom: "No one hears hidden music." Then that brilliant young man [Ariosto] said, "I bid goodbye to that book of mine, which has banished from my mind nearly all good sense. For while I was trying to please our prince, Ippolito, I have been spending all my days and nights at work on it wasting my best hours. It weighs more heavily on me than anything else that you and my other friends think that I have frittered away my most beautiful and, if you and my other friends don't deceive me, elaborately prepared literary studies on French harlots (I don't hesitate to call them that) and on stories that make the

rounds of the piazzas. How much better it would have been if I had prepared these feasts for you! But for the man who has donned the helmet, there is no time to repent the war. Why go looking for advice when already in the arena? But rest assured that when I left the city today to enjoy these pleasures with you, I served notice of divorce to those trifles north of the Po.[12]

Among other things, this exchange emphasizes the decision that Ariosto believes he must now make about which language to use in his poetry, Latin or Italian. Whereas earlier he had written in both, now he feels forced to choose between them. Giraldi's reference to giants and heroes is not just about the subject matter of Ariosto's new project; it is also a comment on Ariosto's engagement with the messy culture of the vernacular. Calcagnini's text for its part is written in elegant Ciceronian Latin, peppered throughout with vocabulary and phrases in Greek (the proverb on hidden music and the word ἄδοξος [unworthy] are printed in Greek). Calcagnini gives us a verbal portrait of the classicizing linguistic culture of the humanists of his day, who were becoming trilingual: perfecting their Latin and respective vernaculars, with growing proficiency in Greek. By focusing on Ariosto's literary project in Italian (in a Tuscanized form of a literary dialect of the Po River valley, to be precise), this passage juxtaposes the learned erudition of the humanists with what was perceived to be the less noble linguistic experience of those committed to the vernacular.[13]

At the time of Calcagnini's dialogue, Ariosto had recently abandoned the path of the Neo-Latinists, riding off, as it were, in a different direction, toward vernacular romance, which Calcagnini criticizes as mere literature of entertainment. Ariosto did take a different path from his humanist companions, but he did not completely reject their world; he developed a new kind of writing that incorporated the classical into vernacular romance in ways that Calcagnini could not accept or perhaps even understand. Calcagnini imagined an either/or literary career for the young humanist poet: either erudite Neo-Latin verse of the sort that he and his peers composed or romance narrative poetry in the vernacular.[14] But Ariosto, it turns out, had another possibility in mind, something more like a blend of the two. Similar to Cervantes and Milton in his wake, he perfected a compositional practice of rendering the classical in a vernacular mode, of blending the Latin and the Greek classics with medieval vernacular sources.[15] And later readers, swayed by this intrinsic quality of Ariosto's poetics, would consequently proclaim his poem a classic in its own right.[16]

Ariosto the Vernacular Humanist

Ariosto struggled with the decision over what kind of poet to become. An anecdote recounted by Giovanni Battista Pigna (not in his *editio princeps* of Ariosto's *Carmina*, 1553, but in his critical work on the genre of romance, *I romanzi*, published in 1554) has it that none other than Pietro Bembo encouraged Ariosto to write in Latin. Pigna reports that the poet responded to Bembo "that he would rather be one of the leading writers in Italian than barely a second-rate author in Latin."[17] On their exchange, Girolamo Baruffaldi, the Ferrarese scholar of the Enlightenment, reflected in rather grandiose terms, "It would have done great harm to the nation and the Italian language if Ariosto had taken Bembo's advice on this account."[18]

We do not have any evidence that reveals the specific details of Bembo's ongoing conversation with Ariosto about the quality of his Latin verse beyond what Pigna reports. But we can speculate on how their exchange might have developed. As a young man, Bembo spent extended periods at the Estense court in Ferrara, first from 1497 to 1499, and again from 1502 to 1503, when he famously courted the recent bride of Alfonso d'Este, Lucrezia Borgia. We can reconstruct Bembo's literary conversation in Ferrara with Ariosto and Ercole Strozzi, among others, for it provides the foundation for the dialogue that Bembo later created in his *Prose della volgar lingua* (1525) on the *questione della lingua*. In fact, we may hear the reverse of Bembo's argument to Ariosto for Latin in the section of his *Prose* where Federico Fregoso convinces Ercole Strozzi, the dialogue's spokesman for Neo-Latin, of the value of writing in the vernacular.

Fregoso argues that the Italian vernacular derives from the corruption of Latin through its mixing with languages brought into the peninsula by barbarian invaders, such as the Goths and Lombards in the first millennium of the common era.[19] Fregoso, as Bembo portrays him, argues that liberation from these and other barbarians near the beginning of the second millennium gave birth to a new political outlook and a new linguistic framework. The vernacular has an inherent value because it was born in an act of liberation and is free to change, to get better or worse, to be more or less noble and dignified, not unlike Pico's chameleon, the human being.

In *Prose della volgar lingua*, Bembo does not imply that one should abandon all composition in Latin for expression in the vernacular. His point is that the humanists should not disdain the vernacular, as the historical Ercole Strozzi had done up to then in his own poetic career. Bembo suggests that the humanists should embrace the vernacular and be a part of the process to make it better, a process, he notes, that began when speakers of different vernaculars in the peninsula first encountered Troubadour and Sicilian writings in the 1100s and 1200s. In Bembo's fictitious work, Strozzi moves to this position fairly quickly. In a passage that recalls the description of Ariosto lost in thought in Calcagnini's *Equitatio*, Bembo depicts Strozzi caught up in his reflections: "What were you so focused on?" "I was thinking about whether or not I should give myself over to writing in the vernacular."[20] Bembo portrays Strozzi in the process of changing his mind about the value of a different form of literary and linguistic expression. Ariosto will make the same decision, but not before he establishes himself as a serious craftsman in Latin with a substantial body of work that deserves our attention.

The Carmina of Ludovico Ariosto in the Sixteenth Century

The autograph manuscript, *Classe* I C, Biblioteca Comunale Ariostea, Ferrara—compiled sometime between 1494 and the end of Ariosto's life in 1533—contains thirty-nine poems by Ariosto, twenty-seven of which are published later in the *editio princeps*.[21] In the *editio princeps* Pigna prints fifty-four poems in total; he rejects twelve poems that first appear in the autograph manuscript and includes an additional twenty-seven, the source of which is uncertain. In the manuscript the poems are not arranged in any discernible order. Many poems are thoroughly rewritten, while twelve are crossed out partially or completely. Pigna excluded these twelve from his final text. The manuscript is essentially a notebook of compositional work in various phases of completion, with only a few polished poems with which the poet appeared to be completely satisfied. Its incomplete status led Catalano to count only thirty-four poems. We do not have the working manuscript that Virginio Ariosto handed over to Pigna as the basis for the first edition of 1553, but *Classe* I C could be a substantive part of that original manuscript. The complete copy that Pigna worked from might have represented Ariosto's ideas on the arrangement of his poems, or at least his son's assumptions about what Ariosto wanted. We have to leap from the rough and incomplete autograph compilation to Pigna's first edition, a book that is not unproblematic or without its own difficulties.

Pigna's edition is an anthology that collects the Latin poems of Ariosto, Celio Calcagnini, and Pigna himself, giving each poet his

own clearly defined section, almost as if it were three separate
books bound into one volume. The positioning of names printed
on the book's title page and the varied typefaces suggest a hierar-
chical order, with the first of the four names standing out as the
most important: IO. BAPTISTAE / PIGNAE CARMINUM / LIB.
QUATUOR (Giovanni Battista Pigna's Poems in Four Books).
Moving down the page, one comes to the remaining names in this
order: AD ALPHONSUM FERRARIAE / PRINCIPEM. / His adi-
unximus / CAELII CALCAGNINI CARM. LIB. III. / LUDOVICI
AREOSTI CARM. LIB. II. The second name on the page is that
of Prince Alfonso d'Este, the volume's dedicatee, followed by the
other two poets: Calcagnini's poems in three books, and in the fi-
nal slot, Ariosto's poems in two books. The implicit hierarchy is
further emphasized by the typeface that becomes progressively
smaller as one moves from the first to the fourth name, from top
to bottom of the title page, from a font of approximately ten mil-
limeters in height to one of three. There is more of Pigna to this
book than one might expect. Pigna's poetry runs from pages 5 to
170 in the volume, Calcagnini's from 171 to 269, and Ariosto's from
270 to 312. Pigna's work fills over half the volume (precisely 53.7
percent of the 307 pages dedicated to poetry, not counting the
pages dedicated to front matter and the index and *errata corrigenda*
at the end); Calcagnini's fills just under a third (31.9 percent); and
Ariosto's barely one-eighth (13.6 percent). It may be that the verso
of the title page is meant to provide a visual and typographical cor-
rective to this implicit hierarchy, for while it lists the three poets
in the same order as the title page, omitting the name of the dedi-
catee, it presents all their names in a typeface of the same size,
lending them an appearance of equality. It is difficult to under-
stand any other function for this unusual faux title page (of which
there do not seem to be similar examples in the output of the
printer, Vincenzo Valgrisi); it cannot be construed as a table of

contents, at least not an effective one, since it does not include page numbers.

One of the ways that Pigna structures the volume is to open each section with a dedicatory poem to the leader of Ferrara at the time of each respective poet. For his part, Pigna dedicates each of the four sections of his poetry to Prince Alfonso II, born in 1533, dedicatee in 1553, and in line to succeed as the fifth duke of Ferrara at the death of his father, Ercole II, which occurred in 1559. The dedicatory poems space the opening half of the volume, appearing on pages 5, 44, 73, and 100, with a fifth "book" of satirical poems also beginning with a poem to Prince Alfonso, on page 116. Alfonso II would rule from 1559 till 1597, when he died without an heir, prompting the devolution of Ferrara to the papacy under Clement VIII. The handsome portrait by Girolamo da Carpi of the young Estense prince with his right hand on an open book, now in the Prado Museum, Madrid, was painted at about the time Pigna's volume was published. Moving back a generation, each section of Celio Calcagnini's poems opens with a poem to Ercole II, Alfonso's father (pp. 171, 193, 223). And back further still, as the reader progresses deeper into the book and comes to the final two sections, which include Ariosto's poetry, each *liber* opens with poems to the man who was duke during the second half of Ariosto's life: AD ALPHONSUM FERR. DUCEM III. But here we have a disconnect. Alfonso I d'Este, referred to here as the third duke of Ferrara, held that position from 1505 to 1534, the year after Ariosto's death, but when our poet wrote the better part of his Neo-Latin verse, especially the longer occasional poems, the leader of the state actually was Ercole I, father of Alfonso I. Probably a decade before the death of Ercole in 1505, Ariosto wrote the long poem in hexameters that Pigna uses to open Ariosto's section of the book, *Extollit clamor patrem, pars murmure laudat.*[22] The second section opens with a poem about the death of Ippolito (p. 292), an event which, as the poem tells it, saves the life of Alfonso I. Neither of these poems fits the pattern Pigna first establishes to organize the structure of the book. It is neater, perhaps, to have dedications moving backward chronologically over three generations from Alfonso II to Ercole II to Alfonso I, son to father to grandfather. But the first poem Pigna places in Ariosto's Book 1 is actually to Alfonso II's great-grandfather, and the poem at the start of Book 2 is to the memory of his deceased great-uncle. Neither is addressed to the namesake of Prince Alfonso despite the inaccurate dedicatory titles Pigna assigned them.

This is Pigna's book, not Ariosto's or Calcagnini's, and the editor arranges, dedicates, and renames its contents as he sees fit. The Este dedications create a coherent ordering pattern for him, and they may serve his needs as courtier.[23] He also derives a sense of order from other points of connection within the volume's pages. Among his own poems Pigna includes one dedicated to Virginio Ariosto (p. 52) as well as another to Lilio Gregorio Giraldi, in which he mentions Ludovico Ariosto (pp. 111–13). The poems of Calcagnini share many details with those later in the volume by Ludovico himself. The three books of Calcagnini's verse are divided according to meter and theme: Book 1 consists primarily of hendecasyllables; Book 2 contains elegiacs of an occasional nature, including many for or about peers to whom Ariosto also writes, for example, Ercole Strozzi (p. 187), Ippolito d'Este (p. 195), and Raphael (p. 205); Book 3 contains longer elegiacs on mythological subjects. Pigna likewise organizes Ariosto's poems by meter: Book 1 contains poems in dactylic hexameter and longer elegiacs (pp. 270–91); Book 2 contains poems in a variety of lyric meters, including shorter elegiacs (pp. 292–312). The collection's final poem is Ariosto's own epitaph, bringing the narrative, such as it is, to an end.

Lilio Gregorio Giraldi, Ariosto's interlocutor in Calcagnini's *Equitatio*, outlived most of his cohort by more than two decades to become the grand old man of Ferrarese letters in the mid-sixteenth century. Giraldi comments on Ariosto's Latin in one of his own dialogues, *Dialogi duo de poetis nostrorum temporum* (1551), published near the end of his life. The first of the two dialogues is set sometime between 1513 and 1515 just as Ariosto is preparing to publish the *Furioso*, to which Giraldi refers (1:1088–89). At 1:1085–87, he notes "that same Ludovico Ariosto [whom Giraldi previously recognized as a master of the vernacular] delights sometimes in composing verses in Latin. I remember having read several of his compositions that seemed to me to bear the sign of talent even if they are a little rough around the edges (*ingeniosa sed duriuscula*)." And he adds a comment about Ariosto's readership: "His epigrams and songs are in circulation (*feruntur illius epigrammata et cantiones*)." This could refer to his Latin poetry on the one hand, in particular the epigrams, and to his vernacular lyric poems on the other, which are circulating widely in the hands of readers. Giraldi does not elaborate his opinion about Ariosto's Latin verse but gives the impression that he thinks the Ferrarese poet made the right choice in veering off from the career of Neo-Latin humanist to take up the path of vernacular poet. How much better we will understand the innovative vernacular classicism manifested in Ariosto's *Orlando Furioso* when we understand the fullness of what he created in his Latin poems, even if they are *duriuscula*.

We are grateful to James Hankins for his support as our project made its way from proposal to final manuscript. Under his direction we have received more generous treatment than Ariosto did at the hands of the Este family.

We are deeply indebted to our editor, Leah Whittington, John L. Loeb Associate Professor of the Humanities in the Department of English at Harvard University, who has been unfailing in her patience and encouragement, and incomparably vigilant in scrutinizing our manuscript. Her comments, criticisms, and corrections have made this a better book. Her fine sense of style led to the swift removal of not a few infelicities. We may yet regret those occasions when we did not follow her advice.

Joseph Tipton, a brilliant Latinist, in both the spoken and the written language, read our manuscript of the Latin text and translation and subjected both to a thoroughgoing critique. He commented in detail, and his observations and suggestions have resulted in improvements to text and translation. We are the beneficiaries of his enviable Latinity and his precision as a translator.

The Packard Humanities Institute website (http://latin.pack hum.org/about), which provides a searchable database of classical Latin texts, is an indispensible resource for the study and analysis of the language of Latin poetry. The importance of this website for our work will be obvious from the Notes to the Translation. We have likewise profited from another online resource, www.poet iditalia.it.

Dennis Looney and D. Mark Possanza

When this project was in its first stages in 2009, N. John Cooper, Dean, Dietrich School of Arts and Sciences, University of Pittsburgh, granted me a sabbatical that enabled me to spend an extended period in Bologna and Ferrara at work on Ariosto. From then to now, Mirna Bonazza, curator of manuscripts and early printed editions, Biblioteca Comunale Ariostea, has been a constant source of information and advice for us. Cristina Zampese (University of Milan), Paolo Trovato (University of Ferrara), and Gianni Venturi (Institute of Renaissance Studies, Ferrara) were important guides as the project took shape. In the land of the generous, Giovanni Contini, who hosted me repeatedly as I traipsed about after Ariosto, stands out for his generosity. I first read Ariosto's Latin poetry in a course on Renaissance Humanism with Aldo Scaglione at the University of North Carolina at Chapel Hill. I am grateful that Scaglione challenged me to study and embrace the fullness of Ariosto's writing.

Dennis Looney

My deepest gratitude belongs to the administrators, staff, and fellows (class of 2015–16) of the National Humanities Center in North Carolina, where, as Frank H. Kenan Fellow, I had the privilege of conducting my research in a supportive and generous environment in which even lunch-table conversations opened up new lines of investigation or helped to clarify old problems. I owe a special debt to the Center's Director of the Library, Brooke Andrade, and the Assistant Librarian, Sarah Harris, who had a detective's instinct in searching out books and a bulldog's tenacity in having them delivered to the Center. I hope that the spirit of humanism that flourishes at the Center and the efforts of those who work so hard to sustain it are somehow present in these pages.

I also want to thank the Dietrich School of Arts and Sciences at the University of Pittsburgh, its Dean, N. John Cooper, and the University's Provost, Patricia Beeson, for granting me a Faculty Leave for Professional Enhancement, which allowed me to take up my fellowship at the National Humanities Center. While working on this project, I had the great good fortune to receive an invitation from Francesco Citti, Professore ordinario in the Dipartimento di Filologia Classica e Italianistica at the University of Bologna, to participate in his summer Classics program in Bologna. His invitation brought me close to Ferrara and provided me with the unexpected opportunity to restore myself with the rich cultural traditions of these two illustrious cities and to make easy trips to the Biblioteca Comunale Ariostea, whose librarians were always courteous and helpful. Professor Citti also provided me with a copy of the hard-to-find first edition of Bolaffi's

Ludovici Areosti Carmina and introduced me to an invaluable online resource, www.poetiditalia.it. Professor Citti and his colleagues, Professor Bruna Pieri and Professor Lucia Pasetti, were wonderful hosts, and I am most grateful to them for their warm hospitality. The wisdom and craftsmanship of Maurizio Nanetti and Ermanno Bartoletti have taught me much about the soul of Emilia-Romagna.

A work like this is built on the labors of generations of predecessors who have made contributions great and small to transmitting the Latin text of these poems in a form as correct as the evidence will allow and to interpreting and annotating them both in relation to the Classical literary tradition and in relation to the vibrant and experimental literary culture of their day. Our errors and omissions come with an open invitation to be corrected.

Ours has been a happy collaboration. Our friendship of many years, dating back to graduate school, survives intact. As Ennius said, *amicus certus in re incerta cernitur*.

D. Mark Possanza

Tibi, Ferraria, civitas illustrissima et patria dulcissima Ludovico Areosto, poetae divino ingenio summaque virtute, qui aeternis te carminibus in caelum sustulit, hunc libellum auctores dono dederunt.

NOTES

1. Ariosto's brother Gabriele claims in the eulogy he writes at Ludovico's death that *De laudibus sophiae* was delivered to open the academic year; see Catalano (*Vita*, 1:100–103), who contests the date of 1495, whereas Carducci (*La gioventù* [1905], 137–44) and Segre (Ariosto, *Opere minori*, 14) follow it.

2. "[N]on mediocre desiderium studiosis incidit habendi libros Marsilii et aliorum qui aliquid de hac secta a Graecis scriptum latine transtulerunt" (*Lettere*, 131).

3. *Parva, sed apta mihi, sed nulli obnoxia, sed non / sordida, parta meo sed tamen aere domus* (Bolaffi 1938, 56). Some scholars attribute the inscription to Bartolomeo Cavalieri, who owned the house before the poet; see Chiappini, "The *parva domus.*"

4. At the end of his first year in the Garfagnana, Ariosto recalls nostalgically the time he spent as a younger man in the house of his cousin, the poem's dedicatee, Sigismondo Malaguzzi. The Malaguzzi family, to whom Ariosto was related on his mother's side, had a villa outside Reggio, where Ariosto stayed in 1496–97 and 1502–3: "Cercando or questo et or quel loco opaco / quivi in più d'una lingua e in più d'uno stile / rivi traea sin dal gorgoneo laco" (Seeking there now one and now another shady retreat, in more than one language and style, I called forth rivulets from the Gorgonian lake; *Satires*, trans. Wiggins, 105) (*Sat.* 4.127–29).

5. Ezio Bolaffi's critical edition of the *Carmina* (1934), republished with corrections in 1938, is the basis for all subsequent editions. Bolaffi depended on the two primary authorities for establishing his text: Ariosto's autograph manuscript, which contains thirty-nine poems, and the first printed edition, edited by Giovanni Battista Pigna (1553), which contains fifty-four poems; the manuscript contains poems that are not in the *editio princeps*, and the *editio princeps* prints poems that are not found in the manuscript. See "A Note on the Text and Its Textual History" for a fuller discussion.

6. The best critical response to these poems remains Carducci's nineteenth-century contribution, which he first entitled *Delle poesie latine edite ed inedite di Ludovico Ariosto* (1875) and then changed to reflect substantial revisions, *La gioventù di Ludovico Ariosto e la poesia latina in Ferrara* (1905). We cite from the 1905 edition. See Casari for a useful analysis of how Carducci moved from his original intention of writing a biography of Ariosto to focusing more generally on Ferrarese humanism of the late Quattrocento.

7. *Memorie* XVI: "Non fu molto studioso, e pochi libri cercava di vedere. Gli piaceva Virgilio; Tibullo nel suo dire: Ma grandemente commendava Orazio, e Catullo; ma non molto Properzio." Barotti, *Memorie istoriche*, I:225.

8. On how Ariosto ironically used Horace's feigned madness, see Durling, *Figure of the Poet*, 174–76.

9. "Circa l'oda che voi mi dimandate, la cercherò tra le mie mal raccolte composizioni, e le darò un poco di lima al meglio che io saprò e manderòllavi" (*Lettere*, 172).

10. "Io fo pensier ancho di stampare alcune altre mie cosette" (*Lettere*, 461).

11. ". . . fare ristampare il libro et tutte l'altre composizioni sue latine et volgari" (71v).

12. *Equitatio* (ed. Antonio Musa Brasavola), 562.

13. For a synoptic discussion of the linguistic options for authors in the vernacular in Ariosto's lifetime, see Hall, *Italian 'questione della lingua.'* For a provocative reassessment of the juxtaposition of Latin and Italian and of the impact of the tension between these two linguistic cultures on Renaissance historiography, see Celenza, *Lost Italian Renaissance*. For a more detailed reading of this passage from the *Equitatio*, see Looney, "Ariosto's Dialogue with Authority in the *Erbolato*," 24–27.

14. This line of interpretation runs all the way to Benedetto Croce, who similarly reads Ariosto's career choices as an either/or move from humanism to vernacular writing (*Ariosto*, 38–39). See Savarese's discussion of Calcagnini's portrait of Ariosto, as well as Prandi's interesting recontextualization of Savarese's reading ("Premesse umanistiche del *Furioso*," 8–10) and his comments on Croce (11).

15. This is the argument in Looney, *Compromising the Classics*, 15–30.

16. See Javitch, *Proclaiming a Classic*.

17. "che più tosto volea essere uno de primi tra scrittori Thoscani che appena il secondo tra Latini" (75).

18. "Sarebbe stato un gran danno alla nazione, e alla Lingua Italiana, se in questa occasione si fosse arreso l'Ariosto al consiglio del Bembo" (*Vita*, 15, n. 20).

19. This position was held by Flavio Biondo approximately one hundred years earlier in his debate with Leonardo Bruni over the source and status of the vernacular.

20. "Ma voi di che pensavate così fissamente?" "Io pensava . . . che se . . . a scrivere volgarmente mi disponessi . . ." (1:12, 105–6).

21. Carducci's description of the manuscript remains the most detailed (*La gioventù* [1905], 13–26). The manuscript also contains poems by Pietro Bembo and a poem by a Roman poet of late antiquity, Pentadius (Pesenti, "La fortuna").

22. See Catalano (following Torraca), who points out that the third section of this poem (poem 4 in Bolaffi's edition) has to refer to Ercole (*Vita*, 1:101).

23. Fatini takes Pigna to task for ordering the poems along these lines (*Lirica*, 349).

LATIN POETRY

LUDOVICI AREOSTI CARMINA

: I :

Ad Philiroen

Quid Galliarum navibus aut equis
paret minatus Carolus, asperi
    furore militis tremendo,
      turribus Ausoniis ruinam;
5 rursus quid hostis prospiciat sibi,
me nulla tangat cura, sub arbuto
    iacentem aquae ad murmur cadentis,
      dum segetes Corydona flavae
durum fatigant. Philiroe, meum
10 si mutuum optas, ut mihi saepius
    dixisti, amorem, fac corolla
      purpureo variata flore
amantis udum circumeat caput,
quam tu nitenti nexueris manu;
15   mecumque caespite hoc recumbens
      ad citharam suavis canito.

: Ia :

Ode. de vita quieta ad Philiroen (F)

Quid Galliarum rex Carolus paret
minatus, ut qui militis optime
    vim noverit sui, tremendam
      turribus Ausoniis ruinam;

2

POEMS OF LUDOVICO ARIOSTO

To Philiroe

What preparation Charles is making with the ships and horses of
France to threaten destruction to the towers of Ausonia with the
dreaded ferocity of his violent soldiers, and what steps his enemy
is taking in turn—let not a single worry touch me as I lie under a
strawberry tree by the murmur of falling water, while the golden
grain crop gives hardy Corydon a workout. If you desire, Philiroe,
to share my love, as you have told me again and again, make sure
there's a garland variegated with purple flowers, made by your fair
hands, around your lover's drunken head and, lying here on the
ground with me, sing sweetly to the lyre.

: Ia :

Ode on the Tranquil Life to Philiroe (F)

What preparation Charles, King of France, is making, since he
knows very well the might of his soldiers, to threaten dreaded de-
struction to the towers of Ausonia, and what steps his enemy is

5   rursus quid hostes prospiciant sibi,
    me nulla tangat cura, sub arbuto
      iacentem aquae ad murmur cadentis,
        dum segetes Corydona flavae
    durum fatigant. O miseri, quibus
10 vesana mens est vendere sanguinem
      auro suum! Quicum relicto
        corpore postquam anima effluit, nec
    parata tantis arva laboribus
    iuvare possunt, nec Pario domus
15   Laconico simulque et Afro et
      omnigeno lapide enitescens.
    Haec, hoc et auri quicquid aenea
    stipatur arca, prodigioribus
      linquenda posteris propinquis
20   omnia sunt, avido aut tyranno
    magis. Tyranno nam mala principi
    inest cupido qua bona liberis
      relicta parvis in profanos
        diripiat male gratus usus,
25 oblitus olim quid tulerit pater
    facturus ense in perniciem suam
      potentiorem erum superbum.
        Sint miseri, ut libet esse; non mihi
    haec sit libido. Philiroe, meum
30 si mutuum optas, ut mihi saepius
      dixisti, amorem, fac corolla
        purpureo variata flore
    mero uda amantis tempora vinciat,
    quam tu nitenti nexueris manu,
35   mecumque caespite hoc recumbens
      ad citharam cane multicordem.

4

taking in turn—let not a single worry touch me as I lie under a strawberry tree by the murmur of falling water while the golden grain crop gives hardy Corydon a workout. O they are unhappy, those who have the mad idea to sell their blood for gold. After the soul, along with the blood, leaves the body behind and escapes, fields worked with tremendous effort can be of no help, nor a house that sparkles with Parian stone, Laconian, African, and every kind all together. All these and whatever gold is stashed in the bronze strong box must be left to descendants who will squander them, or instead to a greedy tyrant. For there comes naturally to the tyrannical prince the wicked desire that causes him to plunder, in perverse gratitude for service rendered, the inheritance of small children for his unholy purposes, forgetting what their father endured when he was ready with his sword, at the risk of his own death, to make his arrogant master more powerful. Let them be unhappy, as it pleases them to be; not for me this hungry craving. If you desire, Philiroe, to share my love, as you have told me again and again, make sure there's a garland variegated with purple flowers, made by your fair hands, that binds your lover's temples drunk with wine, and, lying here on the ground with me, sing to the many-stringed lyre.

: II :

Ad Pandulphum

Dum tu prompte animatus, ut
se res cumque feret, principe sub tuo,
 Pandulphe, omnia perpeti,
quaeris qui dominae crinibus aureis
5   Fortunae iniicias manus;
nos grati nemoris, rauca sonantium
 lympharum strepitus prope,
umbrosas vacui quaerimus ilices
 canna non sine dispari,
10 quae flavae Glyceres reddat amoribus
 cantatis suaves modos,
queis Panum invideat capripedum genus;
 nos longum genio diem
sacramus, penitus quid face postera
15   mater Memnonis afferat
securi, roseis humida curribus.
 Qui certantia purpurae
dum vina in tenero gramine ducimus,
 vincti tempora pampino,
20 aut serto ex hedera, sanguinea aut rosa,
 quod vel candida nexuit
Phyllis vel nivea Philiroe manu,
 tum praedivitis haud movent
me vel regna Asiae, vel ferus Adria
25   quicquid puppe vehit gravi.
Quare saepe minas aequoris horream,
 ut me fictilia, in quibus
ulnis Philiroe candidulis mihi

: II :

To Pandolfo

While you, Pandolfo, resolved and ready to endure everything under your prince, whatever the situation may be, look for a way to lay your hands on the golden locks of mistress Fortune, I at my ease seek out shady holm oaks in an attractive grove near the low murmuring of rippling waters with my pan pipe, its reeds of unequal length, to play soft music for songs of my love for fair-haired Glycere, music which the tribe of goat-footed Pans would envy. The livelong day I consecrate to creative inspiration, utterly untroubled by what the mother of Memnon, wet with dew in her rose-colored chariot, will bring with tomorrow's sun. While I drink my wine — it rivals purple in its hue — on the soft grass, my temples circled with vine leaves or a garland of ivy or bloodred roses woven by lovely Phyllis or Philiroe with snow-white hands, then the kingdoms of rich Asia or whatever precious cargo rides the wild Adriatic in laden ships doesn't concern me. Why should I time and again shudder in fear at the dangers of the sea, since I take more pleasure in the earthenware vessels, in which beautiful Philiroe with her white arms has curdled milk for me, than in the

lac formosa coegerit,
30 delectant potius quam Siculi dapes
regis, quas teneat nitens
aurum, sede licet collocer aurea,
quem circum pueri integri
adsint, ut veteris pocula Massici
35 propinent? Docilis tulit
fontis quae rigui lympha, bibentibus
inter laeta rosaria
tristis cura magis tempora Syrio
unguento madida insilit
40 et saevit penitus, si furor, Alpibus
saevo flaminis impetu
iam spretis, quatiat Celticus Ausones.
Hic est qui super impiam
cervicem gladius pendulus imminet.

: III :

Epitaphium Fulci Areosti (F)

Stirps Areosta fuit, Ferraria patria, Fulcus
nomen, Roma altrix, Apula humus tegit hic.
Tormento ictus obi, dum Ripae a moenibus arcens
Fernandum Vrsino pro duce praesideo.
5 Octavam vixi trieterida. Cetera, quaeso,
disce aliunde; nefas me mea facta loqui.

banquets of the Sicilian King, served on ware of shining gold—though I be seated in a golden chair with innocent boys around me to serve cups of aged Massic? Rather, for those who drink among rich rose beds fed by the channeled waters of a spilling fountain, melancholy care besets their perfume-drenched heads and stirs turmoil deep within, if Celtic madness makes the Ausonians tremble, scorning the Alps with the savage onslaught of its storm. This is the sword that hangs suspended above treacherous necks.

: III :

Epitaph of Folco Ariosto (F)

My family was the Ariosti, my native land Ferrara, my name Folco. Rome raised me, earth of Apulia covers me here. I was struck and killed by artillery fire while, in command at Ripa for Duke Orsini, I was defending the city walls against Ferdinand. I lived twenty-four years. From others please learn the rest; it is not right for me to speak of my own deeds.

: IV :

*[De laudibus Sophiae ad Herculem Ferrariae
Ducem II]*

*   *   *   *   *   *

Extollit clamor patrem; pars murmure laudat
dicta Iovis tacito iam iam labentis ad aegros
terrigenas: animis adeo caelestibus haeret
cura, licet totiens recidivae in crimina, gentis!
5 Orbe iacet medio, superis tunc hospita, tellus,
cum longo innocuis habitata est gentibus aevo.
Qua Pelusiacos aditus, perque ora Canopi
amne petit gemino sinuosa volumina ponti
Nilus, et in latum cogit succrescere campos,
10 aridaque umenti fecundat iugera limo,
Iuppiter hic claro delapsus ab aethere iussit
numina cuncta epulis positae discumbere mensae,
laetus ut unigenae celebret natalia divae.
Conveniunt superi; tenuit mora nulla vocatos;
15 inde maris terraeque deos simul impiger omnes
Mercurius monuit Phariis accedere mensis,
quos pater omnipotens hilari inter pocula fronte
accipit et meritum cunctis largitur honorem.
O fortunati quorum succedere tectis
20 dignata est haec sancta cohors! Nondum impia tristes
hauserat implacidi Busiridis ara cruores,
tum neque polluerat fraterna caede Typhaon
gramina nec lacrimis fueras quaesitus, Osiri.
Interea Eoas volitat vaga fama per urbes
25 caelicolum visos mortali lumine coetus

: IV :

[In Praise of Wisdom: To Ercole d'Este, Second Duke of Ferrara]

*   *   *   *   *   *

The father of the gods is cheered with shouts of approval. Some praise Jupiter's words with hushed voices as now he glides on his way to the afflicted children of earth. Such concern do divine hearts feel for the human race, though it has fallen back so many times into its wicked ways. The earth, situated in the middle of the celestial sphere, was hospitable to the gods when it was inhabited by innocent people in the long course of the ages. Where the Nile flows with its two branches through the passageway of Pelusium and the mouth of Canopus to the rolling folds of the sea waves, and causes the fields to be replenished far and wide, fertilizing the dry acres with sopping mud, here Jupiter descended from the bright ether and bid all the divinities to recline at a table laid with sumptuous dishes so that he could celebrate the birthday of the goddess who had one parent. The gods assemble; no one delays in responding to the invitation. Then Mercury speedily bids the gods of land and sea to come together to the banquet table in Pharos. The almighty father welcomes them with a smile on his face as the cups go round, and he bestows on all the honor they deserve.

Truly blessed were those whose homes this band of gods thought worthy to enter. Not yet had the altar of savage Busiris drunk the blood of murdered victims, nor had Typhaon then polluted the grass with the slaughter of his brother nor had there been a tearful search for you, Osiris. Meanwhile word flies, making its rounds far and wide throughout the cities of the east, that mortal eyes saw a gathering of the gods holding a banquet together

ducere Niliacis pariter convivia terris.
Tum numerum ex omni properantem parte videres,
hospitis ut praesens veneretur numina tanti.
Par aderat Vulcanus huic, septemflue, proles,
30   Nile, tua, haud Phariis probitate ignota colonis;
affuit et Libya genitus, qui sidera torquet;
deseruit clarae urbis opus ter maximus Hermes;
legifer hinc Moses, illinc pia turba frequentat,
casta quidem, sed rara tamen; namque incluta virtus
35   neglegit infausti foedata examina vulgi.
Hos habuit Iove nata suis penetralibus, urbes
ex illo monitu superum cultura, ministros.

    Tum primum a silice antiquum genus exuit aegram
segnitiem, coepitque rudes deponere cultus.
40   Paulatim ignipedum quis cursus frenet equorum
quaerere, quae mundi fuerit nascentis origo,
mentibus obrepens deturbat cura quietos,
utque, simul fragiles artus prostrarit Anance,
nulla perenne sibi formidet funera nomen.

*   *   *   *   *   *

45   Dexter eris, rediens, hominum iustissime, coeptis.
Namque tuam nunc forte tenet cura altera mentem;
quod procul Insubrum iudex delectus in oris
concilias solitaque animi probitate revincis
pace deum populos inimico Marte furentes.
50   Seu Sophia ulcisci bello, seu pace tueri
flagitet, Herculeam vel opem si poscat utrumque,
iusta quis invicto sumet te fortius arma,
qui tot parta refers propria virtute tropaea?
Vel quis pace frui tribuet sapientius alter,
55   qui mediam Latii servasse laboribus urbem

in the land of the Nile. Then you would have seen people hastening in numbers from every direction to worship face to face the divine majesty of so amazing a guest. Vulcan, Jupiter's equal in rank, was present — your progeny, Nile of the seven streams — well known to the inhabitants of Pharos for his goodness; also present was Atlas, born of Libya, who makes the stars revolve; Hermes Trismegistos left behind his famous city's work; from one direction comes Moses the lawgiver, from another comes the devoted throng, pure indeed, but nonetheless few in number because renowned virtue ignores the filthy hordes of the accursed mob. These the daughter of Jupiter had as attendants in the innermost parts of her sanctuary when, by the gods' command, she went to dwell in cities.

Then for the first time the ancient race made from stone put off its ailing sluggishness and began to abandon its uncivilized way of life. Gradually curiosity crept into their minds, disturbing their tranquil lives, to find out who reins the fiery-footed horses in their paces, what the origin of the world was when it first came into being, and how, once Fate has struck down the fragile body, everlasting fame has nothing to fear from death.

*   *   *   *   *   *

Upon your return, most just of men, you will support these undertakings. Right now your mind happens to be preoccupied with different cares because, chosen as mediator in the distant territory of the Insubres, you, with your customary integrity, are reconciling peoples caught up in the war-crazed fury of Mars and are binding them together with the blessing of the gods. Whether Wisdom demands vengeance in war or protection in peace time or if both require the help of a Hercules, who will more bravely take up just arms than you who are unconquered, you who bring back so many trophies of victory won by your valor? Or who else will bestow the enjoyment of peace more wisely than you who are celebrated in song for single-handedly saving the city in the middle of Italy from

solus inexhausta caneris virtute? Tuum sic
fortunata diu iactet Ferraria munus,
quo rediviva suas reparet Tritonia laudes.

: V :

Epitaphium Regis Ferdinandi (F)

Illa ego laeta olim nunc maerens Itala Virtus
    Fernandi ad tumulum tristis et orba fleo;
vere orba, erepto talis mihi pignore nati,
    cui reliquam merito posthabui sobolem;
5 namque reportavit matri spolia, ah! quibus illos
    degeneres hostis barbarus exuerat.

: VI :

Ad Pandulphum [Areostum]

Ibis ad umbrosas corylos, Pandulphe, Copari,
    murmure somnifero quas levis aura movet.
Me sine sub denso meditabere tegmine carmen,
    dum strepet Aeolio pectine pulsa chelys.
5 Illic silvicolae laudabunt carmina Fauni;
    si forte heroum fortia facta canes,
seu fidibus iuvenum mandabis furta sonoris,
    non ciet arbitrio fistula rauca lyram.
Audiet a viridi Dryadum lasciva rubeto,
10   et bibet amotis crinibus aure melos,

its troubles with your unfailing valor? Thus blessed, let Ferrara long boast of your gift by which Tritonia lives again and will restore her renown.

: V :

Epitaph of King Ferdinand (F)

I am that Italian Valor, once happy, now mourning as I weep, sad and bereft, beside the tomb of Ferdinand, truly bereft now that the boon of such a son has been stolen from me. Deservedly did I prefer him to all other sons, for he brought back to his mother the spoils that (alas!) a foreign enemy stripped from those cowardly men.

: VI :

To Pandolfo [Ariosto]

You will go, Pandolfo, to the shady hazel groves of Copparo, which a gentle breeze shakes with somnolent murmuring. Without me you'll practice your song under a thick cover of shade while your lyre sounds its notes, struck by the Aeolian plectrum. There the wood-dwelling Fauns will praise your songs. Whether you happen to sing the brave deeds of heroes or you entrust young lovers' trysts to the sonorous strings, the shrill pipe will not challenge the lyre to a decision. A pixie of a Dryad will listen from a green bramble thicket and, her long hair drawn back, will drink in your

(cantanti venient suspiria quanta labello!)
 et latebras cupiet prodere tecta suas.
O quid si nimio cantu defessa sopori
 te dare gramineo membra videbit humo?
15 Exiliens taciturna, pedem per gramina tollet,
 optata et propius cernat ut ora petet.
Inde procax tereti timide suspensa lacerto,
 rara tibi furtim suavia rapta dabit;
vel leviter patula decerpet ab arbore ramos,
20 lacteolae ut moveat flamina grata genae.
Fortunate puer, qui inter tua iugera cessas,
 et nemora et saltus liber ab urbe colis!
Me miserum (imperium dominae, non moenia, claudit)
 quod nequeam comitis visere prata mei!
25 Vincior, ah, gracili formosae crine puellae,
 purpurea en vinctum compede servat Amor!
Luce meae tota dominae vestigia lustro;
 dein queror ad tacitas, iudice nocte, fores.
Expers ipse tamen rides mala nostra; caveto
30 sed Nemesim; est fastus saepius ulta graves.
Tempus erit cum te nimium miseratus amantem,
 an iusta haec fuerit nostra querela scies.
Nunc quoniam haud nosti Venerem nec vulnera nati,
 ferre putas omni libera colla iugo;
35 sed mora. Quae nostrae rigidum te tradere turbae
 nititur, in longos non feret illa dies.
Nuper quae aligerum cecinit mihi passer Amorum,
 dum Paphies humili culmine iussa monet
texere Naiadas Veneri nova vincla sub undis,
40 (quem cupiant taceo), si sapis, ipse cave.
Interea optati sine me cape gaudia ruris
 continue et felix vive memorque mei.

song with her ears (what sighs will escape her lips as you sing!)
and though concealed from view, she will be eager to betray her
hiding place. What if she sees you, tired out from all that singing,
fall asleep on the grassy ground? Stepping gingerly over the grass
without a word, she'll try to get a closer look at the face she has
longed to see. Then the flirt, propped cautiously on her shapely
arm, will furtively steal a few kisses or gently pluck branches from
a spreading tree so that she can fan pleasant breezes on your milk-
white cheek. Lucky boy, you who relax among your fields and
dwell in groves and woodlands, free from the city. Unhappy am I
because I can't go and visit the delightful meadows of my compan-
ion (it is my mistress's total control, not the city walls, that con-
fines me). I am fettered, so true, by my beautiful darling's fine
tresses, and Love holds me fast in her tresses' dark sheen. All day
long I follow my mistress's footsteps; with night as my judge I
make my complaint to a silent door. Though you yourself have no
experience in this, yet you laugh at my troubles. But beware Nem-
esis; again and again she avenges unrelenting disdain. The time
will come when you, pitying yourself for being too much in love,
will know whether this complaint of mine was justified. Now, be-
cause you have no knowledge of Venus and the wounds inflicted
by her son, you think that you can strut about, head unbowed by
the yoke of bondage; but it's merely a postponement. The goddess,
who is devising a way to deliver you up to my tribe, despite your
hard resistance, won't endure it for long. If you're smart, you your-
self beware of what the sparrow of the winged *Amores* recently
sang to me while from his low perch he issued the Paphian god-
dess's orders: the Naiads are weaving new fetters for Venus under
the waves (who their target is, I do not say). In the meantime, take
uninterrupted pleasure in your cherished countryside without me.
Live happily, with me in your thoughts.

: VII :

Ad Petrum Bembum

Me tacitum perferre meae peccata puellae?
    Me mihi rivalem praenituisse pati?
Cur non ut patiarque fodi mea viscera ferro
    dissimulato etiam, Bembe, dolore iubes?
5   Quin cor, quin oculosque meos, quin erue vel quod
    carius est, siquid carius esse potest.
Deficientem animam quod vis tolerare iubebo,
    dum superet dominae me moriente fides.
Obsequiis alius faciles sibi quaerat amores,
10   cautius et vitet tetrica verba nece,
qui spectare suae valeat securus amicae
    non intellecta livida colla nota,
quique externa toro minimi vestigia pendat,
    dum sibi sit potior parve in amore locus.
15   Me potius fugiat nullis mollita querelis,
    dum simul et reliquos Lydia dura procos.
Parte carere omni malo, quam admittere quemquam
    in partem; cupiat Iuppiter ipse, negem.
Tecum ego mancipiis, mensa, lare, vestibus utar;
20   communi sed non utar, amice, toro.
Cur ea mens mihi sit, quaeris fortasse, tuaque
    victum iri facili me ratione putas.
Ah pereat qui in amore potest rationibus uti!
    Ah pereat qui ni perdite amare potest!
25   Quid deceat, quid non, videant quibus integra mens est;
    sat mihi, sat dominam posse videre meam.

: VII :

To Pietro Bembo

To think that I'm to endure my girl's cheating in silence! That I'm to endure a rival outshining me! Why not command me, Bembo, to suffer my guts to be carved out with a blade and hide the pain to boot? Why not pluck out my heart, my eyes, or some more vital organ, if there is one? I will command my failing spirit to endure what you want, provided my mistress remains faithful as I lay dying. Let another man seek out a love affair that runs smooth for him by his acts of servile compliance, and let him avoid harsh words more carefully than death, a man who has the ability to look without worry at his girlfriend's neck bruised with a mark he doesn't recognize, a man who doesn't give a second thought to signs of a stranger in his bed, as long as he holds a greater or an equal place in her love. As for me, I'd rather hard-hearted Lydia, if she won't be softened by my prayers, stay away from me, as long as she stays away from the rest of her suitors as well. I prefer to do without the whole package than to let anyone have a piece of it. Should Jupiter himself want part of her, I'd say no. With you I would share my servants, my table, my house, my clothes, but, my friend, my bed is not common property. You might ask why I think that way and imagine that you'll get the better of me with a ready piece of logic. May the man perish who can use logic in love, and the same for the man who can love without loving desperately. Let clearheaded people be concerned about proprieties. For me it's enough to be able to see my mistress, it's enough.

: VIII :

Francisci Areosti Epitaphium (EP) sine inscriptione (F)

Hic Franciscum Areostum uxor natusque superstes
    nataque confectum composuit senio,
quantivis equitem pretii tot et aspera vitae
    emensum illaesis usque rogum pedibus;
5 qui claram ob probitatem efferri totius urbis
    singultu et lacrimis ad tumulum meruit.

: IX :

Ad Albertum Pium

Alberte, proles incluta Caesarum,
utraque nam tu gente propagini
    ostendis Augustos fuisse
      nobile principium tuorum,
5 hac luce mecum laetitiam cape,
sed quae sit omni libera compede;
    ne sit mero frontem severam
      exhilarare pudor Falerno;
nimirum amamus si genio diem
10 sacrare, cum sint digna licentia
    exuberantis gaudii atque
      immodicum petulantis oris
quae mane nobis nuntius attulit,
fidelitatis nuntius integrae,
15   a Gallico qui nuper orbe
      principibus rediit Latinis.

: VIII :

Epitaph of Francesco Ariosto (EP) no title (F)

Here Francesco Ariosto, worn out by old age, was laid to rest by his surviving wife, son and daughter. He was a knight of the utmost worth, who traversed life's rough roads all the way to the grave without stumbling. Because of his famous integrity he deserved to be carried out for burial accompanied by the sobs and tears of the whole city.

: IX :

To Alberto Pio

Alberto, renowned scion of Caesars (for you prove to your descendants that *Augusti* were the noble origin of your people on both sides of the family), revel in happiness with me today, a happiness free of every restraint; let there be no shame in gladdening a stern visage with unmixed Falernian wine. It's no surprise if we take pleasure in consecrating the day to the spirit of merriment since this news warrants free expression of overflowing joy and reckless, rowdy banter—news which a messenger of unimpeachable reliability brought to us this morning, who recently returned from the realm of France to the princes of Italy. He said that he had seen

Vidisse dixit Lugdunii meum
Gregorium, illum cui per Apollinem
   uterque nostrum debet ample,
20   quamvis ego magis et magis te.
Tu litterae quod multum Echioniae
calles, tenentur primi aditus viro
   huic; ast ego plus debeo, nam est,
      siquid inest mihi clari, ab illo.
25 Parantem aiebat quam citius pote
transferre se ad nos, cui timui miser
   'vale' ultimum dixisse, cum olim
      ad gelidas veheretur Alpes.
Io! redibit qui penitus rude
30 lignum dolavit me et ab inutili
   pigraque mole gratiorem
      in speciem hanc, Pie, me redegit!
Io! videbo qui tribuit magis
ipso parente, ut qui dedit optime
35   mihi esse, cum tantum alter esse
      in populo dederit frequenti!
Virum, boni di, rursus amabilem
amplectar! An quid me esse beatius
   potest beatum, o mi beate
40   nuntie, qui me hodie beasti?

: X :

[Epitaphium Nicolai Areosti]

Molliter hic Nicolaum Areostum composuere
   uxor cum caris Daria pignoribus,
quam neque honorati solata est fama mariti

my Gregorio at Lyon, that man to whom both of us are deeply
indebted for our Apolline studies, although I am ever more in-
debted than you. Your initiation into Echionian letters, in which
you are now expert, belongs to this man. But I owe him more; for
if I possess any brilliance, it comes from him. The messenger said
that he was preparing to come to us as soon as he could. On the
day when he traveled to the cold Alps, I feared in my sadness that
I had said goodbye to him for the last time. Now great news! He
will return, the man who hewed me into shape from top to bot-
tom when I was a rough timber; he trimmed me down, Pio, from
a useless and lazy lump into this attractive figure. Great news! I
will see the man who bestowed on me more than my own father,
because he was the one who made possible my success, while my
father gave me only a life amid masses of people. Once again,
blessed gods, I will embrace this delightful man. Who that is
happy can be happier than I am, oh my happy messenger, who
today has made me happy?

: X :

[Epitaph of Nicolò Ariosto]

Here Nicolò Ariosto was gently laid to rest by his wife Daria and
their beloved children. She has found no comfort in her honored
husband's fame and will find none in her wealth or her children

nec faciet vel opum copia vel sobolis,
5   donec, decurso spatio vitae, ossibus ossa
aeternum atque animam miscuerint animae.

: XI :

De Quincti Valerii uxore (EP) sine inscriptione (F)

Molliter hic Quincti Valeri complectitur umbram
compos voti uxor Quinctia facta sui,
quam nunquam abrepti probitas laudata mariti
solata est nec opum copia nec sobolis,
5   donec, decurso spatio vitae, ossibus ossa
miscuerit caris atque animas animis.

: XII :

De Nicolao Areosto

Has vivens lacrimas, sed qui odio miser
tristem vitam habeo, dono, pater, tibi,
vitae sollicitis functe laboribus;
    has dono, pater optime,
5   sincerae monimentum illius, illius
quam noras pietatem, imperiis tuis
sanctis a tenera huc usque puertia
    cum semper fuerim obsequens.
Saevum munus habe, seu liquidi aetheris
10 cultor vana hominum nunc studia improbas,

24

until, the course of her life completed, her bones are mingled with his bones and her soul with his soul in eternity.

: XI :

On the Wife of Quinzio Valerio (EP) no title (F)

Here his wife Quinzia gently embraces the shade of Quinzio Valerio, her prayer fulfilled. She never found comfort in the celebrated integrity of her deceased husband or in her wealth or in her children until, the course of her life completed, she mingled her bones with his dear bones and her soul with his.

: XII :

On Nicolò Ariosto

These tears, father, I give to you, I who go on living, yet in my grief hate this wretched life, now that you have passed on from its toil and trouble. These tears, best of fathers, I give you as a reminder of that pure devotion, which you have known from the tender years of my childhood up to now, since I have always been obedient to your revered commands. Receive the offering of my grim sadness, whether as a denizen of the clear ether you now reject human pursuits as fruitless in comparison to what you

praequam extra nebulas instabilis plagae
    tute intelligis et vides;
seu lucos steriles et nemus Elysi
incedis vacuum perque silentia
15 iucundos comites quos prior abstulit
    hora agnoscis et osculo
occurris tacito. Do, pater, ultimum
munus, quod, Stygios si qua lacus volat
ad vos fama, reor gratius affore,
20   quam si quicquid opum ferant
vel messes Arabum vel Cilicum tuo
ussissem tumulo. Iam, genitor, vale,
aeternumque vale. Has molliter imprimat
    tellus reliquias precor.

: XIII :

Nicolai Areosti Epitaphium

Nicolaus Areostus, insignis comes,
hanc, pridie quam abiret, urnam emit ⟨sibi⟩,
ubi secuturos brevi heredes manet.

: XIV :

Ad Albertum Pium

Fama tuae matris crudeli funere raptae
dudum terrifico nostras, Pie, perculit aures
murmure; sed me adeo stravit dolor improbus, inquam,

understand and see beyond the haze of this inconstant realm, or whether you walk among the barren woods and empty groves of Elysium, recognizing through the silence boon companions, who were taken away at an earlier time, and meeting them with a quiet kiss. This final offering I give you, father. If any word reaches you among the Stygian pools, I think it will be more pleasing than if I had burned all the rich harvest of perfumes from Arabia or Cilicia on your tomb. Now, father, goodbye, and forever goodbye. I pray the ground may press gently on these remains.

: XIII :

Epitaph of Nicolò Ariosto

Nicolò Ariosto, distinguished Count, bought himself this urn on the day before he passed away, where he awaits his heirs who will soon follow.

: XIV :

To Alberto Pio

I was shocked, Pio, when I heard the terrible news that your mother had just been carried off by cruel death. Relentless grief

me, me, Alberte, tuae motus quoscumque sequentem
5   fortunae, ut subito correptus frigore membra
torpuerim, ut gelido titubans vox haeserit ore,
ut stupor insolitus mentem defixerit aegram,
deprensus veluti sub querno tegmine pastor,
cuius glandiferos populatur fulmine ramos
10 Iuppiter, ut rutilo reteguntur lumine silvae
et procul horrenti quatitur nemus omne fragore,
labitur ille impos mentis, rigor occupat artus,
stant immoti oculi, ora immota, immobile pondus.
      Quod tum me censes potuisse effingere carmen
15 ardentique tuo solacia ferre dolori,
vulnere paene pari misere graviterque iacentem?
Ast ubi iam sese desertis sedibus infert,
tristia qui celeri obsedit praecordia cursu
sanguis et exclusos vocat ad sua munia sensus,
20 haec tibi, quae forsan tarda intempestaque sordent
— ne refuge — haud duri canimus solacia casus,
sed potius tacitos renovantia carmina fletus.
Ipse tuis lacrimis lacrimas miscere, gravique
usque etiam cupio tecum certare dolore.
25   An quicquam dignum lacrimis an flebile quicquam
impia pectoribus poterunt immittere nostris
⟨posthac Fata, tuae si non iactura parentis
flebilis et lacrimis non est dignissima nostris,⟩
seu venit in mentem venerandae gratia frontis,
30 qua me quaque alios quoscumque benignus amares,
excipere illa tui merito studiosa solebat;
seu subit illius gravitas condita lepore
eloquii, qua sueta tui placare tumultus
est animi, quondam cum ageret fortuna sinistre
35 cum rebus male fida tuis, ut limina supplex
exutus regno tereres aliena paterno

laid me so low, Alberto—me, the companion of your life's chang-
ing fortunes—that cold gripped my limbs, and I grew numb, my
voice stuck faltering in my icy mouth, my mind in its distress was
stricken with a paralysis like never before. I was caught by surprise
like a shepherd under an oak's leafy canopy when Jupiter ravages
its acorned branches with lightning and the woods light up with a
red glow, and in the distance the whole forest shakes with dread
thunder cracks; the shepherd collapses senseless, his limbs stiffen,
eyes stare fixed, his face does not move, his body a motionless
mass.

What kind of poem do you think I could have composed to
bring consolation to the torment of your grief, when I lay in sor-
row and misery, stricken with a wound almost equal to yours? But
now that the blood, which settled quickly in my sad heart, is re-
turning to the abodes it deserted and summons my baffled senses
to their proper functions, I am composing this poem for you—
which perhaps seems unworthy being slow in coming and un-
timely (don't turn your back on it)—not to console you for this
harsh misfortune but rather to renew your silent weeping. I myself
want to mingle my tears with yours and even to be your constant
rival in deep sorrow.

Is it possible for the evil fates to inflict on our hearts anything
worthy of tears or anything deserving lamentation if the loss of
your mother is not lamentable and not most worthy of tears? No,
not when I remember the grace of her dignified countenance, with
which she, deservedly devoted to you, was accustomed to welcome
me and whoever else enjoyed your generous affection. Or when I
remember her way of speaking with that combination of serious-
ness and wit, with which she was in the habit of soothing your
emotional turmoil at the time when treacherous fortune mali-
ciously upset your affairs so that you were stripped of your father's
kingdom and had to wear down with frequent visits the thresholds

(et quamvis per te multum tibi consulis ipse
nec documenta parum sophiae, quibus impiger omne
impendis studium, prosint, tamen usque fateris
40 iuverit auditae quantum te cura parentis);
sive Pudicitiam tumulo spectamus eodem
exanimem condi, Probitas ubi clara Fidesque,
Religio, Pietasque tua cum matre teguntur?
    Heu, morum exemplar, columen, tutela bonorum,
45 Pica iacet veteris demissa ab origine Pici,
Laurentis Pici, qui te, Saturne, parentem
rettulit (antiqui tu sanguinis ultimus auctor),
Pica atavis generosa, animo generosior alto,
Pica potens opibus, virtute potentior ipsa.
50 Indicium cum saepe sui, tum protulit ingens
prudentis vis illa animi, decor ille modesti,
extincto genitore tuo cum sola relicta est
et formosa et adhuc vel in ipso flore puella,
te puero nondum bimo commune tenente
55 regnum cum patruo et populi Carpensis habenas,
ah! male diversis amborum flexibus aptas,
te puero pueroque simul cognomine patris
fratre Leonello, cuius vix sedula nutrix
invalidum denis numerabat solibus aevum.
60 Tunc tibi, tuncque tuis adeo Pica optima rebus
cavit, ut illi etiam deberi gratia possit
quod validus sceptris et honore fruaris avito.
Tuncque adeo bene consuluit probitate pudori,
tunc et perpetuos quoscumque exegerit annos,
65 ut decus id, laudes hae sint, ea gloria parta,
quae rediviva suas reparant post funera vires.
    Hinc optare proci conubia tanta frequentes,
aut genere aut opibus freti; dein poscere fratres,
primores populi ambire ⟨atque⟩ domestica matrum

of strangers as a suppliant. (And although you yourself are very much your own source of counsel, and the teachings of philosophy, to which you actively devote all your interest, are of no little value, nevertheless you admit all the time how much you were helped by listening to your mother). Or again when we consider that Chastity lies dead and buried in the same tomb where radiant Goodness and Honesty, Reverence and Devotion lie buried with your mother.

Alas, that paragon, pinnacle, guardian of good character, Pica lies dead, descended from the stock of ancient Picus, Picus of Laurentum, who called you, Saturn, father (you are the earliest progenitor of the ancient bloodline). Pica, noble in her ancestors, nobler in her lofty spirit, Pica, powerful in wealth, more powerful in virtue. While she often gave proof of a mind strong in wisdom and decorous in modesty, she did so especially when, after the death of your father, she was left alone, still a girl in the very flower of youth and beauty. You were a child not yet two years old, ruling jointly with your uncle and holding the reins of power for the people of Carpi (sadly, reins poorly suited to changes in direction from two people). You were a child, and so was your brother Leonello, named after his father, an infant barely ten days old according to his diligent nurse's reckoning. Then Pica guarded you and your interests so well that thanks to her, your position is strong, and you enjoy the scepter and the official dignity of your ancestors. Then, and for as long as she lived, she attended so well to her sense of decency in her virtuous behavior, that she won the kind of renown, praise, and glory that live on after death and grow in strength.

From that time forward, crowds of suitors, relying on birth or wealth, desired such a prestigious marriage; they importuned her brothers, they lobbied the leading men of the people, and they availed themselves of their mothers' private counsel and the

70 consilia et crebros monitus adhibere faventum.
Mille petunt; petit ante alios et fervidus instat
ille Bianorei procerum ditissimus agri,
Rodulphus Gonzaga, potens maioribus armis,
inclutus Italia et toto celeberrimus orbe.
75 Tunc cupiunt fratres taedas crepitare secundas
et sibi Rodulphum geniali foedere iungi.
Ergo illam precibus tangunt, rationibus urgent,
utilitate movent sobolis, cui maxima tanti
accedat tutela viri, seu mollius aevum
80 claris formari exemplis, seu regna tueri
consiliove opibusve armisve poposcerit usus.
Quid faciat? tenerae iam primum commoda prolis
anxia pertentant tenerae praecordia matris;
sic tua nimirum vestrae ratione salutis
85 cogitur a viduo genetrix discedere lecto.
Cuius, ubi supra muliebrem provida captum
plenius inspecta a prudenti coniuge mens est,
sic regni ut thalami consors est sumpta virago.
    Tum genetrix tua, cui clare est data copia agendi,
90 iustitiae vindex incorruptissima sacrae,
dura malis, clemens miseris, gratissima iustis,
propositique tenax atque imperterrita recti,
perque gradus cunctos virtutis clara refulsit,
clara refulsit, onus pariter subeunte marito.
95 Clarior at multo vacua cum tristis in aula
magnanimi immatura viri post fata relicta est:
namque diem multa Gallorum caede cruentus
extremum cum laude obiit Mavortius heros
ad vada purpureo spumantia sanguine Tarri,
100 tempore quo spoliis rex agmina onusta Latinis,
rex Carolus, magni Caroli generosa propago,
ad gelidas Sequanae ripas populator agebat.

repeated advice of their supporters. A thousand strong they seek her hand. One man before all others courts her and passionately presses his suit, the richest of the suitors from the territory founded by Bianor, Rodolfo Gonzaga, powerful in mighty arms, famed in Italy, and renowned in the whole world. Then her brothers are eager for auspicious marriage torches to crackle with flame and to join Rodolfo to themselves by the bond of marriage. And so they move her with their entreaties, ply her with their arguments, and impress upon her the advantage for her children, who would come under the preeminent guardianship of so great a man — whether their tender age needed to be molded by famous models or necessity required the defense of the kingdom by good counsel or wealth or arms. What is she to do? Now for the first time the advantages for her young children begin to play on your tender mother's anxious heart. Not surprisingly, consideration of your welfare and that of your siblings compels her to leave her widow's bed. And when her wise husband saw that her intelligence far exceeded a woman's capacity, he took that dauntless lady as the consort both of his kingdom and of his bedchamber.

Then your mother, who was given the opportunity of acting nobly, became an incorruptible defender of sacred justice, pitiless to the wicked, merciful to the unfortunate, kind to the just, steadfast of purpose, and fearless in the right. She shone brightly in every aspect of virtue, a shining light, and her husband bore his responsibilities with equal integrity. But the light of her virtue shone more brightly when she was left mourning in the empty palace after the untimely death of her greathearted husband. That hero, son of Mars, met his final hour with honor, covered in blood from butchering many Frenchmen by the waters of the Taro that foamed with the purplish froth of blood, when King Charles, that plunderer, noble scion of Charles the Great, was leading his ranks, laden with Latin spoils, to the cool banks of the Seine. That day

33

Matribus et trepidis lux detestata puellis,
illa nimis lux saeva, nota signanda perenni,
105   prae cunctis sed, Pica, tibi saevissima luxit.
     En vidua et tutrix iterum maestissima prolis
bis geminae superas; melioris pignora sexus
namque duo et totidem diversi parva fovebas.
An pupillarem prius eloquar auxeris ut rem?
110 An cultu assiduo natorum ut corda paternos
indueris mores? certe rumore secundo
utrumque et multo laudari carmine dignum.
Praeteream sed et ista, sed et connubia natae;
atque his plura sciens, nec possem singula nec fas
115 dicere vel rudibus praesertim nota colonis,
limpidus Ocneis quacumque aut Mincius arvis
inter harundineas it flexo limite ripas
quaque sinus, Benace, tuos imitatus apertos
fluctibus et fremitu et spumantibus aestuat undis;
120 aut Venetas quacumque Padus perlabitur oras,
multa mole minax multoque labore docendus
pinguibus et cultis et aprico parcere ruri.
An quisquam summa virtutum deneget arce
insedisse tuam, generose Alberte, parentem?
125 Aut virtus sermo merus est et inutile nomen
aut opere et claro penitus dignoscitur actu,
cum medio rerum immersabilis enatat aestu.
Heu, heu! quae sceleri debentur digna nefando,
talia virtutum si praemia Pica reportat?
130   Sed quid inepta tuos renovabit Musa dolores?
Sed duce me in lacrimas iterum cur ibis inanes?
Sed quid hians medicae tractabo nescius artis
vulnus, opis quicquam nil post laturus amicae?
Sed quid ego ereptae crudelia fata parentis
135 in medium proferre loquaci carmine nitar,

was cursed by mothers and trembling girls, that cruel day, forever branded with a black mark, but cruelest for you, Pica, beyond all other women.

Now once again a widow, you were left in your grief to care for four children; two of the stronger sex and two of the opposite sex, the tender pledges of marriage, you cradled in your love. Shall I describe first how you increased the property of those fatherless children? Or how through careful education you instilled their father's character in their hearts? Both, to be sure, deserve public praise and celebration in poetry. But let me pass over these things, and the marriage of your daughter as well. And though I know there is far more to tell, I would not be able to describe everything in detail — nor would it be right to do so, especially since your actions are known even to coarse farmers, wherever the crystal clear Mincius goes its winding way between reed covered banks in the fields of Ocnus; or where, taking the shape of your expansive lake, Benacus, it swells with the resounding surge of foaming waves; or wherever the Po glides through Venetian territory, menacing in its massive flow, a river which must be trained with great effort not to harm the fertile farms and the sunny countryside. Is there anyone, noble Alberto, who would deny that your mother was a towering bastion of virtue? Either virtue is nothing but talk and an empty name, or it appears in our distinguished acts and deeds as we float on the sea of troubles. Alas, alas! What fit penalty is there for unspeakable crimes, if this is the reward Pica reaps for her virtues?

But why shall my Muse thoughtlessly renew your pain? Why shall I be the cause of your crying unavailing tears again? Why shall I, who know nothing of the healer's art, handle your open wound, when afterward I will not be able to bring any helpful assistance? Why shall I strive to make public your mother's fate — snatched by a cruel death — in a prattling poem, when I can offer

cum neque succurrat ratio solaminis ulla,
qua tot deinde queam fluctus, quos ipse citarim
imprudens, animique graves componere motus?
　At reticenda nec est ea mors, cui maxima virtus
140　causa fuit: nec enim vas exitiale cicutae
vult Aniti latuisse reus, nec Virbius axes,
ancillae nec Pica feros quibus occidit ausus.
Liberius iam iam res ut sit facta docebo,
unde queant magnum venientia ducere saecla
145　exemplum, humano leviter quam fidere quisquam
ingenio possit; documento nec fuit illa
absque aliquo moriens, cuius dum vita manebat
omne olim fuerat studiis imitabile factum.
Illa severa adeo cultrix Italique pudoris
150　custos, illa adeo vindex labentis honesti
extitit, ut facto turpi curaret ab omni
et levibus licet opprobriis pulchrasque sodales
ancillasque domumque omnem servare pudicam,
nedum se similemque sui, castissima, prolem;
155　cui dum se digno ferventius haeret et instat
proposito, in sese muliebris suscitat iram
flagrantem ingenii, quod amor furiavit iniquus
et male suada Venus. Quid non vesana libido
mersa cupidinibus mortalia pectora cogit?

: XV :

Ad Herculem Strozzam

Audivi et timeo ne veri nuntia fama
　sit quae multorum pervolat ora frequens.
Scin verum, quaeso? scin tu, Strozza? eia age, fare;

no solace to quell the many painful waves of turmoil in your heart
that I myself thoughtlessly stirred up?

But I cannot keep silent about her death, when highest virtue
was its cause. The defendant accused by Anytus does not want the
fatal cup of hemlock to be a secret, nor Virbius his deadly chariot
ride, nor Pica her maid's savage schemes by which she met her
death. Now I will openly tell how it happened so that coming ages
may draw an important lesson from it: how little we can trust hu-
man nature. As in life her every deed had once been a model for
eager imitation, so even in death she had a lesson to teach. She
showed herself to be such a strict keeper and guardian of Italian
moral decency, such a defender against lapses in goodness that she
took care to keep her noble companions, her maidservants, and
her entire household—not to mention herself and her children—
so like herself, the model of chastity, pure from every kind of
shameful behavior and from causes of reproach, however slight.
While she held to this purpose, true to her character, and intent
upon it with passionate urgency, she aroused against herself the
burning anger of a woman's heart that was driven mad by wrong-
ful love and cozening Venus. To what does mad passion, sunk
deep in lustful desires, not drive human hearts?

: XV :

To Ercole Strozzi

I've heard and I fear that the rumor making the rounds on many
people's lips brings a true message. Do you know the truth? Please
tell me. Do you know, Strozzi? Come, tell me. Your word would

maior quam populi, Strozza, fides tua sit.

5   An noster fluvio misere. . . ? Heu, timeo omnia! at illa,
     di, prohibete et eant irrita verba mea,
et redeat sociis hilari ore suasque Marullus
     ante obitum ridens audiat inferias.
Fama tamen vatem, sinuoso vortice raptum,
10   dulciloquam fluvio flasse refert animam.
Scin verum, quaeso? scin tu, Strozza? eia age, fare;
     maior quam populi, Strozza, fides tua sit.
Vt timeo! nam vana solet plerumque referre
     fama bonum; at nisi non vera referre malum.
15   Quamque magis referat saevum, crudele, nefandum,
     pro superi! est illi tam mage habenda fides.
Quid potuit gravius deferri hoc tempore nobis,
     qui sumus in Phoebi Pieridumque fide,
quam mors divini (si vera est fama) Marulli?
20   Iuppiter, ut populi murmura vana fluant!
Scin verum, quaeso? scin tu, Strozza? eia age, fare;
     maior quam populi, Strozza, fides tua sit.
Nam foret haec gravior iactura mihique tibique,
     et quemcumque sacrae Phocidos antra iuvent,
25   quam vidisse mala tempestate (improba saecli
     condicio!) clades et Latii interitum,
nuper ab occiduis illatum gentibus, olim
     pressa quibus nostro colla fuere iugo.
Quid nostra an Gallo regi an servire Latino,
30   si sit idem hinc atque hinc non leve servitium?
Barbaricone esse est peius sub nomine, quam sub
     moribus et ducibus — di, date digna — malis.
Quorum quam imperium gliscente tyrannide tellus
     Saturni Gallos pertulit ante truces!
35   Et servate diu doctumque piumque Marullum,

mean more than the crowd's. Can it be that our friend in a river
pitifully. . . ? Oh, I am afraid to say the rest. You gods, avert it and
let my words prove empty. And let Marullus return to his com-
panions with a cheerful face, and, laughing, hear his own funeral
rites before his death. But rumor reports that the bard was
snatched up in a swirling whirlpool and breathed forth his sweet-
voiced soul in the river. Do you know the truth? Please tell me.
Do you know, Strozzi? Come, tell me. Your word would mean
more than the crowd's. How fearful I am! Rumors that bring good
news are usually false; but a rumor bringing bad news is usually
true. The harsher, the crueler, the more unspeakable the news it
brings, good God, the more it must be believed. What more griev-
ous news could come now to those of us in the care of Phoebus
and the Pierian Muses, than the death, if the rumor is true, of
divine Marullus? Jupiter, if only the mutterings of the crowd
would drift idly away. Do you know the truth? Please tell me. Do
you know, Strozzi? Come, tell me. Your word would mean more
than the crowd's. For this loss would weigh more heavily on you
and me and on all who love the grottoes of sacred Phocis than
when we saw the devastation and destruction of Italy in a ruinous
storm of strife (shameless condition of the age!) recently inflicted
by the western peoples whose necks once bore our yoke. What
does it matter to us whether we are slaves to a French or an Italian
king if the enslavement — no easy burden — is the same in either
case? Is it worse to live under a foreign name than under corrupt
morals and bad leaders? — you gods, give them what they deserve!
How the land of Saturn endured their rule, as their tyranny
swelled, long before the savage French! Keep Marullus safe — that

redditeque actutum sospitem eum sociis;
    qui poterit dulci eloquio monitisque severis,
        quos Musarum haustus plurimo ab amne tulit,
    liberam et immunem, vincto etsi corpore, mentem
40   reddere et omne animo tollere servitium.
    Sit satis abreptum nuper flevisse parentem;
        ah, grave tot me uno tempore damna pati!
    Tarchaniota aura aetheria vescatur; et inde
        cetera sint animo damna ferenda bono.
45 Scin verum, quaeso? scin tu, Strozza? eia age, fare;
        maior quam populi, Strozza, fides tua sit.
    At iuvat hoc potius sperare, quod opto: Marullum
        iam videor laeta fronte videre meum.
    An quid obest sperare homini dum grata sinit res?
50   Heu, lacrimis semper sat mora longa datur.

: XVI :

Cosmici Epitaphium

Hospes, siste parumper hocque munus
habe et parva brevis morae repende
damna, quod patris elegantiarum,
Romanae patris eruditionis,
5 vides Cosmici Apolline et sororum
urnam Pieridum choro frequentem.
Sed munus tenue est, sed est pusillum,
prae quod vate frui, manente vita,
tam comi et lepido tibi fuisset.
10 Rursus nec tenue est nec est pusillum,
cui non contigerit, manente vita,

learned and pious man — and return him instantly to his compan-
ions unharmed. With his sweet eloquence and stern warnings,
drunk in from the bountiful stream of the Muses, he can make
our minds free and unfettered, even if our bodies are bound, and
banish slavery from our spirits. Let it be enough to have wept re-
cently for a father who was taken from me. Oh, it is a grievous
thing for me to endure so many losses at one time! If only Marul-
lus Tarchaniota still feeds on the upper-air breezes: then I could
bear the other losses with a resolute heart. Do you know the
truth? Please tell me. Do you know, Strozzi? Come, tell me. Your
word would be worth more than the crowd's. Yet, it does more
good to hope for what I desire; now I seem to see my Marullus
looking happy. Does it do a man any harm to hope as long as fa-
vorable circumstance permits? Alas, there is always time enough
for tears.

: XVI :

Epitaph of Niccolò Cosmico

Stop a moment, stranger: take this gift and receive recompense for
the small loss of a short delay. For you look upon the urn of the
father of elegant expression, the father of Roman learning, Cos-
mico, attended by Apollo and the chorus of Pierian sisters. It is a
small gift, a mere trifle compared to what you would have had, if
you had been able to enjoy the living presence of so cultured and
charming a poet. On the other hand, for a person who did not
have a chance to enjoy one so cultured and charming while he was

tam comi et lepido frui, videre
saltem Cosmici Apolline et sororum
urnam Pieridum choro frequentem.

: XVIa :

Epitaphium (F)

Paulum siste, viator, et tibi sit
munus, quod patris elegantiarum
et cultae simul eruditionis
Laeli Cosmici amabilem videbis
5 urnam et Pieridum choro frequentem.
Est munus tenue, est nimis pusillum,
prae quo vate frui, manente vita,
tam comi et lepido tibi fuisset.
Rursus nec tenue est nec est pusillum,
10 cui non contigerit, manente vita,
tam comi et lepido frui poeta,
saltem reliquias videre; nam quae
rari notitia et boni et probati
detur quantulacumque amanda est.

: XVII :

De Megilla

Illius timidis spes sit amoribus,
qui formae comitem ferre superbiam,
   centenamque repulsam

alive, to look, at least, upon the urn of Cosmico, attended by Apollo and the Pierian sisters, is a gift neither slight nor small.

: XVIa :

Epitaph (F)

Stop a moment, traveler, and let this be your gift, that you will look upon the urn of the father of elegant expression and refined learning, Lelio Cosmico, a lovely urn attended by the chorus of Pierian goddesses; it is a small gift, quite a trifle compared to what you would have had, if you had been able to enjoy the living presence of so cultured and charming a poet. On the other hand, for a person who did not have a chance to enjoy so cultured and charming a poet while he was alive, to look, at least, upon his remains is a gift neither slight nor small. For what is given in recognition of a rare, good and estimable man, however small it may be, deserves to be loved.

: XVII :

Megilla

Let the fearful lover have hope, if he has been able to bear with a light heart the conceited *hauteur* that is beauty's companion and to

leni pectore quiverit;
5 qui surdos tulerit tot querimoniis
postes, dum glomerat trux Boreas nives,
    miraturque suam vim
      tantis vincier ignibus;
qui rivalem animo viderit integro
10 offensum, totiens limen amabile
    noctu praetereuntem,
      quod vel iurgia spreverit,
iras, nequitias, instabilem fidem,
et quicquid dominae saevities tulit.
15   Illum mater Amorum,
      mater blanda Cupidinum,
tandem audit, precibus victa diutinis,
et finem tepidis luctibus imperat,
    durae corda puellae
20   divino insiliens pede,
non oblita facis quam Cinyreius
excivit iuvenis, quam Phrygius prope
    Idaeum Simoenta,
      quam Mars bellipotens pater.
25 Illi fert gremio pleno Amathuntia
lusus, illecebras, delicias, iocos,
    risus, quicquid et almo est
      regno dulce Cupidinum.
En me, quem lacrimis, quem miseris modis
30 mersum ludibrio longum habuit puer,
    spretor divum hominumque,
      en hac luce beat Venus.
O signanda dies non modo candida
nota de veteri more Cydonio,
35   sed sacro celebranda
      nobis iugiter annuo!

bear being rejected a hundred times; if he has endured doors deaf to so many complaints, while brutal Boreas was piling on the snow and was marveling that love's flames survive his onslaught; if he has seen his rival again and again crossing his beloved's threshold at night and has met him calmly because he has renounced quarrels, angry outbursts, naughty behavior, inconstancy, and whatever else his mistress's cruelty has inflicted. At last, the mother of *Amores*, the sweet mother of Cupids hears him, won over by his persistent prayers, and orders an end to his warm tears. Striding with a goddess's step, she leaps onto the unfeeling girl's heart, recalling the flames kindled by the youthful son of Cinyras, by the Phrygian shepherd beside the river Simois near Mount Ida, and by father Mars mighty in war. From her overflowing bosom, the goddess of Cyprian Amathus brings him games, allurements, pleasures, playful banter and laughter, all the sweet delights that come under the gracious reign of the Cupids. Now look at me! For so long that boy — Cupid, despiser of gods and men — made me a laughingstock, drowning me in tears and misery. See how Venus smiles on me today. O day that we will not only note with a white mark after the ancient Cydonian custom but that we will celebrate

Lux, qua plena meis amplaque gaudia
commuto lacrimis, quaque laboribus
   munus grande reporto!
40   O solacia suavia!
Fallorne? An placida somnus imagine
ludit me, ut miseris questibus obviet?
   An haec vera Megilla
     cuius detineor sinu?
45 Haec, haec vera mea est; nil modo fallimur,
mi anceps anime: en sume cupita iam
   mellita oscula, sume
     expectata diu bona.

: XVIII :

De Iulia

Qualem scientem carminis et lyra
Sappho sonantem molliter aurea,
   expertem amorum atque integellam
     floris adhuc nimium caduci,
5 vocavit altis e penetralibus
pubentis agri conspicuus nitor,
   herbaeque flosculique hiantes
     flatibus egelidis Favoni;
mox dithyrambos Aeoliae impulit
10 testudini committere spiritus
   strepens per altas ilices et
     murmur aquae prope defluentis;
qualemve doctam Calliopen modos,
cui rex deorum sistere tinnula

ever after with yearly rites! Day on which I trade my tears for full
and copious joys and bring back a splendid reward for my labors!
O sweet satisfaction! Am I deceived? Is this a dream that mocks
me with its calming sights to appease my pitiful complaints? Or is
this the real Megilla who holds me in her arms? Yes, yes, it's really
her and she's mine. I am not at all deceived, my doubtful mind. So
now, take honey-sweet kisses long desired, take joys long awaited.

: XVIII :

Julia

Like Sappho, skilled in song and playing gently on her golden lyre,
inexperienced in love and still whole in virginity's all too fleeting
bloom—Sappho, whom the arresting splendor of the flourishing
field and the grass and the flowers opening under cool western
breezes called from deep within her room; whom the breeze whis-
tling through the tall holm oaks and the murmur of the water
flowing nearby soon inspired to compose dithyrambs on her Aeo-
lian lyre. Or like Calliope, learned in musical measures, to whom
Jupiter, king of the gods, gave the power to stop rivers with her
ringing voice in recognition of her fair-haired mother's service—
Calliope whom the company of the gods at banquet heard (at ease

15   permisit amnes voce flavae
          Iuppiter ob meritum parentis,
      audivit olim libera caelitum
      iam iam fugatis mensa Gigantibus
          manum Tonantis et deorum
20   praesidium ad citharam canentem,
      audivi eburno pollice Iuliam
      chordas moventem Threiciae fidis,
          et arte iucundos magistra
              ad numerum strepitus citantem,
25   et ora vernis aemula floribus
      solventem acutis vocibus in modum,
          nervosque vocales decenter
              carminibus sociantem Etruscis,
      cantusque presso gutture mobiles
30   ducentem ad auras per tremulas prius
          flexosque concisosque fauces,
              murmure nunc tacito volutos,
      nunc plena in aurem voce refractulos,
      quibus nigranti cedit ab arbore
35   in roscidis quicquid virectis
              vere canit volucrum tepente.
      Vt ut canoros quaero iterum modos!
      Vt ut mihi me surripuit melos!
          Nec mecum adhuc sum; adhuc hiulco
40   nescit abire animus labello!
      Nec si sciat, vult mitti; adeo et bona et
      grata tenetur compede. Iam mihi est
          adempta libertas nec haustu
              Elysiae reparanda Lethes.
45   Si tale Siren, stirps Acheloia,
      nautis canebat praetereuntibus,
          nil miror aversas carinas

now that the Giants had been put to flight), as she sang with her lyre of the violent handiwork of Jupiter the Thunderer and his divine defenders. Julia was like Sappho or Calliope, when I heard her play the strings of her Thracian lyre with an ivory plectrum. With art as her guide, she brought forth delightfully rhythmical sounds and uttered trilling melodious words with lips like spring flowers, gracefully accompanying her tuneful notes with Tuscan verses, as, with throat compressed, she guided her song through her quavering lips to the shifting breezes, at first modulated in pitch and staccato, now *legato* and *sotto voce*, now echoing *fortissimo* upon the ear — with such songs the birds singing in the dewy greenery in spring's warmth take flight from the tree's deep woven shade. How I keep searching for that melodious music again! How her song robbed me of my own self! I am still not in possession of myself; my soul still cannot turn from her open lips — and even if it could, it would not wish to, so strong and so pleasing is the chain that holds me. My freedom has been taken from me and cannot be restored with a drink from Elysian Lethe. If the Siren, offspring of Achelous, was singing such a song as this to sailors as they sailed by, I do not wonder that hollow ships changed course

sponte cavas adiisse rupes.
Nescis tu, Vlysseu, qui fugis illitis
50   cera Pelasgi remigis auribus,
        inter puellarum choros tam
            dulce canentium obire felix.

:   XIX   :

De vellere aureo

O pubis iuvenes robora Thessalae,
perculsi toties qui pelagi minis,
        pellem avertere Colchis
            auratam cupitis tamen,
5   olim pollicita est vobis ut innuba
Pallas velivolam cum daret aequori
        pinum, quam sub opaci
            flexit vertice Pelii,
cur non lecta manus fortiter occupat
10   portus Phasiacos, dum Boreae silet,
        vestris saepe sinistri
            votis, spiritus impotens?
En vobis spolium tempus apiscier
famosae pecudis limine, quod diu
15   servavere dracones
            Martisque ignivomi boves.
Insomnes etenim destituit vigil
serpens excubias, ut fera beluis
        olim infensa marinis,
20   post terrestribus aspera
et nunc vipereas in latebras ruens,

and of their own accord sped toward the rocks. You, Ulysses, who escape because your Pelasgian rowers have their ears stopped with wax, don't know how to meet a happy death amid that chorus of girls singing so sweetly.

: XIX :

The Golden Fleece

You young men, backbone of Thessaly's manpower, you who, though battered so many times by the menacing sea, still long to carry off the golden fleece from Colchis, as the virgin goddess Pallas promised long ago when she launched the sail-flying ship of pine on the sea, which she fashioned beneath the summit of shadowy Mt. Pelion—young men, why is a band of picked men not making port at the river Phasis, while the wild blasts of Boreas, often harmful to your enterprise, lie silent? Yes, now is the time for you to seize from its precinct the legendary ram's fleece, which serpents and Mars's fire-breathing bulls have long guarded. For the watchful serpent now abandons its sleepless vigil because a wild beast, once hostile to sea creatures, then savage to creatures on land, is now attacking the serpent in its lair and driving it off,

illum sanguineis unguibus undique
    pressum turbat et ore
      semper caedibus oblito.

: XX :

De catella puellae

Quis solaciolum meum, meos quis
lusus, quis mea gaudia, heu, catellam,
erae mnemosynon meae catellam,
quis, ah, quis misero mihi involavit?
5 Quis, ah, quis malus, improbus, scelestus
tam bellam mihi tamque blandientem,
tamque molliculam abstulit catellam?
Furum pessime et omnium malorum
quisquis candidulam mihi catellam,
10 erae mnemosynon meae catellam,
meas delicias, meique amoris
et desiderii mei levamen,
nostras praeteriens fores, dolose
manu sub tunicam rapis sinistra!
15 At di dent mala multa, di deaeque
dent omnes tibi, quisquis es, sceleste,
actutum mihi ni meam catellam,
erae mnemosynon meae, remittis.

clenching it with its bloody talons and with its mouth ever smeared with gore.

: XX :

His Girlfriend's Puppy

Who was it? Who swooped down and stole from me my little bundle of comfort, my playful darling, my delight, alas my puppy, my puppy, keepsake from my mistress? Who, O who stole my puppy from me and made me miserable? What creep, what crook, what criminal stole so cute, so affectionate, so soft a puppy? Wickedest of thieves and worst of all bad men, whoever you are, who passing by my door sneakily filch my white puppy with thieving hand under your tunic, my puppy, keepsake from my mistress, my pet, solace of my love and my longing. Well then, may the gods, may all the gods and goddesses give you troubles aplenty, whoever you are, you criminal, if you don't return to me right away my puppy, keepsake from my mistress.

: XXI :

[In lenam] sine inscriptione (F)

Abi, vorax anus, tuis cum blandulis
istis susurris; cognita est mihi satis
superque vestra (serius licet) fides.
Non sum ille ego in quem impune vobis ludere
5   fas iugiter sit feminis rapacibus.
Vt ut piget me tam diu fallaciis
vestris retentum, dum miser dari reor
dulces mihi fructus amoris unice,
quos comperi post, cum pudore maxumo,
10 illi datos et illi et illi et omnibus
ementibus pernicioso munere
adulterarum coitus foedissimos!
Viden ut audax me rogat, tamquam inscium
eius probrosi criminis? Recede, abi,
15 abi, impudica, abi, scelesta et impia,
impura lena, venditrix libidinum,
meorum amorum prostitutrix lurida.
Vt ira suadet unguibus nocentia
proscindere ora! Vt gliscit impetus ferox
20 inferre canis crinibus truces manus!
Impunis anne abibit haec venefica?
Iam iam cupidini morem geram meo
et torva lumina eruam isti primulum,
linguam deinde demetam dicaculam,
25 quae me misellum effecit et pessumdedit
et perdidit nullumque prorsus reddidit.
Quid me, sodales, detinetis pessumi?
Dimittite; est certum obsequi iustissimo

: XXI :

[Against the Procuress] no title (F)

Enough, you insatiable old crow! Enough with those wheedling
whispers of yours! I know your honesty well enough, too well,
though it's too late. I'm not the kind of man that a greedy woman
like you is free to dupe again and again and get away with it. How
it disgusts me that for so long I was held in thrall by your tricks,
all the while thinking in my misery that the sweet enjoyments of a
love were being given to me alone, when, as I later found out with
the greatest shame, they were given to this guy and that and an-
other, to everybody who buys vile intercourse with adulterous
women at a ruinous price! Do you see what nerve she has to ask
me, as if I were unaware of her disgraceful behavior? Get out of
my sight. Go. Go, you slut. Go, you infamy and desecration, slag,
pander, peddler of lusts, sallow prostitutor of my love. How anger
urges me to rend your guilty face with my nails! How a wild im-
pulse swells in me to lay violent hands on your pasty white hair!
Or will this witch get away unpunished? At this moment I'm on
the verge of following my instinct; first, I'll rip out those cruel eyes
of hers, then I'll cut off the smart-talking tongue that has made
me miserable, has ruined me, destroyed me, has made me an utter
wreck. Why do you hold me back, disloyal friends? Let me go. I'm

    meo furori; debitas poenas luat
30 mihi scelesta. An huic, rogo, favebitis,
    fortasse nescii quam inexpiabile
    scelus patretis hanc iuvantes impiam,
    quam saepe nocte repperi obscurissima
    sacros cadaverum eruentem pulveres,
35 diroque carmine evocantem pallidas
    umbras ab Orci tristibus silentiis?
    Haec noxio infantes tenellos fascino
    interficit. Discedite, ut poenas luat.
    At si meae vos nil preces iustae movent,
40 in pessimam crucem recedat pessima;
    non usque habebit vos paratos subsides.

: XXII :

sine inscriptione (F)

    ⟨Infelix a⟩nime et miser, quid ultro
    ipsum te crucias? tuos quid ultro,
    ah vere miser, excitas fovesque
    ignes? nec minimae tibi quietis
5 tantillum esse sinis, vigil diesque
    noctesque ad nitidos hians ocellos,
    os ad purpureum genasque molles,
    ad guttur niveum manusque leves,
    formam denique ad integram puellae,
10 formam non tamen integrae puellae,
    ausae delicias meosque lusus . . .
    Dicamne an sileam? Ah quid ah silebo?

determined to give vent to my justified rage. Let the infamous woman pay the penalty owed to me. Or will you, I ask, support her, ignorant perhaps of what an unpardonable crime you commit by helping this desecrator? Often I have found her in darkest night digging up the sacred dust of dead bodies and, with fearful incantations, summoning pale shades from the gloomy silence of Orcus. This woman kills tender little infants with her evil spells. Leave me so that she may pay the penalty. But if my just prayers don't move you at all, may the damnable woman drop into the deepest damnation. She will not have you at the ready to help her all the time.

: XXII :

no title (F)

My heart, so very unhappy and suffering, why do you deliberately torture yourself? Why do you deliberately stir up and fan the fires, o miserable heart? You don't allow yourself the smallest bit of rest, awake day and night, intently gazing at her radiant darling eyes, her crimson mouth, her soft cheeks, her snow-white neck and delicate hands—in short, at the girl's untouched beauty. But it's the beauty of a girl who is not untouched, who took the pleasures of lovemaking that were mine and dared to . . . Should I speak or

Ausa est perfida et improba et scelesta,
ausa est delicias meosque lusus
15   auro vendere, nec deum potentem
pavit fallere saepe deieratum.
Infelix anime, ecquid impudica,
ecquid te meretrix avara perdet?
Respira atque tibi potens vigensque
20   te redde, utque lubet sine impudicam
moechis vivere cum suis. Tibine
os spurca placet oblitum saliva
et livens memori nota perenne
foedae, pro dolor!, osculationis?
25   An te illi ebrioli movent ocelli
illi quos movet hic et hic et ille et
quisquis dedecorum putetur emptor?
Obdura, mi anime, improba et puella
cum moechis valeat suis, puella
30   igne indigna tuo. Potestne, quaeso,
quod felicius ardeas deesse?

∶   XXIII   ∶

De Lydia

Haec certe Lepidi sunt Regia moenia, quae sic
  grata mihi paucos ante fuere dies,
Lydia dum patrios coleret formosa penates,
  redderet et forma cuncta serena sua.
5   Nunc, ut ab illis immutata! quid illius, eheu!
  illius amota luce decoris habent,
illius a cara quae me genetrice domoque

keep silent? Oh, why keep silent! Treacherous, wicked, unscrupulous, she dared to sell the pleasures of lovemaking that were mine for gold and wasn't afraid to betray the mighty god by swearing oaths again and again in his name.

Unhappy heart, it can't be, can it, that a filthy, greedy courtesan—it can't be, can it, that she will destroy you? Take a moment, recover your strength, take control of yourself and let the filthy woman live as she please with her adulterers. Is her mouth pleasing to you, smeared with slimy saliva and discolored with a mark that constantly reminds you of her gross kissing? It kills me to think of it! Or do those tipsy darling eyes excite you, those eyes that are excited by this guy and that and another and whoever is considered a buyer of disgraceful acts. Be firm, my heart and let that wicked girl thrive with her adulterers; she's not worthy of your passion. Can it be, I ask you, that there's no chance you'll have a happier love?

: XXIII :

Lydia

This is indeed the city of Reggio, founded by Lepidus, which just a few days ago was so welcome to me, while the beautiful Lydia was living in her father's house, making everything around her bright with her beauty. But now how changed the city is from what once it was! What attraction does it hold when the radiance of that woman—ah, that woman—is gone, that woman who for so many harvests had the power to keep me far away from my dear

tot valuit messes detinuisse procul?
Tu sine me tacitis excedere, Lydia, portis,
10   tu sine me potis es rura videre tua?
Cur comitem me, dura, negas admittere? Curve
   sarcina sum raedae visa onerosa tuae?
In tua non adeo peccarem commoda demens,
   artius ut premerem terga latusve tuum!
15 Conductus non deerat equus, non deerat amicus
   iuvisset mannis qui mea vota suis.
Ipse pedes validis potui decurrere plantis,
   sive terenda brevis seu via longa fuit.
Ah, ego (vita, modo sineres) quam fortiter irem,
20   sisteret ut nullus crura citata labor!
Corruptum nec iter hieme et pluvialibus austris
   suasisset iustas, te properante, moras.
Sum sine te biduum. An me ultra patieris abesse?
   Heu miserum me! me, quaeso, venire iube.
25 Ecquid habent gelidi montes et inhospita tesqua,
   ecquid habent sine me devia rura boni?
Quaeso, venire iube. Placeant tum lustra ferarum,
   atque feris arces montibus impositae;
tum placeant silvae, tunc sint gratissima saxa,
30   dum latus ipse tegam, duxque comesque, tuum.
Tunc iuvet audaci lepores agitare Lacone,
   caecaque nocturnis ponere vincla lupis,
inque plagas turdum strepitu detrudere edacem,
   et quaecumque hiemes gaudia rure ferunt.
35 Quaeso, venire iube. Quod si mala murmura vulgi
   ne cieam veniens est timor, ipsa redi.

mother and my home. Without me, Lydia, can you go out through the silent gates, without me can you look upon your fields? Why do you, hard woman, refuse to take me as your companion? Why am I seen as a pile of baggage overburdening your wagon? I wouldn't so recklessly offend against your comfort so as to press your back or side too tightly! I even had a hired horse, and a friend who would have aided my prayers with his ponies. Taking to my feet, I could have run on my sturdy soles, whether the road to be traveled was short or long. Oh, how energetically I would have walked (if only, my life, you allowed me), no strain would have slowed my speedy legs. The route, even if rutted by storms and rainy south winds, would not have prevailed on me to justify delay while you were hurrying on. Two days I've been without you. Will you endure my absence longer? I'm so unhappy. Tell me, I beg you, tell me to come. Do the icy mountains hold any enjoyment without me? The inhospitable wilderness? The remote countryside? I beg you, tell me to come. Then the lairs of wild beasts and forbidding mountain peaks would be pleasing; then forests would be pleasing, then rocky scenery would be most welcome, as long as I am at your side to protect you, your guide and companion. Then it would be pleasing to hunt rabbits with a dauntless Spartan dog and to set hidden snares for wolves prowling at night and to drive greedy thrushes into nets, and whatever enjoyable pastimes winter brings in the country. I beg you, tell me to come. But if you fear that my coming will stir up the crowd's malicious mutterings, come back here yourself.

: XXIV :

sine inscriptione (F)

Istos, quaeso, oculos operi, dum cetera lustrem
   spectator formae, Lydia bella, tuae;
namque meos hebetant sensus prohibentque tueri
   quam sit digna oculis pars tua quaeque tuis.

: XXV :

Bacchi statua (EP) sine inscriptione (F)

'Quid causae, aeterna frueris quod, Bacche, iuventa
   vel sene qui multo grandior es Pylio?'
'Est quod vino, hospes, genioque indulgeo; quod non
   ambitio mentem distrahit ulla meam.'
5 'Cur te nulla operit vestis, cum casta puella
   saepe puerque tuos cursitet ante pedes?'
'Vt doceam sic et nudari cuncta mea vi,
   conscia qui multo torqueo corda mero.'
'Aspera quid sibi vult frons cornibus?' 'Indicat ut sim
10   Martia siccato promptus ad arma scypho.'
'Cur Nysa, Thebis, Dia, Citherone relictis,
   Boiardae cordi sunt tibi prela domus?'

: XXIV :

no title (F)

Close those eyes of yours, please, Lydia my belle, while I take a tour of your other attractions. They dull my senses and prevent me from seeing how every part of you complements your eyes.

: XXV :

Statue of Bacchus (EP) no title (F)

(*Stranger*): What is the reason, Bacchus, that you enjoy eternal youth, even though you are older than the old man of Pylos?

(*Bacchus*): The reason is, stranger, that I indulge my penchant for wine and pleasure, and my mind isn't distressed by any form of ambition.

(*Stranger*): Why isn't there a stitch of clothing on you, when innocent boys and girls often run back and forth before your feet?

(*Bacchus*): It's so that I can show, in the buff, that I have the power even to strip everything naked, tormenting hearts that have something to tell when they have had a lot to drink.

(*Stranger*): What does it mean that you have spiky horns on your forehead?

(*Bacchus*): It means that I'm ready for armed conflict when the drinking cup has been drained dry.

(*Stranger*): Why, when you leave Nysa, Thebes, Dia, and Cithaeron behind, do you hold dear to your heart the wine-presses in the house of Boiardo?

'Quod praestant cunctis hic vina, quod impius illic
    pro! mos nunc gelida Massica mutat aqua.'
15 'Cur neque adest satyrus neque lynx trahit esseda pictus
    concitus hic thyrso, concitus ille mero?'
'Ne feritas huius, ne huius petulantia quemquam
    terreat a nostro limine cavit erus.
Sed iam iam ingredere, ut, quem vanum forte putasti,
20   ostendant verum pocula plena deum.'

∶ XXVI ∶

Ad Bacchum (EP) sine inscriptione (F)

Quod semper vino madidus somnique benignus,
    securus pendis nil nisi quod placeat,
laetitia frueris nimirum, Bacche, perenni
    exarat et frontem nulla senecta tuam.
5 Sic quicumque pedem tua per vestigia ponet,
    exiget in multa saecula longa rosa.

∶ XXVII ∶

De Baccho (EP) sine inscriptione (F)

Qui non castus adis Bacchi penetralia, non te
    flumine, sed multo prolue rite mero.

(*Bacchus*): Because the wine here surpasses all others and because over there — heaven help us! — by an unnatural custom Massic wine is spoiled with cold water.

(*Stranger*): Why isn't there a satyr nearby or a spotted lynx drawing your chariot, the lynx stirred up by the thyrsus, the satyr by wine?

(*Bacchus*): The owner has taken care that the savage lynx and the rowdy satyr won't scare anyone away from our threshold. But it's time you step inside so that brimming cups may prove that the god who perhaps you thought was a phony is a real god.

: XXVI :

To Bacchus (EP) no title (F)

Since you haven't got a care in the world, except what pleases you, always soused with wine and fond of sleeping, it's not surprising, Bacchus, that you enjoy uninterrupted happiness, and old age doesn't plow furrows in your brow. So, whoever follows in your footsteps, will live for ages on a bed of roses.

: XXVII :

On Bacchus (EP) no title (F)

You who are unclean and approach Bacchus's inner sanctum, purify yourself according to ritual not with running water but with plenty of wine.

: XXVIII :

sine inscriptione (E)

Vna vivamus, sed sic vivamus, amici,
　　una ut diu possimus una vivere.
et dum nos fata esse sinunt, ut nos decet esse
　　simus, scientes quod diu esse non sinunt.

: XXIX :

De Eulalia (EP) sine inscriptione (F)

Vt bella, ut blanda, ut lepida utque venustula ludit
　　Eulalia, Hispanae filia Pasiphiles!
Vt bene maternos imitatur parvula mores!
　　Incedit, spectat, ridet, agit, loquitur,
5　omnia ut illa facit tandem iam fingere novit
　　et sibi de tenero quos amet ungue legit.
O bona sectatrix matris nata, o bona mater
　　tam bene dilectam quae instituis sobolem,
ut tibi quandocumque obrepat inertior aetas,
10　　cum meretrix nequeas vivere, lena queas!

: XXVIII :

no title (E)

Friends, let us live together, but let us live together in such a way that we can live together for a long time. And while the fates allow us to have life, let us have life as befits us, knowing that the fates don't allow life to last for long.

: XXIX :

Eulalia (EP) no title (F)

How lovely, how charming, how delightful, how delicious Eulalia is when she's having fun! She's the daughter of Pasiphile who comes from Spain. How well the little one imitates the ways of her mother, the way she walks, the way she casts a glance, the way she smiles, the way she gestures, the way she talks; in short, she knows how to fashion herself in every way like her mother and chooses at her tender age who her lovers will be. Child, what an excellent student of your mother you are! Good mother, what an excellent teacher of your beloved daughter you are! You've done your job so well that, whenever old age creeps up on you and slows you down and you can't live as a courtesan, you can live as a procuress.

: XXX :

De Iulia

O rarum formae decus, o lepidissima verba,
  o bene deductum pollice et ore melos!
An Charitum quarta, an Venus altera, an addita Musis
  est decima, an simul haec Gratia, Musa, Venus?
5 Iulia quin sola est, qua cantu Musa, lepore
  Gratia, qua longe est victa decore Venus.

: XXXI :

De Veronica (EP) sine inscriptione (F)

Es Veronicane? An potius vere unica, quae me
  uris, quae mihi me tam cito surpueris?
Vnica nimirum, cui soli est forma decorque,
  gratiaque et quantum est et salis et veneris,
5 quaeque simul casta es, simul et pulcherrima sola,
  o sola, o vero nomine digna tuo!

: XXXII :

De Glycere et Lycoride (EP) sine inscriptione (F)

An Glyceren pluris faciam, plurisne Lycorin,
  si, Cerinthe, scio dicere, dispeream.
Moribus haec atque haec placet, et placet utraque cultu;

: XXX :

Julia

What exquisite beauty, how lovely the sound of her words, how brilliantly played is her song in fingering and voice! Is this a fourth sister of the Graces or a second Venus or a tenth Muse, or Grace, Muse and Venus together? No, it's Julia, a solo act, who far surpasses a Muse in singing, a Grace in charm, and Venus in beauty.

: XXXI :

Veronica (EP) no title (F)

Are you Vera Monique or, shall I say, Miss Truly Unique? You make me feel the fire of love, you've stolen my very soul in an instant. Yes, unique because you alone have beauty and charm and grace and all there is of wit and loveliness; and you alone are chaste, a beauty extraordinaire. O Vera Monique the unique, true to your name!

: XXXII :

Glycere and Lycoris (EP) no title (F)

Does Glycere mean more to me or Lycoris? If I know the answer to that, Cerinthus, may I not live another day. The one has a delightful manner, and so does the other. I like the style of the one,

parque illis lepor est, gratia parque venus.
5   Hanc amo, depereo illam; quin amo depereoque
    utramque et rursum utraque vita mihi.
   Quaeres fortassis qui possim. Nescio; tantum
    novi ego, quod geminas ardeo, amo, pereo.

⁛ XXXIII ⁛

Ad puellam vendentem rosas (F) *Ad puellam* (EP)

Hasne rosas an te vendes an utrumque, puella,
   quae rosa es atque inquis vendere velle rosas?

⁛ XXXIV ⁛

Idem (F) *De eadem* (EP)

Vendere velle rosas inquis. Cum sis rosa, quaero
   tene rosasne velis, virgo, an utrumque dare.

⁛ XXXV ⁛

De lupo et ove (EP) *sine inscriptione* (F)

Fetum invita lupae sed iussu nutrit erili
   et sua lacte suo pignora fraudat ovis,
scilicet ut meritam bene de se perdat adultus.
   Mutare ingenium gratia nulla potest.

and I like the other's too. In charm, grace, and attractiveness
they're equals. I love one, the other I'm desperate for. Truth be
told, I love them both to death, and they're both my reason for
living. How can I do it, you might ask. I don't know. I know only
this, the pair of them are my love and my passion, and I feel it to
distraction.

: XXXIII :

To a Girl Selling Roses (F) *To a Girl* (EP)

Are these the roses you're selling, girl, or yourself, rose that you are
among these roses you want to sell?

: XXXIV :

The Same (F, EP)

You say you want to sell roses. Since you're a rose, my question is
this: Do you want to offer yourself, maiden, or roses or both?

: XXXV :

The Wolf and the Sheep (EP) no title (F)

Against her will but by her master's order a sheep nurses a wolf
cub and cheats her own lambs of her milk, no doubt with this re-
sult: that the wolf, full grown, kills the sheep that served him well.
No kindness can change natural instinct.

: XXXVI :

De Bardo poeta (EP) sine inscriptione (F)

Cuncta memor recitat quae pangit milia Bardus
　carmina, nulla tamen scribere Bardus ait.
Si verum est, bene, Paule, facit, qui perdere chartam
　nolit, cum mentem perdere sat fuerit.

: XXXVII :

De Callimacho

'Heus puer,' imprudens dixi cum pone viderem
　Callimachum. 'O,' dixi, vertit ut ora, 'pater.'

: XXXVIII :

De eodem

Sunt pueri crines, senis ora, tuique videtur
　tam belli occipitis sinciput esse pater.

: XXXVI :

The Poet named Bard (EP) no title (F)

Blabbard recites from memory the poems he's composed by the thousands, every one of them. But Blabbard says he doesn't write down a single word. If that's true, Paolo, then good for him. He doesn't want to waste paper since he's done enough by wasting his brain.

: XXXVII :

Callimachus

"Hello there, boy," I said without thinking when I saw Callimachus from behind. When he turned around, I said, "Hello there, signore."

: XXXVIII :

The Same

You've got the hair of a boy and the face of an old man. The front half of your head appears to be the sire of your beautiful rear.

: XXXIX :

Ad Aulum (F) *In duos loquaces* (EP)

Ne distorque oculos, ne nuta, ne fode surdum,
    ne mihi velle latus, ne pede tunde pedem.
Sensi: te Lalio eripiam vis, Aule, loquaci.
    Dic, age, si id facio, quis tibi me eripiet?

: XL :

Ad puerum (F) *Ad Lygdamum* (EP)

Quod fractus nisu in medio te deserit arcus,
    non tua sed Clarii, Lygdame, culpa dei,
qui prius ut cithara clarum te vidit et ore,
    indoluit cithara victus et ore deus;
5 atque arcum metuens, arcu ne victus abiret,
    fregit et imprudens tam mage victus abit.

: XLI :

De puero mortuo (F) *De puero formoso* (EP)

Exanimum Paphie puerum miserata feretro
    'Eheu, talis,' ait, 'noster Adonis erat!'

∶ XXXIX ∶

To Aulo (F) *Two Chatterboxes* (EP)

Don't roll your eyes, don't nod, don't nudge me (I'm not responding), don't tug at my side, and don't tap your foot on mine. I get it. You want me to rescue you, Aulo, from blabbering Lalio. Come on then, tell me: if I do it, who will rescue me from you?

∶ XL ∶

To a Boy (F) *To Lygdamus* (EP)

Your bow broke when you were in the middle of bending it and left you in the lurch; it's not your fault, Lygdamus, but the fault of the god of Claros. When he first saw your brilliance on the lyre and in song, he felt the pain of being outdone, though a god, in lyre and song. And fearing that he would be outdone in the bow, he broke your bow and unwittingly was outdone so much more.

∶ XLI ∶

A Dead Boy (F) *A Handsome Boy* (EP)

The Paphian goddess, pitying the lifeless boy laid out on the bier, said: "How sad! Such a one was our Adonis."

: XLII :

In Venerem armatam Lacedaemone (F)

'Arma, Venus, Martis sunt haec. Quid inutile pondus,
   mortali bellum si meditare, subis?
Nil opus est ferro, ferri cum nuda potentem
   exueris spoliis omnibus ipsa deum.'
5 'Arma deo sua sunt, hospes, ne fallere; Sparta est
   haec, ubi de patrio sunt data more mihi.
Meque decent saevo in fluctu quae sanguine nata,
   quae sum Martis amor, quae Lacedaemonia.'

: XLIII :

De Trivultia

Quod genere et censu praestes, Trivultia, multis,
   est decus, at decus id pluribus esse vides.
Quod prior innumeris tua sit nullique secunda
   forma, tamen non est unica, rara licet.
5 Quod sis casta, etsi non est te castior ulla,
   tecum alia atque alia est casta puella tamen.
Quod docta atque sciens Musarum es sola, sed olim
   Deiphobe et fidicen Lesbia talis erat.
Quod generosa eadem, dives, formosa, pudica
10   doctaque sis, nulla est par tibi, nulla fuit.

: XLII :

Armed Venus in Sparta (F)

(*Stranger*): These, Venus, are the weapons of Mars. Why shoulder
their useless weight, if you are planning war against a mortal?
You have no need of weaponry, since you in the nude on your
own stripped of all his spoils the god who is master of weap-
onry.

(*Venus*): Gods have their own weapons, stranger; make no mis-
take. This is Sparta where in accordance with ancestral custom
they have been given to me. And they are appropriate for me
because I was born from blood spilled by a savage act on the
sea, because I am Mars's lover, because I am a Spartan.

: XLIII :

Trivulzia

The fact that you surpass many in birth and wealth, Trivulzia,
does you honor; yet, as you see, very many hold that honor.
Granted that your beauty is superior to that of countless women
and is second to none, nonetheless that doesn't mean it is unique,
though it is rare. Granted that you are chaste, even if there is no
one more chaste than you, there are, nonetheless, some girls who
are as chaste as you are. Granted that you alone are well educated
and skilled in the arts of the Muses, yet long ago Deiphobe and
the Lesbian lyre player were equally accomplished. It is because
you are, in one and the same person, noble, wealthy, beautiful,
chaste, and well educated, that no one is now or has been your
equal.

: XLIV :

De Trivultia

Sis dives, generosa, bella, casta,
docta et si ulterius potes quid esse;
si, Trivultia, non simul benigna es,
nulli bella places, pudica nulli,
5 nulli docta videris et beatae
nullos divitiae movent genusve
et si his ulterius potes quid esse.

: XLV :

[Epitaphium Philippae] Camillae Epitaphium (EP)
sine inscriptione (F)

Marmoris ingenti sub pondere clausa Philippa est:
   cavit vir tandem ne ulterius fugeret.

: XLVI :

Epitaphium (F) *Eiusdem* [i.e., Camillae] *Epitaphium* (EP)

Quaeris quae fuerim? Me scito fuisse Philippam.
   Plura rogas? Nolo plura loqui, nisi quod
nil alienum a me mulier muliebre putavi.
   Hoc, heus, in partem accipe, quaeso, bonam.
5 Quid tibi vis? An me interius vis nosse? Quid? Ipsum
   ten noscis? Prior haec sit tibi cura et abi.

78

: XLIV :

Trivulzia

You may be rich, noble, beautiful, chaste, well educated, and whatever beyond that you can be; but if you are not kind as well, Trivulzia, then no one is pleased by your beauty, no one thinks you chaste, no one considers you well educated, and no one pays attention to your splendid wealth or lineage and whatever beyond that you can be.

: XLV :

[Epitaph of Philippa] Epitaph of Camilla (EP)
no title (F)

A massive weight of marble shuts Philippa in. Her husband finally saw to it that she wouldn't run off any more.

: XLVI :

Epitaph (F) *Epitaph of the Same* [i.e., Camilla] (EP)

You ask who I was. Know that I was Philippa. More questions? I don't want to say more except that as a woman I regarded what concerns woman as a matter of concern to me. So please, take this in good part. Is there something more? Do you want to know me better? Well? Do you know your own self? Let this be your first concern and be on your way.

: XLVII :

[Epitaphium Labullae]

Huc oculos, huc verte, Bonae quicumque Parentis
    templa subis, sibi et haec quid velit urna vide.
Flaminis hic uxor Turini funere acerbo
    dulcis ab amplexu rapta Labulla viri est,
5 quae forma et censu innumeras et honore parentum,
    at virtute omnes vicerat una nurus.
I nunc et votis caelum, miser, omne fatiga,
    quando bona haec quanti sint facienda vides.

: XLVIII :

[Eiusdem]

Haec vivens nec certa satis natisque viroque
    si sua curae esset muta futura cinis,
illa, virum quamvis et natos semper amarit,
    uxor quam magis et mater amare potest,
5 esset opes quamvis natis lictura viroque,
    blanda licet natis, blanda viro fuerit,
haec, inquam, coniunx Turini saxa paravit,
    functa quibus voluit luce Labulla tegi.

: XLVII :

[Epitaph of Labulla]

Here, turn your eyes here, you who enter the temple of the Holy Mother, and see what this urn has to say. Here lies Labulla, the cherished wife of *Flamen* Turino. She was snatched from her husband's embrace by bitter death. She surpassed countless women in beauty, wealth, and the high esteem in which her parents were held, but she alone, as a young wife, surpassed all in virtue. Go on your way now and, with heavy heart, assail all heaven with your prayers now that you see how much these good qualities are to be valued.

: XLVIII :

[The Same]

This tombstone, while she was alive, not certain whether her mute ash would be cared for by her children and her husband, even though she always loved her husband and children as much as a wife and a mother could, even though she intended to bequeath her wealth to her children and her husband, and even though she was affectionate to her children and her husband—this tombstone, I say, Labulla, wife of Turino, had made for herself to cover her when she departed the light of life.

: XLIX :

[Epitaphium Manfredini]

'Quis tegitur tumulo?' 'Manfredinus ille, viator,
    Raenaldus qui sub pace dolo occubuit.'
'Sed quae tanta necis tam saevae causa?' 'Sororem
    interfectoris perdite amasse sui.'
5 'Pro scelus! ista tulit quod amarit praemia? Quid si
    odisset? Meriti est dura homini ratio.'

: L :

[Epitaphium]

Claudit Alexandrum fossa brevis urna. Puella,
    cui dare dum nimium vult, nimium eripuit.
Nunc eat et durum demens incuset Amorem.
    Hunc, quia se facilem praebuit, enecuit.

: LI :

[Epitaphium Badini]

Qui iuvenis Martem, senior qui Martis amicam
    temptando aerumnas hinc tulit, inde decus,
Badinus iacet hic. Felix ter ut ante iuventa

: XLIX :

[Epitaph of Manfredini]

(*Traveler*): Who is buried in this tomb? (*Interlocutor*): The re-
nowned Rinaldo Manfredini, traveler, who met his death by
foul play in peace time.

(*Traveler*): What compelling motive was there for so cruel a
murder? (*Interlocutor*): He was desperately in love with the sister
of his killer.

(*Traveler*): What a terrible crime! That's the reward he received
for being in love? What if he had hated? Harsh is the reckon-
ing of what a person deserves.

: L :

[Epitaph]

A small urn encloses Alexander in his grave. His girlfriend, while
she was willing to give him too much, took too much out of him.
Now let her go rave and blame Love for being cruel. By offering
herself too readily, she killed him.

: LI :

[Epitaph of Badino]

Here lies Badino, who as a young man tested himself on the bat-
tlefields of Mars, and as an old man on the battlefields of Mars's
lover; from love he got troubles, from war honor. Three times

si sic et caelebs acta senecta foret!
5 Cetera vir prudens, solers fidusque gerendis
    rebus Atestino carus ob idque duci.

: LII :

Ad Timotheum Bendideum (F)

'Ignaro servum domino promittere quicquam
    posse ratum, mores scriptaque iura vetant.'
Hoc mihi, Timothee, in patriam discedere tecum
    pollicito, intorto verbere dixit Amor.
5 Quid faciam? Iubet ille, rogas tu; terret erilis
    saevitia, ipse fidem poscis; utrumque trahit.
Durus Amor flectique nequit, tu mitis et idem
    exorandus; ad haec tu vir et ille deus.
Iam quid agam teneo: veniam sperare benigne
10   malo, quam promptae tradere colla neci.

: LIII :

Epithalamium

[Ferrarienses]

Surgite, iam signum venientis tibia nuptae
concinuit procul. Ecce venit formosa iugato
qualis olore Venus, cum Memphim aut alta Cythera

84

blessed would he have been, if as earlier in his youth, so also in his old age he had been a bachelor! In other respects, he was a prudent man, clever and trustworthy in managing affairs, and thus dear to the duke of Este.

: LII :

To Timoteo Bendidei (F)

"Custom and written law forbid a servant, unbeknownst to his master, to promise the fulfillment of anything." Love said this to me, Timoteo, twirling his whip, after I had promised to depart for our homeland with you. What can I do? He commands; you request. His domineering cruelty terrifies me, while you demand that I be true to my word; both pull at me in a tug of war. Love is hard-hearted and doesn't give an inch; you are kind and of the sort that can be appeased. Add to that: you're a man and he's a god! Now I know what I should do: I prefer to hope for a kind pardon rather than stick my neck out for a quick death.

: LIII :

Wedding Song

[*Young men of Ferrara*]

Arise, the flute has now sounded the signal for the coming of the bride. Look, she comes, as beautiful as Venus when, drawn by her yoked swans, she makes her way to visit Memphis or lofty Cythera

aut nemus Idalium aut Amathuntis templa revisit.
5 Cernitis ut circumque oculos, circumque decorum
osque genasque umerosque et circum virginis omnem
laudatam speciem volitet Charis utque serenos,
vibratis levibus pennis illi afflet honores?
Cernitis ut circum tenerorum lusus Amorum
10 obstrepat, ut calathos certent invergere florum
in comptum dominae caput, utque hic lilia fronti
componens niveae, hic immortales amarantos
purpureasque rosas malis, mirentur eandem
formam diversos florum superare colores?
15 Cernitis ut iuvenes obducta fronte Latini,
queis est dicta dies reditus, pilenta sequantur?
Cur non audimus tacita quid voce volutent,
reddere et argutis meditamur commoda dictis,
sic ad regales thalamos Hymenaea citantes?
20 Blande Hymen, iucunde Hymen, ades, o Hymenaee.

[Romani]

Aspicite Herculeos iuvenes procedere contra,
o socii, iam iam numeris certare paratos.
Sic certe haud temere veniunt; victoria nobis
difficilis, laetas nam poscunt carmina mentes;
25 nos tristes. Quid enim nisi triste efferre paramus,
culmine deiecti tanto, pulcherrima, cum te
externi invideant thalami, Lucretia, nobis?
Dure Hymen, Hymenaee, piis invise Latinis!

[Ferrarienses]

Aspicite Ausonios meditata requirere vates,
30 victrici qui saepe caput pressere corona.
Quare non facilis stat nobis palma, sodales,

or the Idalian grove or the temples of Amathus. Do you see how Charis flutters around the maiden's eyes, around her graceful mouth and cheeks and shoulders, and around all her prized beauty, and how with the beating of her delicate wings she breathes upon her a calm dignity? Do you see how the tender *Amores* play rowdily around her, how they compete to shower basketfuls of flowers on their mistress's pretty head, and how, as one of them arranges lilies on her snow-white brow and another amaranths and purple roses on her cheeks, they are amazed that the beauty of one woman surpasses the various colors of the flowers? Do you see how the young men of Rome, whose day of return has been set, follow the carriages with downcast faces? Why don't we listen to what they are saying to each other in hushed tones and devise fitting responses that are cleverly worded, thus rousing up the wedding song on the way to the royal bedchamber? Sweet Hymen, delightful Hymen, be present, Hymenaeus.

[Young men of Rome]

Look, my companions: the young men from Ercole's entourage are coming forward to challenge us, now ready to compete in song. It is surely no accident that they are coming our way. For us victory will be hard: songs require happy thoughts, and we are sad. For what are we preparing to express but sadness, miserably cast down from our height, now that a foreign marriage jealously deprives us of you, most beautiful Lucrezia? Cruel Hymen, Hymenaeus, hateful to the pious Romans!

[Young men of Ferrara]

Look, the Ausonian bards are searching their repertoire, and they have often won the crown of victory. For that reason, companions, the victorious palm will not easily be ours since we are entering

qui prima alterno cantu certamina inimus;
gloria sed maior quae multo parta labore
provenit. Hoc agite, huc animum convertite, ne qua
35 sit mora cum docto deceat succedere cantu.
Blande Hymen, iucunde Hymen, ades, o Hymenaee.

[Romani]

Omnia vertuntur. Quae quondam maxima Roma
Ausonias inter tantum caput extulit urbes,
quantum abies inter graciles annosa genistas,
40 aut quantum tenues inter vetus Albula rivos,
seu claris hominum studiis, seu moenibus altis,
nunc deserta vacat, veteri depressa ruina;
atque ubi templa deum et Capitolia celsa fuere,
curiaque et sancto subsellia trita senatu,
45 flexipedes surgunt hederae fruticesque maligni,
et turpes praebent latebras serpentibus atris.
Est levis haec iactura tamen: ruat hoc quoque, quicquid
est reliquum, iuvet et nudis habitare sub antris,
vivere dum liceat tecum, pulcherrima virgo.
50 Dure Hymen, Hymenaee, piis invise Latinis!

[Ferrarienses]

Omnia vertuntur. Modicis quae moenibus olim
hinc viridi ripa, hinc limosa obducta palude
angustas capiebat opes Ferraria pauper
angustasque domos, angustaque templa deorum,
55 apta tamen tenui populo tenuique senatu,
finitimas inter tantum nunc eminet urbes,
quantum inter Bacchi colles pater Apenninus,
Eridanusve inter fluvios, quos accipit infra,
quosque supra e tota Hesperia Neptunus uterque.

our first contest in amoebaean singing. But greater is the renown that is won by great effort. This is what we need to do, to this direct your attention: make sure there is no delay when our turn comes to respond with well-crafted song. Sweet Hymen, delightful Hymen, be present, Hymenaeus.

[Young men of Rome]

All things change. Majestic Rome, which towered over other cities like a fir tree of age immemorial among slender broom shrubs or the ancient Albula among spindly brooks—whether for the renowned endeavors of her people or her lofty walls—now lies deserted and empty, sunk in wasted ruin. Where the temples of the gods and the lofty Capitol stood and the Curia and the worn benches of the sacred Senate, pliant-footed ivy and barren bushes shoot up, providing foul lairs for black snakes. Yet this is a loss that is easy to bear. Let whatever remains standing fall to the ground, and let us be happy to dwell under the bare rock of caves, as long as we may live with you, most beautiful virgin. Cruel Hymen, Hymenaeus, hateful to the pious Romans.

[Young men of Ferrara]

All things change. Lowly Ferrara, once hemmed in on one side by a green river bank and on the other side by a muddy marsh, used to enclose humble resources within its modest walls—humble houses and humble temples of the gods, fit for lowly people and a lowly Senate—but now rises above its neighboring cities as much as father Apenninus surpasses the hills of Bacchus and the Eridanus surpasses all the rivers which both seas receive from the whole

60   Nunc, ubi piscoso pellebant gurgite lintrem
      aut ubi in aprico siccabant retia campo,
      regia templa, domus, fora, compita, curia, turres
      Herculeique decent muri portaeque viaeque
      vixque suo populo ampla, potenti et molibus aequis
65   et paribus studiis generi contendere Martis.
      At nullos tantum iactat Ferraria cultus,
      quam quod te dominam accipiat, pulcherrima virgo.
      Blande Hymen, iucunde Hymen, ades, o Hymenaee.

[Romani]

      Qualis in Ionio magno, bacchantibus Austris,
70   nauta, ubi vel Syria vel Thynna merce gravatam
      illiditque ratem scopulisque relinquit acutis
      naufragus, et multum per caerula volvitur expes,
      nudus et ignotae tandem iactatur harenae;
      dum vacuam querulis contristat fletibus oram,
75   haud procul informi in limo radiare coruscam
      intuitur, quam vertit atrox ad litora gemmam
      tempestas, seque illa opibus solatur ademptis;
      ecce autem mirantem ignes rutilumque decorem
      incautumque potens manus occupat obvia et illum
80   dimittit maria implentem et nemus omne querelis;
      talis Roma, diu casus ubi flevit iniquos
      optavitque dolens veterum decora alta Quiritum,
      dum Vaticano flexisset lumina colli,
      te vidit, clari soboles, Lucretia, Borgae,
85   pulchro ore et pulchris aequantem moribus, aut quas
      verax fama refert aut quas sibi fabula finxit,
      atque novo veteres solata est munere curas.
      O septem colles, Tiberis pater, altaque prisci

of Hesperia, north and south. Now the places where they used to row small boats on waters teeming with fish or where they used to dry their nets on sun-drenched fields, are graced with royal temples, houses, piazzas, crossroads, the Curia, towers, Herculean walls, gates, and streets, all scarcely large enough for the people, capable of rivaling the race of Mars with equal monuments and equal endeavors. Yet, Ferrara, with all its adornments, boasts of none so much as the fact that it receives you as its mistress, most beautiful virgin. Sweet Hymen, delightful Hymen, be present, Hymenaeus.

[Young men of Rome]

Just as, when the south winds rage on the great Ionian sea, a sailor dashes his ship, laden with the wares of Syria or Bithynia, on jagged rocks and, leaving it shipwrecked, is rolled again and again over the dark expanse of water, bereft of hope, naked, and at long last is cast up on a strange beach, and while he makes the empty shore moan with his woeful weeping, not far off he sees the glow of a sparkling object in a muddy glob, a gem which the wild storm carried to the shore, and finds consolation in it for the riches he lost, but while he marvels at its fiery gleams and flickering beauty, a band of powerful men comes upon him unaware and leaves him filling the sea and all the forest with his complaints. Just so is Rome: for a long time she wept for her harsh misfortunes and in her sorrow longed for the lofty glories of the ancient Quirites, until she turned her eyes to the Vatican Hill and saw you, Lucrezia, progeny of illustrious Borgia, who equal in beauty and character both real women whose fame is deserved and women who are the creations of fable — and with this new gift Rome consoled her sorrows. O Seven Hills, father Tiber, and lofty monuments of imperii monimenta, graves intendite luctus:

90 nuper Atestini fratres proceresque propinqui,
Herculeus iuvenis patria quos misit ab urbe,
quod pulchri fuerat nobis impune tulere
externoque decus nostrum iunxere marito.
Dure Hymen, Hymenaee, piis invise Latinis.

[Ferrarienses]

95 Vt qui perpetuis viret hortus consitus umbris
mobilibusque nitet per quadrua compita rivis,
laudetur licet Idaeae sub sidere Caprae,
seu cum Libra oritur, seu cum sata Sirius urit,
est tamen egelidos Tauro referente tepores

100 gratior; erumpunt tum lento e vimine frondes,
tum pingunt variis decorantque coloribus herbas
liliaque violaeque rosaeque brevesque hyacinthi;
sic quae regali fulsit Ferraria cultu,
aedibus aut sacris aut auctae molibus urbis

105 aut mage privatis opibus luxuque decenti,
vel studiis primum ingenuis iuvenumque senumque,
nunc pulchra est, nunc grata magis, cum, Borgia, tauro
vecta tuo referes auratis cornibus annum.
Vere novo insuetos summittit terra colores

110 Herculeique nitent nativis floribus horti;
arte tibi qua quisque valet blanditur honesta,
et nos, qui teneris Musas veneramur ab annis,
alternis laetos numeris canimus Hymenaeos.
Blande Hymen, iucunde Hymen, ades, o Hymenaee.

[Romani]

115 Dure Hymen, Hymenaee, piis invise Latinis,
qui potes e lacrimis miserorum auferre parentum

ancient imperial power, hear our mournful cries. The Este broth-
ers and their high-ranking relatives, whom Ercole's young descen-
dant dispatched from his native city, have taken without punish-
ment what beauty we possessed and have married our glorious
adornment to a foreign husband. Cruel Hymen, Hymenaeus,
hateful to the pious Romans.

[Young men of Ferrara]

Just as a garden that, planted in constant shade, grows verdant and
shimmers with streams rolling along the paths between square
plots, although it wins praise under the constellation of the Idaean
Goat or when Libra is rising or when Sirius scorches the crops,
nevertheless is more attractive when Taurus brings back warm
weather (then leaves sprout from the pliant branches, then lilies,
violets, roses and short-stemmed hyacinths paint and dapple the
grass with various colors), so Ferrara, which shone with royal mag-
nificence, with hallowed temples, with structures that enlarge the
city, or, what is more, with private wealth and tasteful opulence, or
above all with the liberal studies of men young and old, is now
more beautiful, now more gracious since you, Borgia, conveyed by
your bull with gilded horns, renew the season. When spring is
new, the earth sends up unusual colors, and the gardens of Ercole
are bright with native flowers. Each person pays tribute to you in
the noble art in which he is skilled, and we, who have worshiped
the Muses from boyhood, sing the happy wedding song in alter-
nating verses. Sweet Hymen, delightful Hymen, be present, Hy-
menaeus.

[Young men of Rome]

Cruel Hymen, Hymenaeus, hateful to the pious Romans, you
who can drag a trembling girl from the tears of her unhappy

ardentique viro trepidam donare puellam
et procul a patria longinquas ducere ad oras!
Dure Hymen, Hymenaee, piis invise Latinis!

[Ferrarienses]

120 Blande Hymen, iucunde Hymen, ades, o Hymenaee,
qui cupido iuveni cupidam sociare puellam
tendis, qui tacitos questus miseraris amantum,
qui nympham haud pateris viduo tabescere lecto
longinquasque urbes geniali foedere iungis.
125 Blande Hymen, iucunde Hymen, ades, o Hymenaee.

[Romani]

O quondam gratae pulchro candore puellae,
quae Phaethontëi colitis vada conscia casus,
quid Latiae nuptae iucundo occurritis ore?
Nec sensistis uti potioris luminis ortu
130 vester hebet languetque decor spectabilis olim,
Arctos ut Eoo veniente Hyperionis axe?
Dure Hymen, Hymenaee, piis invise Latinis!

[Ferrarienses]

O longum incultae tenuique in honore puellae,
pinguia quae colitis testantia culta labores
135 Herculeos, ubi multiplicem Dux inclutus hydram
contudit ignavis foedantem flexibus agros,
virginis adventu Romanae exporgite frontem.
Nam pulchra ut rerum facies celatur opaca
in nocte et picea sordens caligine nullos
140 oblectat torpetque alienae obnoxia culpae,
quae mox cum thalamo Tithonia surgit ab Indo,

parents and give her to a husband burning with desire and lead her far from her birthplace to distant shores! Cruel Hymen, Hymenaeus, hateful to the pious Romans.

[Young men of Ferrara]

Sweet Hymen, delightful Hymen, be present, Hymenaeus, you who strive to unite a passionate girl with a passionate young man, who take pity on the silent complaints of lovers, who do not allow a maiden to waste away in a bed without a husband, and who join distant cities in the bond of marriage. Sweet Hymen, delightful Hymen, be present, Hymenaeus.

[Young men of Rome]

O girls once admired for the beautiful whiteness of your complexions, you who dwell by the river that knew firsthand Phaethon's crash, why are you hurrying so cheerfully to meet the Roman bride? Do you not realize how your beauty, once a sight to look upon, is dulled by the rising of a stronger light and grows dim like Ursa Major when the sun comes from the east on his chariot! Cruel Hymen, Hymenaeus, hateful to the pious Romans.

[Young men of Ferrara]

O girls, long neglected and held in low esteem, who inhabit the rich tilled fields that bear witness to Herculean labors, where the renowned duke crushed the sinuous hydra that fouled the land with its sluggish coils, unfurrow your brows at the arrival of the Roman maiden. For just as the beauty of the visible world is hidden in the dark of night and, covered in pitch black, delights no one, languishing at the mercy of another's fault, but when Aurora, wife of Tithonus, rises from her bed in India, that beauty soon

apparet meritasque audit clarissima laudes;
sic vos ingrata resides latuistis in umbra
heroe Herculeo post vincula prima tot annos
145 caelibe, at Aurora nunc exoriente Latina,
gratae estis capiturque decor non visilis ante.
Blande Hymen, iucunde Hymen, ades, o Hymenaee.
    At vos, Romulei vates, ne tendite contra;
iam numeris satis est lusum, iam tecta subimus
150 regia, nec pigeat concordi dicere cantu:
Blande Hymen, iucunde Hymen, ades, o Hymenaee.

⁝ LIV ⁝

De diversis amoribus

Est mea nunc Glycere, mea nunc est cura Lycoris,
    Lyda modo meus est, est modo Phyllis amor.
Primas Glaura faces renovat, movet Hybla recentes,
    mox cessura igni Glaura vel Hybla novo.
5 Nec mihi diverso nec eodem tempore saepe
    centum vesano sunt in amore satis.
Vt sum si placeo, me, me sic utere, virgo,
    seu grata es, seu iam grata futura mihi.
Hoc olim ingenio vitales hausimus auras,
10   multa cito ut placeant, displicitura brevi.
Non in amore modo mens haec, sed in omnibus impar,
    ipsa sibi longa non retinenda mora.
Saepe eadem Aurorae rosea surgente quadriga
    non est, quae fuerat sole cadente mihi.
15 O quot tentatas illa est versata per artes
    festivum impatiens rettulit unde pedem!

96

becomes visible and, now clear in the daylight, hears its well-deserved praises, so too you have languished out of sight in the shade while the Herculean hero was for so many years a widower after his first marriage bond. But now that the Roman Aurora is rising, you are attractive and your beauty, not visible earlier, is perceived. Sweet Hymen, delightful Hymen, be present, Hymenaeus.

But you, bards of Romulus, do not strive in competition. We have now had our fun with verses; we are now entering the royal house. Be not displeased to give voice to a harmonious song. Sweet Hymen, delightful Hymen, be present, Hymenaeus.

: LIV :

A Multiplicity of Loves

Glycere is now my passion, now it's Lycoris, one minute Lyda is my love, the next it's Phyllis. At first Glaura sparks the flame of desire, Hybla fans it afresh, Glaura or Hybla soon makes way for a new fiery *amour*. A hundred women at different times or all at the same time aren't enough for me in my crazy fits of love. Take me, sweet damsel, as I am, if you like what you see, whether you're attractive to me now or soon will be. Long I've lived and breathed with this temperament, quick to like many things that I'm just as quick to dislike. My mind is flighty not only in love, but in all else as well — it never lingers for long over any one thing. Often the intention I have when Aurora is rising in her rose-colored chariot is not the same that I had when the sun was setting. Oh, how many professions my mind tried engaging in, only to retreat cheer-

Cum primum longos posui de more capillos
    estque mihi primum tradita pura toga,
haec me verbosas suasit perdiscere leges
20   amplaque clamosi quaerere lucra fori;
atque eadem optatam sperantem attingere metam
    non ultra passa est improba ferre pedem,
meque ad Permessum vocat Aoniamque Aganippen
    aptaque virgineis mollia prata choris;
25   meque iubet docto vitam producere cantu
    per nemora illa, avidis non adeunda viris.
Iamque acies, iam facta ducum, iam fortia Martis
    concipit aeterna bella canenda tuba.
'Ecce iterum male sana,' inquit, 'quid inutile tento
30   hoc studium? Vati praemia nulla manent.'
Meque aulae cogit dominam tentare potentem
    Fortunam obsequio servitioque gravi.
Mox ubi pertaesum est male grati principis illam,
    non tulit hic resides longius ire moras.
35   Laudat et aeratis ut eam spectabilis armis
    et meream forti conspiciendus equo.
Et mihi sunt aptae vires patiensque laborum
    corpus et has possunt tela decere manus.
Nec mora; bellator sonipes et cuncta parantur
40   instrumenta acri commoda militiae;
iuratusque pio celebri sub principe miles,
    exspecto horrisonae Martia signa tubae.
Iam neque castra placent, rursus nec classica nobis.
    Ite procul, Getici tela cruenta dei.
45   Humanone trucem foedabo sanguine dextram,
    ut meus assiduo sub bove crescat ager?
Et breve mortis iter sternam mihi, ut horridus umbram
    horreat immitem portitor ipse meam
atque aliquis, placida aspiciens a sede piorum

fully out of impatience! As soon as I styled my long hair in the customary fashion and assumed the *toga pura*, my mind persuaded me to study long winded legalese and to make a rich profit in the loudmouthed law courts. Yet, while I was hoping to attain my desired goal, that very same mind, in flagrant disregard, refused to allow me to proceed further on that path and calls me to Permessus and Aonian Aganippe and to soft meadows suited to choruses of dancing maidens, and it bids me lead my life in learned song among those groves that the avaricious are not to enter. Now my mind imagines armies in battle array, now the derring-do of commanders, now heroic wars of Mars worthy to be sung with trumpet calls everlasting. "Here I go again with my madness," it says. "Why do I attempt this useless pursuit? There are no lasting rewards for the poet." So it compels me to try my Fortune—that powerful lady—at court with obedience and burdensome service. But when it grew weary of an ungrateful prince, it could not bear lingering any longer here in idle waiting. It recommends that I go around decked in bronze weaponry, a sight to see, and earn my pay as a soldier, a striking figure on a brave steed. My strength is equal to the job, my body can endure the toil, and my hands are well-suited to weapons. Straightaway a thundering-hoofed warhorse and full panoply fit for tough army service are procured; I swear an oath to be a soldier under a loyal and renowned prince and wait for the blaring trumpet's call to battle. But already I dislike both the camp and the trumpet call. Keep away, bloody weapons of the god worshipped by the Getae! Shall I stain my right hand—pitiless now—with human blood just so that I can till my fields with a hardworking plow ox? And shall I pave a short path to my own death to spook the spooky ferryman himself with the sight of my grisly shade, and provoke someone, watching me from the quiet

50 me procul Eumenidum verbera saeva pati,
'En qui Musarum liquit grata otia,' dicat,
'anxius ut raperet munere Martis opes,'
manibus et sociis narret me digna subisse
supplicia haud ulla diminuenda die?
55 Antra mihi placeant potius montesque supini
vividaque irriguis gramina semper aquis.
Et Satyros inter celebres Dryadasque puellas
plectra mihi digitos, fistula labra terat.
Dum vaga mens aliud poscat, procul este, Catones,
60 este quibus parili vita tenore fluit,
quos labor angat, iter cupientes limite certo
ire sub instabili cuncta novante polo.
Me mea mobilitas senio deducat inerti,
dum studia haud desint quae variata iuvent.
65 Me miserum quod in hoc non sum mutabilis uno,
quando me assidua compede vincit Amor!
Et nunc Hybla licet, nunc sit mea cura Lycoris,
et te, Phylli, modo, te modo, Lyda, velim,
aut Glauram aut Glyceren aut unam aut saepe ducentas
70 depeream, igne tamen perpete semper amo.

: LV :

Iani Francisci Gonzagae Epitaphium

Quae fuerant vivente anima olim mortua membra
absque anima tandem claudit humata lapis.
Corporis affecti aerumnas novus incola caeli
spiritus hic gaudet deposuisse graves.
5 Quare animam Iani seu corpus flere, viator,
frustra hoc, sero illud, vanus uterque dolor.

abode of the pious in the distance as I endure the savage lashings
of the Eumenides, to say, "Look, there is a man who abandoned
the pleasing repose of the Muses to anxiously plunder wealth
thanks to help from Mars," and tell his fellow shades that I de-
served the punishment I endured, punishment that will not be
lessened by one day? Instead, let grottoes delight me and gently
sloping mountains and grassy fields that are always flourishing and
well-watered. In the midst of legendary satyrs and wood nymphs
let the plectrum wear down my fingers and the pipe my lips.
When my roaming mind demands something else, keep away, you
Catos, keep away you for whom life flows on an even course, you
who are afflicted with toil, eager to make your way on a fixed path
under the inconstant heavens that shift and change all things. Let
my changeability lead me away from a dull old age, as long as I
don't lack pursuits that please me in their variety. Oh, I am a piti-
able man, because in this one thing I am not inconstant: when
love binds me in its unshakeable fetters. And although now my
passion is Hybla, and now it's Lycoris; now it's you, Phyllis, that I
want, and now it's you, Lyda; and although I'm dying with desire
for Glaura or Glycere, or for one woman or sometimes two hun-
dred, nonetheless I always love with an unquenchable fire.

: LV :

Epitaph of Gianfrancesco Gonzaga

This tombstone encloses dead limbs that once had a living soul;
they lie buried at last without the soul. The spirit, newly relocated
to heaven, rejoices to have left behind here the burdensome trou-
bles of the afflicted body. Wherefore, passerby, to weep for the
soul of Gianfrancesco is unavailing; and it is too late to weep for
his body; grieving in both cases is in vain.

: LVa :

sine inscriptione (F)

Iani Francisci Gonzagae mortua pridem
 membra, animae quamvis iuncta, dies soluit,
hicque iacent: anima ad sedes sublata quietas
 gaudet onus tandem deposuisse grave.
5 Hospes, quaeso, animam flebis corpusve sepulti?
 Serum hoc, saevum illud, vanus uterque dolor.

: LVI :

sine inscriptione (F)

Sum dat *es est,* et *edo* dat *es est:* genus unde, magister,
 Estense? an quod *sit* dicitur, an quod *edat?*

: LVII :

[In Hippolytum Estensem episcopum Ferrariae]

Excita festivo populi Ferraria plausu,
 protulit ex adytis ora verenda sacris,
utque sua Hippolytum prospexit templa tuentem,
 'O claros,' inquit, 'gens mea nacta duces!
Quis patre invicto gerit Hercule fortius arma?
 Mystica quis casto castius Hippolyto?'

⁖ LVa ⁖

no title (F)

The limbs of Gianfrancesco Gonzaga, dead for some time, though once joined to his soul, were undone on his final day, and here they lie. His soul, raised up to its peaceful abode, rejoices to have finally left behind its heavy burden. Tell me, stranger, will you shed a tear for the soul or the body of the buried man? For his body, it is too late; for his soul, it is cruel; grieving in both cases is in vain.

⁖ LVI ⁖

no title (F)

Conjugate the verb "to be" [*sum*], you get "you are"[*es*] and "he is" [*est*]; and "to eat" [*edo*] gives you "you eat" [*es*] and "he eats" [*est*]. Teacher, whence comes the name of the House of Este: is it from "existing" or "feasting"?

⁖ LVII ⁖

[*To Ippolito d'Este, Bishop of Ferrara*]

Ferrara, roused by the joyous applause of her people, brought forth her venerable face from the inner sanctum. As soon as she saw Ippolito taking care of her temples, she said: "O what illustrious leaders my people have found! Who bears arms more courageously than the invincible father Ercole? Who will care for our sacred rites more piously than pious Ippolito?"

: LVIII :

Ludovici Areosti Epitaphium

Ludovici Areosti humantur ossa
sub hoc marmore, seu sub hac humo, seu
sub quicquid voluit benignus heres,
sive herede benignior comes, sive
5 oportunius incidens viator;
nam scire haud potuit futura, sed nec
tanti erat vacuum sibi cadaver,
ut urnam cuperet parare vivens.
Vivens ista tamen sibi paravit,
10 quae inscribi voluit suo sepulchro,
(olim si quod haberet is sepulchrum)
ne, cum spiritus, exili peracto
praescripti spatio, misellus artus,
quos aegre ante reliquerit, reposcet,
15 hac et hac cinerem hunc et hunc revellens,
dum noscat proprium, vagus pererret.

: LVIIIa :

sine inscriptione (F)

Ludovici Areosti humantur ossa
hoc sub marmore, seu sub hac humo, seu
sub quicquid voluit benignus heres;
nam scire haud potuit futura de se,
5 nec tanti vacuum fuit cadaver

: LVIII :

Epitaph of Ludovico Ariosto

Ludovico Ariosto's are the bones buried here under this marble or under this ground or under whatever covering his kind heir wanted or a friend kinder than his heir or a traveler who happened along at the right time. He could not possibly have known how things would turn out. But his dead body's husk, as far as he was concerned, was not worth the bother of preparing an urn while he was alive. Nonetheless, while alive, he prepared these words which he wished to be inscribed on his tomb (if, that is, he would ever have a tomb), so that when his poor little spirit, the allotted span of its exile ended, claims the body it reluctantly abandoned, it will not wander in uncertainty, tearing up here and there this or that person's ashes, until it recognizes its own.

: LVIIIa :

no title (F)

Ludovico Ariosto's are the bones buried here under this marble or under this ground or under whatever covering his kind heir wanted. He could not possibly have known how things would turn out for himself, and his dead body's husk was not worth bothering

illi urnam ut cuperet parare vivens.
Signari voluit tamen sepulchrum,
ne, cum spiritus ultimo dierum
in membra haec veniet redire iussus,
10   inter tot tumulos diu vagetur.

: LIX :

Herculis Strozzae Epitaphium

Qui patriae est olim iuvenis moderatus habenas,
    quique senum subiit pondera paene puer,
quem molles elegi ostendunt, seu grandia mavis,
    sive canenda lyra carmina, quantus erat,
5 Herculis hic Strozzae tegitur cinis: intulit uxor
    Barbara, Taurellae stemmate clara domus.
Quale hoc cumque suo statuit sacrum aere sepulchrum,
    iuncta ubi vult cari manibus esse viri.

: LX :

Ad Fuscum

Antiqua Fusci claraque Aristii,
puer, propago, forsitan et meum
   ductum unde nomen et meorum,
      nunc Ariostum, at Aristium olim,
5 te vix triennem iam comitem vocat
suum imperator, grandia iam tibi
   virtutis elargitur ultro

to prepare an urn for while he was alive. Nonetheless, he wanted the tomb to be inscribed so that when his spirit comes on the Last Day, ordered to return into these limbs, it will not roam about for a long time among so many graves.

: LIX :

Epitaph of Ercole Strozzi

Here lie covered the ashes of Ercole Strozzi, who in the flower of his youth once held the reins of his country's government and, when he was but a boy, carried a weight suited to older men. His sweet elegies, or if you prefer his longer poems or his songs that are to be sung to the lyre, show his greatness. His wife Barbara, from the illustrious lineage of the Torelli family, buried him. She erected this tomb, such as it is, with her own money, where she wants to be united with the spirit of her cherished husband.

: LX :

To Fusco

Little boy, ancient and illustrious offspring of Fusco Aristio (from whom perhaps my name and my family's name—today Ariosto but Aristio back then—also come), the emperor has already named you one of his counts, though you are barely three years old. On top of that he has already bestowed upon you great

praemia, tergeminos honores,
virtus prius quam (nam tenera impedit
10   aetas) tuo se iungere pectori
     possit, sed Augustus futuram
       mox videt adveniente pube.
Hoc spondet illi nota parentium
virtus tuorum, patrui et optima
15   Thomae institutio et quod ista
     omnibus indole polliceris.
At quantum honoris, tantum oneris datur,
quippe elaborandum est tibi maximam
     tui omnium expectationem et
20   Caesaris indicium tueri.

: LXI :

De Raphaele Vrbinate (EP) sine inscriptione (F)

Huc oculos (non longa mora est) huc verte; meretur
   te, quamvis properes, sistere qui iacet hic,
cuius picta manu te plurima forsan imago
   iucunda valuit sistere saepe mora.
5   Hoc, Vrbine, tuum decus; hoc tua, Roma, voluptas;
   hoc, Pictura, tuus marmore splendor inest.
Marmor habet iuvenem exanimum, qui marmora quique
   illita parietibus vivere signa facit,
os oculosque movere, pedes proferre manusque
10   tendere; tantum non posse deditque loqui;
quod dum qui faciat meditatur opusque perenne
   reddat, monstra Deae talia morte vetant.
Hospes, abi, monitus mediocria quaerere, quando
   stare diu summis invida Fata negant.

rewards of virtue — the triple honors — before heroic virtue can find a place in your heart (your tender age prevents this), but our Augustus anticipates the virtue you will have when you become a young man. His decision is warranted by the esteemed virtue of your relatives, the excellent guidance of your paternal uncle, Tommaso, and the promise that your character holds for everyone. But with so much honor comes an equally onerous burden, for you must make every effort to maintain everyone's high expectations of you and Caesar's mark of faith in your future.

: LXI :

On Raphael from Urbino (EP) no title (F)

Here — it won't take long — look over here. Even if you are in a hurry, he who is buried here merits your time. It may be that many images painted by his hand made you take more than one pleasant pause. Here in this marble tomb is your glory, Urbino; Rome, your delight rests here; in here, Painting, is your splendor. This marble holds a lifeless young man who gave life to marble and to figures daubed on walls. He made mouths and eyes move, feet step forth, hands stretch out; he empowered art to do everything but speak. But while he was planning how he might do even that and render his work eternal, the Fates thwarted such miracles with his death. Stranger, be on your way, and be forewarned to seek out the middle path, since the jealous Fates prevent the best from living long.

: LXII :

Ad Alphonsum Ferrariae ducem III

Cum desperata fratrem languere salute
  et nulla redimi posse putaret ope,
Dis vovet Hippolytus, Getico dum currit ab orbe,
  Manibus ipse suum, vivat ut ille, caput.
5 Vota deos faciles habuere: Alphonsus ab Orco
  eripitur, fratris fratre obeunte vices.
Morte tua, Pollux, redimis si Castora, munus
  accepturus idem das, nec obis, sed abis.
Quod dedit hic, nunquam accipiet, nec lusus inani
10 spe reditus avidi limina Ditis adit.

: LXIII :

Zerbinati Epitaphium

Paulum siste, mora est brevis. Rogat te
Zerbinatus in hoc situs sepulchro,
si sis forte sciens, ut et scientem
se reddas quoque, quis furor Leonem
5 Tassinum impulerit, quem amabat et quem
erat pluribus usque prosecutus
magnisque officiis domi forisque,
ut ipsum insidiis agens necaret.
Quod si scire negas, abi et tibi sit
10 exemplo, ingenium malum feroxque
lenire ut benefacta nulla possint.

: LXII :

To Alfonso, Third Duke of Ferrara

Believing that his brother's health was failing and that there was no hope for recovery, and that he could not be restored by any remedy, Ippolito, while traveling fast from the land of the Getae, promised his own life to the spirits below so that his brother might live. His vow reached gods that were amenable. Alfonso is snatched away from Orcus, with brother taking the place of brother. Pollux, if you redeem Castor with your death, you give the same gift that you will receive: you do not die, you only depart. What this one gave, he will never have again, and he does not go to the threshold of greedy Death deluded by the vain hope of return.

: LXIII :

Epitaph of Zerbinato

Pause a moment; it will not take long. Zerbinato, who lies in this grave, asks you, if you happen to know, to let him know too, what madness drove Leone Tassino, whom he loved and whom he constantly attended with many great services at home and abroad, to set a trap and kill him. But if you say that you do not know, be on your way, and let this be a lesson for you: good deeds cannot soften a fierce and evil heart.

: LXIV :

Oliva (EP) sine inscriptione (F)

Hicne rosas inter Veneris bulbosque Priapi
    et Bacchi vites, Palladis arbor, ero?
Immeritoque obscaena et adultera et ebria dicar,
    sobria quae semper casta pudensque fui?
5 Hinc me auferte aut me ferro succidite, quaeso,
    ne mihi dent turpem probra aliena notam.

: LXV :

De paupertate (EP) sine inscriptione (F)

Sis lautus licet et beatus, hospes,
et quicquid cupis affluens referto
cornu Copia subministret ultro,
ne suspende humilem casam brevemque
5 mensam naribus hanc tamen recurvis,
si nec, Bauci, tuam, tuam, Molorche,
tuamque, Icare, pauperem tabernam
et viles modica cibos patella
sprevit Iuppiter, Hercules, Lyaeus.

: LXIV :

An Olive Tree (EP) no title (F)

Will I, the tree of Pallas Athena, exist here among the roses of Venus, the bulbs of Priapus, and the vines of Bacchus? Undeservedly will I be said to be indecent, adulterous, and drunk, I who have always been sober, pure, and modest? Take me away from here or cut me down at the ground with an ax, please, so that the shameful acts of others won't leave their filthy mark on me!

: LXV :

Poverty (EP) no title (F)

Guest, though you may be rich and lucky, and the overflowing goddess of abundance may supply you with a horn brimful of whatever you desire, nevertheless don't turn up your nose at this lowly house and its meager provisions, if Jupiter did not disdain your poor hut and paltry vittles served in an ordinary dish, Baucis, nor Hercules yours, Molorchus, nor Bacchus yours, Icarus.

: LXVI :

De populo et vite (EP) sine inscriptione (F)

Arida sum vireoque aliena populus umbra,
  sumque racemiferis undique operta comis;
gratae vitis opus, quae cum moritura iaceret,
  munere surrexit laeta feraxque meo.
5 Nunc nostri memor officii, docet unde referri
  magna etiam possit gratia post obitum.

: LXVII :

sine inscriptione (F)

Quae frondere vides serie plantaria longa
  et fungi densae saepis opaca vicem,
lucus erant, horti latus impedientia dextrum
  e regione domus, e regione viae,
parta viderentur septena ut iugera frustra,
  prospectus longi cum brevis esset agri.
Non mites edi fetus, coalescere ramos,
  crescere non urens umbra sinebat olus.
Emptor ad hos usus Ariostus vertit et optat
  non minus hospitibus quam placitura sibi.

: LXVI :

The Poplar and the Vine (EP) no title (F)

A withered poplar, I flourish in another's shade, and I am covered all over with cluster-bearing foliage. This is the work of a grateful grapevine, which, lying on the verge of death, was resurrected happy and fertile thanks to me. Now, in recognition of my service, it gives a lesson in how great recompense can be rendered even after death.

: LXVII :

no title (F)

Those seedlings you see putting forth their leaves in a long row, doing the job of a thick hedge with their shade, used to be woods. The woods were blocking the right side of the garden looking from the house and street, so that the seven acres seemed to be a wasted purchase since the view of the full extent of the field was so minimal. The withering shade didn't allow fruit to ripen, branches to build their strength, vegetables to grow. The buyer, Ariosto, turned his acres to this use, and he hopes that they will be pleasing no less to his guests than to himself.

CARMINA INCERTA

Epitaphium Francisci Gerbinati

Paulum siste, mora est brevis. Rogat te
Gerbinatus in hoc situs sepulchro,
ut, si forte sciens es, et scientem
se reddas quoque, caede cur cruenta,
5   dum nil tale timet, meretur et dum
nil tale, in nitido beatioris
aevi flore sit optimaeque matri
fratrique unanimi omnibusque amicis
sic ereptus. Amasse quippe ait se
10 omnes, quin nec habere clam palamve
quos umquam oderit atque prosecutum
semper quos potuit fuisse magnis
clarisque officiis domi forisque.
Quod si scire negas, abique habeque
15 quae serves documenta vindicare
a fatis benefacta nulla posse.

: II :

Epitaphium Marchionis Piscariae

'Quis iacet hoc gelido sub marmore?' 'Maximus ille
   piscator, belli gloria, pacis honos.'
'Numquid et hic pisces cepit?' 'Non.' 'Ergo quid?' 'Vrbes,

POEMS OF UNCERTAIN ATTRIBUTION

Epitaph of Francesco Gerbinato

Stop a moment; it will not take long. Gerbinato, the man laid to rest in this tomb, asks you, if by chance you know, to let him know as well why, while he feared no such thing and deserved no such thing, in the bright flower of his blessed youth, he was snatched away by bloody murder from his excellent mother and his brother, a kindred spirit, and all his friends. For he says that he loved everyone, and, what is more, that he did not have anyone that he ever hated either in private or in public and that he always supported those whom he was able with important and well-known services at home and abroad. But if you say that you do not know, go on your way, and take and keep this as proof that good deeds are no protection against the fates.

: II :

Epitaph of the Marquis of Pescara

(A): Who lies buried under this cold marble? (B): That great Fisherman, renowned in war and honored in peace. (A): I suppose this Fisherman didn't catch fish as well? (B): No. (A): Well then,

magnanimos reges, oppida, regna, duces.'
5 'Dic, quibus haec cepit piscator retibus?' 'Alto
consilio, intrepido corde, alacrique manu.'
'Qui tantum rapuere ducem?' 'Duo numina, Mars, Mors.'
'Vt raperent quisnam compulit?' 'Invidia.'
'Cui nocuere?' 'Sibi, vivit nam fama superstes,
10 quae Martem et Mortem vincit et Invidiam.'

: III :

Franciscus Maria Molsa Mutinensis

Concineret blandos dum Molsa disertus amores,
    ardua Paelignae gloria Molsa lyrae,
servitium sero gravis excutiebat amicae,
    mortis adesse videns signa propinquae suae.
5 Ipsi difficilis Venus immedicabile vulnus
    attulit, at nomen Musa perenne dedit.

: IV :

sine inscriptione

Nomina bina habui, geminos Pia Prisca maritos
    et geminam sobolem mors geminata tulit,
me febres geminae; claudunt geminata sepulcra,
    coniugis incolumis pectus et iste lapis.

what did he catch? (*B*): Cities, stouthearted kings, towns, king-doms, commanders. (*A*): Tell me, what nets did the Fisherman use to bring in that catch? (*B*): Penetrating judgment, a fearless heart, a hand ready to act. (*A*): Who carried off so great a com-mander? (*B*): Two divine powers, Mars and Death. (*A*): Who drove them to carry him off? (*B*): Envy. (*A*): Whom have they harmed? (*B*): Themselves. For his reputation survives and lives on; it conquers Mars and Death and Envy.

: III :

Francesco Maria Molza from Modena

While Molza, towering glory of the Paelignian lyre, was singing skillfully of sweet love, he tried too late to shake off his enslave-ment to a hard-hearted girl, seeing that the signs of his death were close at hand. Obdurate Venus inflicted an incurable wound on him, but the Muse has given him a name everlasting.

: IV :

no title

I had two names, Pia and Prisca, and two husbands, and my twin offspring were taken away by a double death, and two fevers took me. Two tombs are my resting place, the heart of my husband, who survives me, and this stone.

: V :

sine inscriptione

Fessa gravi morbo cum iam mea Mamma iaceret
   certavere diu Mors, Amor et Charites.
Impia formosum ventrem Libitina premebat,
   os Charites, oculos ipse fovebat Amor;
5 fax erat pulchris oculis, argutus in ore
   sermo; dabant Charites verba, Cupido facem.
Dum tamen aegrotam Mors saeva ferocius urget,
   nec minus hinc Charites hincque repugnat Amor.
Illa simul Charites et Mammam et perdit Amorem
10   scilicet et victrix bina tropaea refert.
Ah nimis insignes tituli celeberque triumphus,
   praeda Necis Charites, Mamma, Cupido iacent!

: V :

no title

When my mother lay dying, weakened and worn by a wasting disease, Death, Love, and the Graces battled for a long time. Callous Libitina sat heavily on her fine abdomen, the Graces brought soothing relief to her mouth, and Love did the same for her eyes. A bright light came from her beautiful eyes and clear speech from her mouth; the Graces provided the words and Love the bright light. While cruel Death fiercely pressed its attack on her as she lay ill, the Graces on one side and Love on another fought back no less forcefully. Death overcame the Graces and my mother and Love all together and in victory brings back two trophies. How sad! The Graces, my mother, and Love lie dead. What a grand claim to fame, what a glorious triumph, what plunder for Death!

CARMINA APOCRYPHA

: I :

De domo sua rustica

Parva sed apta mihi, sed nulli obnoxia, sed non
    Sordida, parta meo sed tamen aere domus.

: II :

De Victoria Columna

'Non vivam sine te, mi Brute,' exterrita dixit
    Porcia et ardentes sorbuit ore faces.
'Avale, te extincto,' dixit Victoria, 'vivam,
    perpetuo maestas sic dolitura dies.'
5 Vtraque Romana est sed in hoc Victoria maior:
    nulla dolere potest mortua, viva dolet.

: III :

Castanea

Arbor inest silvis quae scribitur octo figuris;
fine tribus demptis, vix unam e mille videbis.

APOCRYPHAL POEMS

: I :

His House in the Country

It's small, but just right for me, at no one's beck and call, not shabby, yet purchased with my own money, my house.

: II :

Vittoria Colonna

"I will not live without you, my Brutus," said Porcia in a fit of dread and swallowed down the red-hot firebrand. "Avalo," said Victoria, "though you are dead, I will live on, grieving day after day in sadness without end." Both women were Roman but Victoria was the greater in this: a dead woman cannot grieve, a living one can.

: III :

Chestnut Tree

There is a tree in the woods that is spelled with eight letters [*castanea*, "chestnut tree"]. Take away three from the end, and you'll scarcely find one among a thousand [*casta*, "chaste woman"].

APPENDIX

Order of poems in Ferrara manuscript (F) according to Bolaffi's numeration	Order of poems in *Editio Princeps* 1553 (*EP* 1553) according to Bolaffi's numeration
10	*Liber I*
29	4
11	14
39	53
40	7
33	15
34	6
52	23
3	54
5	25
41	*Liber II*
1a (1–18)	62
64	29
65	31
66	32
67	64
1a (19–36)	66
55a	42 (5–8)
35	26
36	27
50	30
42 (1–4)	43
58a	37
24	38
49	39
25	40
26	43

Order of poems in Ferrara manuscript (F) according to Bolaffi's numeration	Order of poems in *Editio Princeps* 1553 (*EP 1553*) according to Bolaffi's numeration
27	34
22	35
21	36
16a	42 (1–4)
57	61
8	41
32	11
31	55
51	8
47	45
45	46
46	59
61	*Incertum* 2
	9
	60
	17
	1
	2
	18
	19
	12
	21
	13
	20
	65
	44
	63
	16
	58

Note on the Text and Its Textual History

The key consideration for understanding the transmission of Ariosto's Latin poems from manuscript to print is the discouraging reality that the poems were published posthumously and that — from the evidence of the autograph sheets, entitled *Aliquot carmina autographa Ludovici Areosti Ferrariensis*,[1] containing thirty-nine of the *carmina* — the poet had not prepared a fair copy of the corpus of his Latin poems with the intention of publishing them as a book. As a result, the selection and arrangement of the poems in the first printed edition are not authorial, and the print versions of at least some of the poems may be based on manuscript versions that were still in the process of revision. Moreover, the absence of authorial review, and diligent editorial review, of the printed text has resulted in challenging questions about the wording and punctuation of the poems that still require discussion. The *carmina* were first printed nearly twenty years after the poet's death, in a one-volume collection, edited by Giovanni Battista Pigna (1530–75) and published at Venice in 1553. This *editio princeps* contains the poetry of three Ferrarese poets, Pigna himself in four books, Celio Calcagnini (1479–1541) in three books, and Ariosto in two books (hereafter referred to as EP 1553); Ariosto's poems occupy pages 270 to 312. In his preface (p. 4), Pigna gives a brief statement of his editorial activity: "For when my father-in-law Antonio Musa Brasavola entrusted to my discretion and judgment the poetic compositions of his teacher in humane letters [Celio Calcagnini] and when Virginio Ariosto, my close friend bound to me by the bond of literary and intellectual culture, did likewise with his father's poetic compositions, I selected those poems which in my view showed themselves to be of higher quality." Pigna printed fifty-four poems; of these, two (42.1–4 and 42.5–8) are a single poem, and one is now regarded as of uncertain authorship (*Incertum* 2). Pigna arranged the poems according to meter.

Book 1 contains nine poems: the poems written in dactylic hexameter (4, 14, 53) come first, the canonical meter of ancient Greek and Roman epic. Their placement at the beginning of the collection was intended no doubt to impress with their elevated style, subject matter, and length and to put on display Ariosto's continuation of the Latin hexameter tradition in the footsteps of Lucretius, Vergil, Ovid, Lucan, Silius Italicus, and Statius. These are followed by Ariosto's longest poems in the elegiac meter, specifically the love elegies (7, 6, 23, 54) and the lament on the death of Michele Marullo (15). The book ends with a shorter poem in the elegiac meter (25), an inscriptional epigram for a statue of Bacchus. In the longer elegies the influence of Tibullus, Propertius, and Ovid is clear. Book 2 contains forty-five poems in four metrical groupings, in the following order: twenty-nine (including *Incertum* 2) in elegiacs, eight in lyric meters, two in iambics, and six in hendecasyllables. The elegiac poems fall into two subgroups: the majority of them (twenty) are relatively short, witty epigrams on a variety of themes taken from social life and personal encounters; the nine poems that form the second group are funerary epigrams, several of which are in the form of the talking inscription that addresses the passerby. In the epigrams, the spirit of Catullus and Martial boldly asserts itself. The final grouping of lyric, iambic, and hendecasyllabic poems highlights Ariosto's engagement with the works of Catullus and Horace.

The classical precedents for the metrical arrangement of poems — both occasional pieces and longer compositions — in a collection are Catullus's *libellus* and Book 4 of Statius's *Silvae*. Both are examples of poetry books in which meter is the primary ordering principle. For the sequence of meters, Statius's *Silvae* 4 offers the closer parallel: it begins, like the other four books of the *Silvae*, with poems in the hexameter, the predominant meter in the *Silvae*, and ends with a poem in hendecasyllables, as do Books 1 and 2; in between are two lyric compositions, 4.5 and 4.7; Statius does not use the elegiac couplet. For variety of meter, subject matter, and length, however, Catullus's *libellus* is the better parallel. Although the metrical arrangement of the poems in EP 1553 is an editorial construction, it is a thoughtful and creative way of organizing the collection. It focuses attention on the poet's metrical virtuosity, his mastery of different types of poetry, themes, and subjects (epideictic, consolation, epithalamium, love elegy, epigram, funerary epigram, and lyric) and on the living continuity of his poetry with his classical models. Pigna's decision to end the collection with the epitaph (poem 58) that the poet composed for himself gives the collection a sense of closure. It seems entirely appropriate to conclude on a humorous note that asserts the primacy of poetry: come Judgment Day, the poem asserts, Ariosto's soul will need the help of a poetic epitaph, in Catullan hendecasyllables, to locate and be united with his mortal remains. But until that Day arrives, the epitaph will keep the name and the poetry of Ludovico Ariosto alive.

The unsatisfactory state of the text of many of the poems is due in all likelihood to the condition of the manuscript material that Ariosto's son entrusted to Pigna and from which Pigna made his selection of poems. The thirteen manuscript sheets that compose the *Aliquot carmina*, hereafter referred to as F, have thirty-nine of the *carmina* written in Ariosto's hand, on 3r to 5v and 7r to 12r.[2] F and EP 1553 have twenty-three poems in common.[3] F has an additional sixteen poems that were not printed in EP 1553.[4] The reasons for the omission of many of these poems are clear. Poems 1a, 55a, 58a, and 16a are drafts of poems, the final versions of which were printed in EP 1553. In addition, all of these poems have cancellation strokes through them; in the case of 1a the stroke is through lines 29 to 36. Poem 10, an epitaph for Nicolò Ariosto, was largely repurposed for the epitaph of Quinzia (poem 11) and has a cancellation stroke through it. Poems 3, 5, and 49 have cancellation strokes through them. Poems 24 and 22 have marginal and supralinear revisions, which may have discouraged Pigna from trying to reconstruct a definitive version. In the case of the remaining six poems (52, 57, 50, 67, 51, 47), Pigna may have felt that they did not achieve the artistic standard of the other poems.

Ezio Bolaffi's critical edition of the Latin poems, *Ludovici Areosti Carmina Praefatus est, recensuit, Italice vertit, adnotationibus instruxit Aetius Bolaffi* (Modena, 1938[2]), is recognized as the standard critical text of the *carmina*. It is based on the two primary authorities for establishing the text, Ariosto's autograph manuscript F and EP 1553. The collection of *carmina* printed by Bolaffi contains sixty-seven poems by Ariosto, five poems of uncertain authorship, and three spurious poems; the poems are arranged chronologically, to the extent that the approximate year of composition can be determined. In addition to the manuscript and the *editio princeps*,

Bolaffi also collated the printed editions previous to his own. Since 1938, Bolaffi's edition has served as the textual authority, with correction of misprints and revision of punctuation, for subsequent editions of the *carmina*, most notably, C. Segre, *Opere minori* (Naples-Milan, 1954) and M. Santoro, *Opere: volume terzo, Carmina, Rime, Satire, Erbolato, Lettere* (Turin, 1989). As a result of this complex textual history, *cruces* remain, which the editors have been unable to solve on the basis of the evidence provided by the autograph manuscript and the *editio princeps*; in such cases they have resorted to emendation. It is our hope that the present text of the *carmina*, which is founded on the indispensible efforts of previous editors and commentators, will make a contribution to the improved understanding of Ariosto's Latin poetry.

NOTES

1. Ferrara, Biblioteca Comunale Ariostea, ms. cart., sec. XVI. Classe I C. Catalog description: "Manoscritto cartaceo; guardie cartacee; fascicoli legati; 13cc. in origine sciolte inserite fra cc. bianche di un codice." For the order of the poems in F, see Appendix. The autograph sheets came into the possession of Giovanni Andrea Barotti, who edited Arisoto's *Opere* in 1741 and again in 1766, and from them he printed previously unpublished poems. The sheets were acquired by the public library of Ferrara in 1784 (Barotti, *Memorie istoriche*, 2:368, with n. 1; and 2:353–54, on the two editions of the *Opere*).

2. The following pages are blank: 6r–v, 12v, 13v. On 1r to 2v there are four poems by Pietro Bembo; at the bottom of 2v is a four-line epigram beginning *Crede ratem ventis*, attributed to Bembo in the manuscript but belonging to late antiquity. It is attributed to a Pentadius, an author of the third or fourth century CE, in the *Anthologia Latina*, ed. D. R. Shackleton Bailey (Stuttgart, 1998: no. 262); the poem is attributed in some manuscripts to Quintus Cicero. On 13r are written the dedicatory inscription of Agostino Mosti (Augustinus Mustus) for a marble sepulcher of Ariosto and the accompanying verse epitaph by Lorenzo Frizzoli.

3. Poems 29, 11, 39, 40, 33, 34, 41, 64, 65, 66, 35, 36, 42 (printed as two separate poems in EP 1553), 25, 26, 27, 21.1–17, 8, 32, 31, 45, 46, 61. On the treatment of F's text in EP 1553, see Bolaffi 1938: xxi–xxiii.

4. Poems 10, 52, 3, 5, 1a, 67, 55a, 50, 58a, 24, 49, 22, 16a, 57, 51, 47. Barotti 1741 first printed 52 and 3; Barotti 1766 first printed 57, 50, 47, 67, and 49. On Barotti's editing of the *carmina,* see Bolaffi 1938: xxiv–xxviii. Carducci 1905 first printed 10, 5, 1a, 55a, 58a, 24, 22, 16a, 51.

Abbreviations

❦❧

Based on the *Oxford Classical Dictionary*, where possible.

C.	Ludovico Ariosto, *Carmina*
Erb.	Ludovico Ariosto, *Erbolato*
L.	Ludovico Ariosto, *La Lena*
Let.	Ludovico Ariosto, *Lettere*
OF	Ludovico Ariosto, *Orlando Furioso*
R.	Ludovico Ariosto, *Rime*
Sat.	Ludovico Ariosto, *Satire*

Anth. Lyr. Graec.	*Greek Anthology*
Anth. Pal.	*Anthologia Palatina*
App. Verg.	*Appendix Vergiliana*
Ap. Rhod. *Argon.*	Apollonius Rhodius, *Argonautica*
Aratus *Phaen.*	Aratus, *Phaenomena*
Boccaccio *Dec.*	Boccaccio, *Decameron*
Callim. *Epigr.*	Callimachus, *Epigrammata*
Calp. *Ecl.*	Calpurnius Siculus, *Eclogues*
Catull.	Catullus
Cic. *Fin.*	Cicero, *De finibus*
Cic. *Nat. D.*	Cicero, *De natura deorum*
Cic. *Phil.*	Cicero, *Orationes Philippicae*
Cic. *Tusc.*	Cicero, *Tusculanae Disputationes*
Cic. *Verr.*	Cicero, *In Verrem*
Columella *Rust.*	Columella, *De re rustica*
Enn. *Ann.*	Ennius, *Annales*
German. *Arat.*	Germanicus, *Aratea*
Hes. *Theog.*	Hesiod, *Theogonia*
Il.	Homer, *Iliad*
Od.	Homer, *Odyssey*

Hor. *Ars P.*	Horace, *Ars Poetica*
Hor. *Carm.*	Horace, *Carmina*
Hor. *Epist.*	Horace, *Epistulae*
Hor. *Epod.*	Horace, *Epodi*
Hor. *Sat.*	Horace, *Satirae*
Juv.	Juvenal
Lactant. *Div. inst.*	Lactantius, *Divinae institutiones*
Livy	Livy, *Ab urbe condita*
Luc.	Lucan, *Bellum Civile*
Lucr.	Lucretius
Man. *Astr.*	Manilius, *Astronomica*
Mart.	Martial
Ov. *Am.*	Ovid, *Amores*
Ov. *Ars am.*	Ovid, *Ars amatoria*
Ov. *Fast.*	Ovid, *Fasti*
Ov. *Her.*	Ovid, *Heroides*
Ov. *Ib.*	Ovid, *Ibis*
Ov. *Met.*	Ovid, *Metamorphoses*
Ov. *Pont.*	Ovid, *Epistulae ex Ponto*
Ov. *Rem. am.*	Ovid, *Remedia amoris*
Ov. *Tr.*	Ovid, *Tristia*
Pet. *RVF*	Petrarch, *Rerum vulgarium fragmenta*
Petron. *Sat.*	Petronius, *Satyricon*
Phaedrus *Fab. Aes.*	Phaedrus, *Fabulae Aesopi*
Pind. *Nem.*	Pindar, *Nemean Odes*
Plaut. *Amph.*	Plautus, *Amphitruo*
Plaut. *Asin.*	Plautus, *Asinaria*
Plaut. *Aul.*	Plautus, *Aulularia*
Plaut. *Cas.*	Plautus, *Casina*
Plaut. *Curc.*	Plautus, *Curculio*
Plaut. *Epid.*	Plautus, *Epidicus*
Plaut. *Men.*	Plautus, *Menaechmi*
Plaut. *Merc.*	Plautus, *Mercator*
Plaut. *Mil.*	Plautus, *Miles gloriosus*

Plaut. *Per.*	Plautus, *Persa*
Plaut. *Poen.*	Plautus, *Poenulus*
Plaut. *Pseud.*	Plautus, *Pseudolus*
Plaut. *Rud.*	Plautus, *Rudens*
Plaut. *Stich.*	Plautus, *Stichus*
Plin. *HN*	Pliny the Elder, *Naturalis historia*
Plut. *Vit. Brut.*	Plutarch, *Vitae Parallelae, Brutus*
Pol. *Silv.*	Poliziano, *Silvae*
Prop.	Propertius
Sen. *Agam.*	Seneca, *Agamemnon*
Sen. *Ben.*	Seneca, *De Beneficiis*
Sen. *Dial.*	Seneca, *Dialogi*
Sen. *Ep.*	Seneca, *Epistulae Morales*
Sen. *Herc. Oet.*	Seneca, *Hercules Oetaeus*
Sen. *HF*	Seneca, *Hercules Furens*
Sen. *Ph.*	Seneca, *Phaedra*
Sen. *Q Nat.*	Seneca, *Quaestiones naturales*
Sen. *Tro.*	Seneca, *Troades*
Sil. *Pun.*	Silius Italicus, *Punica*
Stat. *Achil.*	Statius, *Achilleis*
Stat. *Silv.*	Statius, *Silvae*
Stat. *Theb.*	Statius, *Thebais*
Tac. *Ann.*	Tacitus, *Annales*
Tac. *Hist.*	Tacitus, *Historiae*
Ter. *Ad.*	Terence, *Adelphoe*
Ter. *An.*	Terence, *Andria*
Ter. *Eun.*	Terence, *Eunuchus*
Ter. *Haut.*	Terence, *Heautontimorumenos*
Ter. *Hec.*	Terence, *Hecyra*
Theoc.	Theocritus, *Idylls*
Tib.	Tibullus
Val. Flac. *Arg.*	Valerius Flaccus, *Argonautica*
Val. Max.	Valerius Maximus
Verg. *Aen.*	Vergil, *Aeneid*

Verg. *Catal.*	Vergil, *Catalepton*
Verg. *Ecl.*	Vergil, *Eclogues*
Verg. *G.*	Vergil, *Georgics*
Vitr. *De arch.*	Vitruvius, *De architectura*
Xen. *Cyn.*	Xenophon, *Cynegeticus*

Notes to the Text

※※※

The text presented in this edition is a revision of the text in Bolaffi 1938, collated against F and EP 1553; Barotti 1741 and Barotti 1766 were also consulted, along with the other editions listed below. Significant divergences from Bolaffi's text are listed and explained in the notes that follow; for the most part they are revisions in punctuation that materially affect the sense and restorations of readings transmitted by F or EP 1553 that were replaced with editorial conjectures or supplanted by unnoticed substitutions. In four instances (6.20, 12.11, 15.32, 20.8) we have resorted to conjecture, because the transmitted text does not yield a satisfactory sense. Although this is not a critical edition and readers should consult Bolaffi 1938 for full reports of the readings in F, EP 1553, and other early printed editions, an attempt is made here to provide readers with some examples of the poet's revisions in F so that they can have a sense of the historical circumstances of transmission and at the same time see the poet at work.

Ariosto's practice in giving titles to his poems is inconsistent. Of the thirty-nine poems in F, twelve have titles. These titles range in character from the fully descriptive (1a, *Ode de vita quieta ad Philiroen*) to the tersely functional (16a, *Epi.*, the abbreviation for *Epitaphium*, and 34, *Idem*, "the same"). It is possible that the poet also gave titles to at least some of the poems on manuscript sheets that were used as copy-text by the printers but are no longer extant, and that these titles were reproduced in EP 1553, although there is no way to know, in the case of poems for which there is no manuscript testimony, which titles are authorial and which are editorial. EP 1553 provides titles for all the poems in the two-book collection, with the exception of 4 and 62, which stand at the beginning of each book, respectively, under a dedicatory phrase. Comparison of titled poems shared in common between F and EP 1553 shows that Pigna exercised a free hand in creating titles. Here are some examples of the changes made in the titles of F:

F	EP 1553
poem 33 *Ad Puellam Vendentem Rosas*	*De Puella*
poem 39 *Ad Aulum*	*In Duos Loquaces*
poem 40 *Ad Puerum*	*Ad Lygdamum*
poem 41 *De Puero Mortuo*	*De Puero Formoso*

In carrying out his duty as editor of a two-book collection of Ariosto's poems, Pigna appears to have been guided by his own tastes and judgment, as well as printing-house practices, when deciding on the most effective way to represent Ariosto's poems, in the company of his own and Calcagnini's, in print.

In addition to F and EP 1553 as sources of titles, there is a third source: subsequent editors who altered them or created new ones. In the case of poem 21, which is untitled in F, EP 1553's title *In Meretricem* is mistaken, as the content of the poem clearly indicates, and was corrected by Polidori 1857 to *In Lenam*, which is now accepted in the print tradition. Likewise, poem 4 was given a new title by modern editors (Fatini 1924, Bolaffi 1938) to replace the misleading dedication that had previously served that function. And when Barotti 1766 first published untitled poems (47, 67) in F that were not printed in EP 1553, he created titles for them. In this edition all titles in EP 1553 are printed with the poems, with corrections as needed; they are part of the print and editorial history of the poems, and some of them may be based on Ariosto's manuscript titles. F's titles, where available, are also printed with the poems. This procedure results in the somewhat unusual situation of giving two titles for poems shared by F and EP 1553. However, the typographic strangeness of two titles serves as a reminder that a manuscript, orphaned of its author, is dependent on the kindness of strangers for its survival in print and is especially vulnerable to unauthorized editorial interventions necessitated by the requirements and expectations of appearing in print. Titles introduced by editors into editions published after EP 1553 are enclosed in square brackets.

In matters of orthography, we have normalized spelling to the standards of classical Latin, that is, the orthographical conventions of roughly the first century CE, now used in printing the texts of Latin authors. Following the example of the "modern spelling" edition of Shakespeare, we consult the convenience of the reader, who will be using Latin dictionaries and other reference works that employ the standard orthography. In an edition such as this, no useful purpose is served by retaining spellings that are the product of historical accident (e.g., *sylva, foemina, author*; or in the case of proper names/adjectives, *Cinareius* [17.21], *Cytherone* [25.11]), and *Cherinte* [32.2], for which we print *Cinyreius, Citherone,* and *Cerinthe*); in fact, such spellings can be a distraction. The texts in the early printed editions of Latin authors reproduced what might be called a debased orthography, which was found in the late manuscripts that were readily available and served as printer's copy for editions. Ariosto's orthographical habits will have been formed by what he saw in contemporary editions of Latin poets and prose writers; and what he saw as a reader he reproduced as a writer, even though the faulty orthography of the early printed editions was not a true element of the classical works he so carefully sought to imitate. In a sense, the standard spelling brings the poems closer to their classical models. We by no means underestimate the importance of an accurate historical understanding of the orthographical system in use for the printing and writing of Latin in the Renaissance; it is an essential study for the transmission of texts and for humanist debates about the spelling of Latin words. For the purposes of this edition, however, we want to assist readers in their understanding and enjoyment of the Latin poems and to bring out as sharply as possible their continuities of form, meter, theme, and diction with classical Latin poetry.

Metrical mistakes in EP 1553 are not corrected (see below in notes on 1.16, 2.11, 9.17, 9.20, 14.102, 19.5–6), except where they are regarded as errors of transmission, not of meter (2.38, 12.11, and 23.36). On balance, the greater probability is that the former group is not the product of the process of transmission but belong to the apprentice author who, as the evidence of F indicates, had difficulties when composing in metrically demanding lyric meters. All of the problematic lines, with one exception (14.102), occur in the asclepiadean or alcaic meter. One must also take into consideration the possibility that some of the manuscript sheets that Pigna used as printer's copy contained drafts of poems that were still in the process of revision and had not yet reached their final form at the poet's hands. There is no compelling evidence to suggest that metrical corrections introduced into early editions published after EP 1553 are anything more than conjectures. Metrical lapses in F are left unchanged (see below in notes on 21.11, 21.12, 32.6, 49.1).

The primary purpose of the following notes is to explain major differences in reading and punctuation between the ITRL text of Ariosto's *carmina* and the text in Bolaffi's second edition, which has served as the base text for subsequent editions. In brief compass we want to inform readers of the evidence for the text and the reasoning behind our editorial decisions.

ABBREVIATIONS

F	*Aliquot carmina autographa Ludovici Areosti ferrariensis,* ms. cart., sec. XVI. Ferrara, Biblioteca Comunale Ariostea, Classe I C.
EP 1553	*Io. Baptistae Pignae carminum lib. quatuor, ad Alphonsum Ferrariae principem. His adiunximus Caelii Calcagnini carm. lib. III. Ludovici Areosti carm. lib. II.* Venetiis, Ex Officina Erasmiana, Vincentii Valgrisi. M. D. L. III: 270–312.
Fabricius 1567	Petrus Fabricius, ed., *Horti Tres Amoris Amoenissimi Praestantissimorum Poetarum Nostri Seculi . . . : Pars Prima.* (Francofurti ad Moenum, 1567), 268r–76v. (A selection of seventeen poems in the following order: 53, 7, 23, 54, 29, 31, 32, 30, 43, 33, 34, 42.1–4, 41, 17, 1, 18, 44.)
Toscanus 1577	*Carmina illustrium poetarum Italorum.* Io. Matthaeus Toscanus conquisivit, recens., bonam partem nunc primum publicavit. 2 vols. (Lutetiae, vol. 1, 1576; vol. 2, 1577). Vol. 2, 263v–72v. (Same selection as in Fabricius 1567.)

Gherus 1608   Ranutius Gherus, ed., *Delitiae CC Italorum Poetarum Huius Superiorisque Aevi Illustrium: Pars Prima.* ([Francofurti ad Moenum], 1608), 273–87. (Same selection in the same order as in Fabricius 1567.) Ranuntius Gherus is the anagrammatic pseudonym of Ianus Gruterus.

Bottarius 1719   J.-G. Bottarius, ed., *Carminum Illustrium Poetarum Italorum*, vol. 1 (Florence, 1719). (A selection of eighteen poems in the following order: 53, 23, 54, 31, 32, 30, 43, 42.1–4, 41, 1, 18, 4, 14, 15, 62, 55, 8, 9.)

Orlandini 1730   Stefano Orlandini, ed., *Opere di M. Lodovico Ariosto*, vol. 2 (Venice: Orlandini, 1730), 389–400.

Barotti 1741   *Opere di Lodovico Ariosto con dichiarazioni*, vol. 4 (Venice: Francesco Pitteri, 1741), 857–98.

Barotti 1766   *Opere di Lodovico Ariosto con dichiarazioni*, vol. 6 (Venice: Francesco Pitteri, 1766), 425–72.

Pezzana 1784   Pezzana, Giuseppe, ed., *Opere di Ludovico Ariosto*, vol. 3 (Paris: G. G. Mérigot, 1784), 261–321.

Polidori 1857   *Opere minori in verso e in prosa di Lodovico Ariosto*, vol. 1 (Florence: Le Monnier, 1857), 315–66.

Carducci 1905   Giosuè Carducci, *La gioventù di Ludovico Ariosto e la poesia latina in Ferrara*, in *Opere*, 3rd ed., vol. 15, *Studi su Ludovico Ariosto e Torquato Tasso* (Bologna: Zanichelli, 1905), 3–260.

Fatini 1924   Giuseppe Fatini, ed., *Ludovico Ariosto: Lirica* (Bari: Laterza, 1924).

Sabbadini 1924   Remigio Sabbadini, "Recensioni orali a L. Ariosto-*Lirica* (G. Fatini)," *Rendiconti Reale Istituto lombardo di scienze e lettere* 57 (1924): 708–9.

Gandiglio 1926[1]   Adolfo Gandiglio, "Contributo alla revisione del testo dei carmi ariostei," *Annuario Liceo-Ginnasio di Fano* (Fano, 1924–25): 3–17.

Gandiglio 1926[2]   Adolfo Gandiglio, "Intorno al testo di alcuni carmi latini dell'Ariosto," *Giornale Storico della Letteratura Italiana* 88 (1926): 194–200.

Bolaffi 1938	*Ludovici Areosti Carmina. Praefatus est, recensuit, Italice vertit, adnotationibus instruxit Aetius Bolaffi,* 2nd ed. (Modena: ex Officina Typographica Mutinensi, 1938).
Segre 1954	Cesare Segre, ed., *Opere minori* (Milan-Naples: Ricciardi, 1954).
Mariotti 1959	S. Mariotti, "Per il riesame di un'ode latina dell'Ariosto," *Italia Medievale e Umanistica* 2 (1959): 509–12. (= Scevola Mariotti, *Scritti medievali e umanistici,* 3rd ed., ed. Silvia Rizzo [Rome: Edizioni di Storia e Letteratura, 2010], 295–300.)
Mariotti 1961	S. Mariotti, "Cronologia di congetture e congetture superflue," *Studi e problemi di critica testuale* (Bologna: Commissione per i testi di lingua, 1961), 359–68. (= Scevola Mariotti, *Scritti medievali e umanistici,* 3rd ed., ed. Silvia Rizzo [Rome: Edizioni di Storia e Letteratura, 2010], 301–12.)
Santoro 1989	*Opere,* vol. 3, *Carmina, Rime, Satire, Erbolato, Lettere,* ed. Mario Santoro (Turin: UTET, 1989).

LUDOVICI AREOSTI CARMINA

Title. The relevant line in the title page of EP 1553 reads *Ludovici Areosti Carm⟨inum⟩ Lib⟨ros⟩ II.*

1.16. *suavis canito* Fabricius 1567] *suavis caneto* EP 1553 *canito suave* Toscanus 1577, Bolaffi 1938. EP's *suavis caneto* is faulty in form and meter; *caneto* should be *canito* and does not fit the metrical pattern, and *suavis* is treated as a trisyllabic word, with *sua-* as a sequence of two short vowels, *u* and *a*; it is a single syllable, the *u* is consonantal and the *a* long. Early on these faults were recognized, and attempts were made to correct them. Fabricius 1567 corrected *caneto,* presumably a misprint, to *canito.* Toscanus 1577 printed *canito suave,* transposing the two words to solve the metrical problem (but only apparently, since now *sua-* is scanned as an iamb with a short *u* and a long *a*) and altering the form of *suavis* from feminine nominative singular to neuter accusative singular, functioning as an adverb, "sweetly." In 2.11, EP's reading *suaves* is again scanned as a trisyllable, with *sua-* as a sequence of two short vowels, and is also unmetrical. Editors since Barotti 1766 have replaced *suaves* in 2.11 with the metrically correct *teneros*. It should be noted that at 17.40 (*O solacia suavia*) the adjective scans correctly. Since there are two occurrences of the adjective *suavis* treated as a trisyllable in the text of EP 1553 and in both occurrences the *u* and the *a* are treated as short vowels, it is reasonable to conclude that at the time he wrote these two poems Ariosto misunderstood the prosody of this word and that therefore it should not be corrected at 1a.16 and 2.11. Though *suavis* and *canito* are unmetrical, they are printed here in the belief that this text has the best chance of being what Ariosto actually wrote.

1a. Transmitted in F only (4v and 7r); first edited by Carducci 1905, 151–52. The sheets containing the draft of this poem were not inserted into F consecutively: lines 1–18 are on 4v, and lines 19–36 on 7r. There is a diagonal cancellation stroke through lines 19–36.

1a.11. *quicum* Mariotti 1959, 510 n.3] *qui cum* F and editors. Mariotti correctly interpreted the reading in F, *qui cum*, as *qui,* the old form of the ablative of the relative pronoun governed by the preposition *cum*; both are usually written as one word. The antecedent of *qui* is *sanguinem*. Attempts to emend *qui* are unnecessary.

1a.13–20. These lines are heavily revised in F. The poet transformed what was initially a group of five lines by adding three lines in the lower right-hand margin to create two complete alcaic stanzas of four lines each. Italic type in the following represents Ariosto's revisions:

Sheet 4v:

Parata tantis arva laboribus *Laconico*		13
nec Pario domus || *simulque et Afro et*		
Iuvare possunt ~~nec quod in arcula~~		14
arca *omnigeno lapide*		
Stipatur ~~auri~~ / prodigioribus *enitescens*		[15] 18
haec hoc et auri quicquid		
~~arcula~~		
aenea		

Sheet 7r:

| Linquenda posteris propinquis | [16] 19 |
| Omnia sunt avido aut tyranno | [17] 20 |

Before revision, Ariosto had written a sequence of three alcaic hendecasyllables (13, 14, [15]), one alcaic enneasyllable [16], and one alcaic decasyllable [17], or what amounts to one alcaic stanza (14, [15], [16], [17]) and one extra-stanzaic line (13). Out of this initial attempt, Ariosto expanded 13–14 into a complete stanza with the addition of *nec Pario . . . enitescens* (14–16), and likewise [15]–[17] into a complete stanza with the addition of *Haec . . . aenea* (17).

1a.15. *Afro et* F] *Afro* Bolaffi 1938, Segre 1954, Santoro 1989. Although *et* is clearly written after *Afro* in F and is reproduced by Carducci 1905, 152, in his transcription of the poem, it is not printed in Bolaffi 1938.

1a.29. *Philiroe* F Segre 1954] *Passiphile* F corrected, Bolaffi 1938, Santoro 1989. In F the name *Philiroe* is canceled (P̶h̶i̶l̶i̶r̶o̶e̶) and *Passiphile* written above it. See Notes to the Translation.

2.11. *suaves* EP 1553] *teneros* Barotti 1766. *Suaves* is unmetrical (see note on 1a.16 above) and was replaced by Barotti with the metrically correct *teneros*, perhaps a conjecture inspired by *tenero* in line 18. Though unmetrical, *suaves* is retained on the high probability that it is what Ariosto wrote.

2.26–35. *Quare . . . horream . . . ut. . . ?* ITRL editors] *. . . quare . . . horream. Vt. . . !* editors. EP 1553 punctuates with a period at the end of 25 (admittedly EP's punctuation does not inspire confidence). *Quare . . . horream* makes much better sense as a deliberative question than as a dependent clause, especially since the poet has already said in 24–25 that he is not anxious about the fate of rich cargoes on a stormy sea. Editors understand *ut* in 27 as exclamatory ("how"), beginning a new sentence. The absence of punctuation in EP after *horream* suggests that the *ut* clause is a continuation of the question in 26. Accordingly, *ut* is here taken in its causal sense, "since" or "seeing that," and introduces the poet's reason for not subjecting himself to the worries attendant on the pursuit of wealth in mercantile ventures on the sea.

3. Transmitted in F only (4r); first published by Barotti 1741. Lines 1–2, before Ariosto's revisions, are written as follows (his spelling and punctuation are retained):

> Stirps Areosta mihi: patria est Ferraria. Fulci
>   Nomen. Roma altrix. Daunia sarcophagus

There is a diagonal cancellation stroke through the poem.

4. The poem begins abruptly; there is no mention of the occasion celebrated in the poem, and no background is provided for the action that commences in line 1. Apparently, there has been a council of the gods on Olympus, at which Jupiter spoke; some of the gods cheer approvingly (*clamor*, 1) in response, others express their approval more quietly (*murmure . . . tacito*, 1–2). It seems that some course of action was decided on, presumably in connection with the birthday celebration for Minerva; the phrase *ex illo monitu* (37) suggests that a decision was made at the council of the gods and is now being carried out by Minerva. Since there is no indication in the text of the convening of the gods or of what Jupiter said, Bolaffi 1938 reasonably posits a lacuna; see his discussion (xxxix). On the verbal level, one can assume that a form of the noun *pars*, or equivalent, coordinated with *pars* in line 1, occurred earlier in the lacuna.

4.40–44. *Paulatim . . . deturbat . . . nomen.* Mariotti 1959 n. 3] . . . *paulatim . . . deturbet . . . nomen.* EP 1553, . . . *paulatim . . . quae turbet . . . nomen* Bolaffi 1938. Mariotti's conjecture *deturbat* for EP's *deturbet* and his repunctuation of these lines, which makes *cura* govern *quaerere*, result in a remarkable transformation of what was once obscure in syntax and meaning. There is no reason now to adopt Bolaffi's conjecture, *quae turbet*.

4.44. The poet's account of the development of human intellectual curiosity and the beginnings of natural philosophy ends suddenly and is followed in 45 by an address to Duke Ercole and praise of his success in negotiating a peace. It is reasonable to assume that the poet had more to say about the development of intellectual pursuits, with Minerva's assistance, and that he devised a transition that connected those pursuits specifically to the cultural life of Ferrara and Duke Ercole's patronage. In line 45 *coeptis*, which has no reference in the extant text, is strong evidence that there was mention of the city's vigorous cultivation of Minerva's *artes*. Accordingly, Bolaffi 1938, xl–xli, posits a lacuna between 44 and 45.

5. Transmitted in F only (4r–v); first published by Carducci 1905, 158. There are four diagonal cancellation strokes through lines 1–4 and three cancellation strokes through lines 5–6.

5.2. Ariosto wrote *vere orba erepto* . . . ; he later deleted the participle (~~erepto~~) and wrote *et tristis* above it, apparently seeking emotional intensity through the repetition of *tristis et orba* in line 2. However, the change to *et tristis* does not fit the syntax of the sentence, as noted by Carducci 1905, 158.

6.5–8. EP 1553 and editors punctuate 5–6 and 7–8 as two separate sentences. This punctuation disrupts the syntax of the alternative conditionals *si . . . seu*, which specify through subject matter (epic and lyric) and instrument (lyre) the general reference of *carmina* in 5 and set up the mention of the Fauns' pipe of pastoral poetry in 8. In 5 the poet compliments Pandolfo's poetry with the praise of the *Fauni*; in 6–8 he deploys the generic markers of their respective types of poetry to establish Pandolfo's poetic identity and to recognize his poetic preeminence in the pastoral landscape. Bolaffi's conjecture *sin* for EP's *seu* in 7 is based on a misunderstanding of the text.

6.11. *cantanti* EP 1553] Bolaffi 1938 prints Gandiglio's 1926[2], 197 n. 1, conjecture *cuntanti*, a nonce word for the correct form *cunctanti*. *Cantanti* gives excellent sense. Failure to understand the construction, the dative pronoun *tibi*, referring to Pandolfo, understood with *cantanti*, has led to unnecessary conjecture.

6.20. *lacteolae . . . genae* ITRL editors] *lacteolae . . . viae* EP 1553 and editors. This may be the most puzzling crux in the text of Ariosto's Latin poems. *Lacteola via* means, literally, "milky way," more commonly, *via lactea*. No convincing explanation of what the words may mean in this context has been given. Since the nymph is enamored of the sleeping Pandolfo's face (*ora*), and Pandolfo is addressed as a *formose puer* (compare Verg. *Ecl.* 2.14–17), presumably suggesting that he has not yet developed a beard, we conjecture *lacteolae . . . genae* (milk-white cheek). Compare

Politian, *Eleg.* 5.26, *lacteolas . . . genas,* although there referring to the complexion of his mistress.

6.23. (*imperium dominae, non moenia, claudit*) Printed without parentheses by EP 1553 and editors. The *quod-* clause following in 24 gives the reason for the exclamation *me miserum;* the parenthesis (*imperium . . . claudit*) provides the explanation for the poet's inability to leave town.

6.24. *prata* Gandiglio 1926², 197 n. 1] *grata* EP 1553, editors. *Grata* is clearly an accidental repetition of *grata* in 20 and does not provide a satisfactory object for *visere.* Gandiglio's conjecture *prata* gives excellent sense, is appropriate to the pastoral setting, and further emphasizes the poet's urban confinement.

6.35–36. *sed mora. Quae* ITRL editors] *sed mora, quae* EP 1553, editors. *mora,* as the antecedent of *quae,* is an odd subject for *nititur,* and for the main verb *feret* (Bolaffi 1938; first printed by Barotti 1766 for EP's *foret*) in the context of Venus's inevitable assault on Pandolfo's freedom. Moreover, the referent of *illa* in 36 is unclear, and various candidates have been suggested. These problems are solved when *sed mora* is interpreted as a separate sentence, tersely undercutting Pandolfo's confidence in his freedom, and *illa,* the antecedent of *quae,* is taken to refer to Venus, who is, as we learn in 37–40, working to ensnare the innocent youth.

6.39. *Naiadas* ITRL editors] *Naiades* EP 1553, editors. The accusative plural of this Greek noun ends in *-as,* not *-es,* the Latin termination. That Ariosto knew the Greek termination is confirmed by *Dryadas* (54.57).

6.40. *si sapis, ipse cave* Gandiglio 1926², 197] *si sapis ipse, cave* EP 1553, editors. The intensifier *ipse,* taken with the imperative *cave,* gives proper emphasis to the experienced lover's admonition to one as yet untouched by the travails of amour.

8. Transmitted in EP 1553, and in F (10v), with a diagonal cancellation stroke through the whole poem.

8.3. *tot et aspera vitae* EP 1553] *per tot mala vitam* F, Bolaffi 1938. Two considerations strongly suggest that EP's *tot et aspera vitae* is the poet's revision of *per tot mala vitam,* the text in F. First, EP's text replaces the generic *mala* with a phrase, *aspera vitae* (life's rough roads), which introduces an image that is neatly consistent with *emensum . . . pedibus*: Francesco Ariosto traversed life's rough roads without stumbling, that is, was uncorrupted. Such a thoughtful revision of F's text is difficult to explain as the result of editorial or print house intervention. The second consideration is that there is a diagonal cancellation stroke through the poem in F; this may be a sign that Ariosto composed a revised draft of the poem that contained the phrase *tot et aspera vitae*, and from this revised draft the text of EP was set.

9.17. The form *Lugdunii* is metrically and morphologically problematic. The *u* in the second syllable is treated as short; it is long. The form should be *Lugduni*, the locative of *Lugdunum*; the poet has added an extra syllable at the end. Since ancient metrical practice allows for some flexibility in the treatment of vowel quantities in proper names, the lengthening of the *u* is not without precedent. As for the addition of an extra syllable, it is possible that Ariosto came across the form *Lugdun⟨i⟩um* in a printed source or that he simply made it up.

9.20. *quamvis*, a spondee, is treated as an iamb.

10. Transmitted in F only (3r); first published by Carducci 1905, 165. There is a diagonal cancellation stroke through the poem.

10.6. *atque* Sabbadini] *at* F. The reading in F is clearly *at*, which is unmetrical and without meaning; *atque* is required both by meter and by sense. Since Ariosto wrote *atque* in 11.6, in a similarly phrased sentence, it seems certain that here we have nothing more than an authorial slip of the pen.

11. Transmitted in EP 1553 and F (3r).

12.9. *saevum* EP 1553] *serum* conjectured by Bolaffi 1938. Compare, in a funerary context, Stat. *Silv.* 5.1.179, *saevo planctu*; and 5.1.198, *saevo clamore*.

12.11. *praequam* ITRL editors] *praeque* EP 1553, editors. No satisfactory explanation of the meaning of *praeque* (the preposition *prae* + the enclitic connective *-que*) has been given. The conjecture *praequam* is based on the assumption of a misreading of Ariosto's abbreviation for *-quam* as *-que*, the same misreading that occurred in 25.17 (see note below).

instabilis Barotti 1766, editors] *immobilis* EP 1553. EP's reading *immobilis* is unmetrical and looks like a deliberate editorial substitution based on a misinterpretation of the sense. According to the geocentric model of the universe, the phrase *immobilis plaga*, referring to the earth, is correct; the earth is suspended immobile at the center. But Ariosto is not giving a lesson in astronomy; as the context makes clear, he is contrasting the human realm of error and mutability (*vana, nebulas*) with the immortal abode where his father now dwells. The poet's perspective is a philosophical, not an astronomical one. Barotti 1766 replaced *immobilis* with *instabilis*, a reading that is metrical and gives excellent sense. It is a safe assumption that Barotti found this reading in the manuscript sheet containing this poem, which was once in his possession. Cf. poem 54.62.

12.12. *tute* ITRL editors] *tu te* EP 1553, editors. The accusative *te* gives poor sense; Ariosto's father will not have been contemplating and looking at himself up in the *ether*. The emphatic form of the nominative, *tute*, is an appropriate form of address to a father who, after death, lives on in another realm.

13.2. In EP 1553 the text of line 2 lacks two syllables to complete the iambic trimeter. The reflexive pronoun *sibi* was supplied by Sabbadini 1924 and Gandiglio 1926[1], 15.

14.27–28. These lines were omitted in EP 1553; they were restored to the text by Barotti 1766. The cause of the omission was eye-skip from *nostris* at the end of line 26 to *nostris* at the end of line 28, tricking the compositor into going directly from the end of 26 to the beginning of 29. Barotti's restoration of these lines provides evidence that he had in his possession at some time more autograph sheets of Ariosto's Latin poems (i.e., at the very least a copy of poem 14) than those he finally gave to the Biblioteca Comunale Ariostea in Ferrara.

14.102. *Sequanae*, a cretic (‾ ˘ ‾), is treated as an anapest (˘ ˘ ‾).

14.142. *axes, / ancillae nec . . . ausus* Barotti 1741, Gandiglio 1926[1], 11] *axes / ancillae, nec . . . ausus* EP 1553, editors. The genitive *ancillae* is dependent on *feros ausus*, "the outrageous cruelty of the maidservant," that is, the murderer of Pica. Previous editors have taken *ancillae* with *axes*, "the chariot of the maidservant," maidservant being interpreted as an insulting name for Phaedra, stepmother of Hippolytus / Virbius, a very unlikely interpretation.

15.31–32. *sub / moribus et ducibus (di, date digna) malis?* ITRL editors] *sub / moribus? At ducibus, di, date digna malis;* EP 1553, editors. In EP's text *moribus* stands without an epithet and the adversative *at* has no context. Clearly, lines 31 and 32 form a single question, and the comparison is between being under foreign rule or under the corrupt morals and bad leadership of native princes.

15.38. *haustus* Bolaffi 1938] *haustu* EP 1553. The masculine plural relative pronoun *quos* has no antecedent; *eloquio* and *monitis* are neuter. The sense, however, requires that *quos* refer to those nouns. Bolaffi's emendation *haustus* solves the problem; *quos* is attracted into the gender of the predicate *haustus*, a regular construction: literally, "which he took in as drafts from . . ."

16a. Transmitted in F only (10r); first edited by Carducci 1905, 207–8. The poem is crossed out.

16a.7. In F *prae quod* is corrected to *prae quo*, with the deletion of the *d*. The poet may have been uncertain about the syntactic construction with *prae*. His first instinct was correct; *prae quod* is an elliptical expression for *prae ⟨eo⟩* [i.e., *munere*] *quod*, the antecedent *eo* being omitted. It appears the poet came around again to the correct construction in the revised version.

17.18. *tepidis* EP 1553] *trepidis* Bolaffi's 1938 conjecture. Compare Ov. *Met.* 4.674, *tepido . . . fletu*.

19.5–6. *vobis ut innuba / Pallas* Sabbadini 1924, 709, Gandiglio 1926[2], 198] *vobis et innuba / Pallas* EP 1553; *Pallas et innuba / vobis* Barotti 1766, Bolaffi. There are two problems here. First, EP's reading is unmetrical; *vobis* is a spondee, where a trochee is required. Barotti 1766 restored the meter by transposing *vobis* and *Pallas*. The question remaining is whether Barotti corrected a transmissional error or the author himself. Sabbadini, Gandiglio, and Mariotti think that Ariosto is responsible for the faulty meter. Perhaps the fact that *innuba Pallas* is the ending of a hexameter precipitated the mistake (Val. Flac. *Arg.* 1.87). The second problem concerns *et.* As either conjunction ("and virgin Pallas once promised") or adverb ("virgin Pallas too once promised"), it is difficult to explain: the conjunction provides a very weak connection with the preceding address to the *iuvenes,* and the late postponement in the sentence is odd; the adverb likewise results in a tenuous link with what precedes, and the additive sense can be explained only if one is to think of Juno's role in supporting the voyage of Jason and the Argonauts. The emendation *ut,* proposed by Sabbadini 1924, 709, and Gandiglio 1926², 198, provides a clear connection with lines 1–4 ("as virgin Pallas once promised") and strengthens the poet's exhortation to drive the mission to its conclusion.

19.9. *occupat* EP 1553] This third-person singular form is out of place in the context of direct address to the *iuvenes* (*cupitis* [4], *vobis* [6], etc.) and especially in connection with *vestris . . . votis* (11–12). The Vergilian parallel (*o lecta manus . . . incumbite,* Aen. 10.294) is suggestive; *lecta manus* may be a vocative, and *occupat* a misprint for *occupas,* a collective singular.

20.8. *et* ITRL editors] *es* EP 1553, editors. Since *pessime* is a vocative, the verb *es* has no complement. In addition, *omnium malorum* is an all-inclusive phrase and should not be restricted to *furum.* See Hor. *Sat.* 1.4.3 for the combination *malus ac fur.*

21. Transmitted in EP 1553 and in F (9v). In F the text of this poem breaks off after line 17, which is the last line at the bottom of sheet 9v; the sheet containing the remainder of the poem is lost. There are some interesting variants between the manuscript and printed versions of lines 1–17.

21.4. *in* F] omitted by EP 1553.

21.4. *vobis* F] *votis* EP 1553.

21.7. *miser* F] *miseri* EP 1553.

21.11. *pernic-,* a trochee (– ∪), is treated as a spondee (– –).

21.12. *coitus,* a spondee (– –), is treated as a cretic (– ∪ –).

22. Transmitted in F only (9r–v); first published by Carducci 1905, 195–96.

22.1. ⟨*Infelix a*⟩*nime* was restored by Carducci 1905, 195, from line 17. A small piece was torn off the upper left-hand corner of sheet 9.

22.15–16. *deum potentem* (F in the margin) *. . . deieratum* (F, *deieratos* corrected)] *deos potenteis* (F, in the text) *. . . deieratos* (F's original reading). It is unclear what prompted Ariosto to change these forms from plural to singular.

22.22–27. There is substantial revision of these lines in F. The first ver-
sion of lines 22–26 is written thus, with horizontal cancellation strokes
through each line:

~~Spurcatum amplius os potest placere~~	22
~~Moechorum undique basiatione~~	23
~~An te illi ebrioli movent ocelli~~	24
~~Qui cuncto populo huc et huc vagantes~~	25
~~Arrident precium male aucupantes~~	26

(Can her mouth, filthy with kissing adulterers from all over, please
you any longer? Or do those tipsy darling eyes excite you, eyes roam-
ing about here and there, a delight to all and sundry, dishonestly try-
ing to snare a buck.)

A revised version of 22–24, itself with revisions, is written in the
right-hand margin adjacent to the original lines; 22a and 23a have hori-
zontal cancellation strokes (translations are purely for the sake of exam-
ple, since it cannot be known how the syntax might have developed):

Os spurca placet oblitum saliva	22
~~Tantorum memori notaque livens~~	22a
Et livens memori nota perenne	23
~~Tantorum utpote basiatione?~~	23a
Foedae proh dolor osculationis	24

(Is her mouth pleasing to you, smeared with the slimy saliva [and
discolored with the sign that is a reminder of so many men] and dis-
colored with the sign that is a constant reminder [of so many men
naturally because of their kissing] of gross kissing. It kills me to think
of it!)

In the bottom margin of the page, below the canceled line 26 above,
are written lines 25–27:

An te illi ebrioli movent ocelli	25
Illi quos movet hic et hic et ille et	26
Quisquis dedecorum putetur emptor	27

23.17. *pedes* EP 1553] *pedum* editors. *Pedes*, nominative singular, here meaning "one who goes on foot," was at some point in the print tradition misunderstood as *pedes*, accusative plural of *pes* "foot"; then, in order to make it fit the syntax of the line, it was changed to *pedum*, dependent on *plantis* (Pezzana 1784).

23.34. *hiemes* Pezzana 1784] *hiemis* EP 1553. The nominative plural *hiemes* provides a much needed subject for the verb *ferunt* and gives excellent sense. The genitive singular *hiemis* is difficult to construe.

24. Transmitted in F only (8r); first edited by Carducci 1905, 202.

24.1. *lustrans* is deleted; *lustrem* is written in the left margin.

24.2. *sim Telesilla tuae* is deleted; *Lydia bella tuae* is written in the left margin.

25. Transmitted in EP 1553 and F (8v).

25.1. *causae* F] *causa* EP 1553, editors. Although Bolaffi 1938 reports *causa* as the reading of F, there are faint traces of the *e* in the *ae* ligature to confirm *causae* as what Ariosto wrote. Moreover, *quid causae* is the standard Latin idiom.

25.12–13. These lines in their original form were canceled:

~~Boiardis servas condita vina cadis~~
~~Praela haec non illis cedunt rite et impius illic~~

([Why . . .] do you preserve the wines of Boiardo stored up in large jars?
These wine presses rightly do not yield to those and there the unnatural . . .)

Bolaffi 1938 in his transcription reads *cite* instead of *rite* in 13. The revised version of 12–13 is added in the left margin.

25.15–16. These lines in their original form were canceled:

~~Cur tibi non satyrus comes est cur esseda tygris~~
~~Non trahit haec tyrso concita at ille mero~~

(Why don't you have a satyr as a companion, why isn't a tigress drawing your chariot, the one stirred up by the thyrsus, the other by unmixed wine?)

Bolaffi 1938 in his transcription reads *concito* for *concita* in 16. The revised version of 15–16 is written vertically down the left margin.

25.17. *quemquam* F] *quemque* EP 1553, editors. EP 1553 incorrectly expanded Ariosto's abbreviation for *-quam* into *-que* and was followed by subsequent editors.

26. Transmitted in EP 1553 and in F (8v).

26.2. In F *volupe est* is deleted; *placeat* is written in the left margin. The adverb *volup* (*volupe* is an incorrect form that Ariosto probably saw in early printed editions) is confined to the plays of Plautus and Terence.

27. Transmitted in EP 1553 and F (8v).

28. Transmitted in Codex Estensis α. T. 6. 8. (66v), with attribution to *Lod. Areo.*; first edited by Carducci 1905, 244.

29. Transmitted in EP 1553 and in F (3r).

29.5. *omnia . . . tandem . . . novit* EP 1553 (no punctuation in F] *omnia . . . tandem! . . . novit* Bolaffi. Bolaffi's exclamation point interrupts the syntax of the sentence.

31. Transmitted in EP 1553 and in F (10v). There is no title in F. EP's title has the incorrect form of the name *Lycoris*. *Lycori* is the vocative; it should be the ablative, *Lycoride*. The correction *Lycoride* was made in Pezzana 1784.

32. Transmitted in EP 1553 and F (10v).

32.3. In F *forma* is deleted; *parque* is written suprascript.

32.6. *rursum* F] *rursus* EP 1553. F's *rursum* results in an elision that leaves the line short by one syllable. EP's *rursus*, adopted by some editors, restores the meter. However, the possibility that *rursus* is the author's, and not EP's revision, seems unlikely; the absence of a cancellation stroke through the poem and EP's adoption of F's correction in 3, *parque* for *forma*, suggest that this was the final draft of the poem. It seems doubtful, *pace* Bolaffi in his note in the *app. crit.*, that Ariosto deliberately introduced hiatus into the line; *rursus* was ready to hand as a metrical alternative to avoid the hiatus. Since this moment of authorial inadvertence gives us insight into Ariosto's handling of Latin poetic language and meter, *rursum* should not be corrected.

33. Transmitted in EP 1553 and in F (3v).

34. Transmitted in EP 1553 and in F (3v).

35. Transmitted in EP 1553 and in F (7v).

36. Transmitted in EP 1553 and in F (7v).

39. Transmitted in EP 1553 and in F (3v).

40. Transmitted in EP 1553 and in F (3v)

42. This poem is printed as two separate poems in EP 1553: 1–4 on p. 296 (titled *De Venere Se Armante*) and 5–8 on p. 294 (titled *De Spartanis*). Only 1–4 are preserved in F on 7v. Since line 4 is the last line on 7v in F, lines 5–8 must have been written at the top of the recto of a new sheet. Either Pigna did not realize that the poem continued onto the next sheet, or perhaps more likely, the autograph sheets, in this particular case, were not arranged in the proper order and the no-longer extant sheet with lines 5–8 did not follow immediately after 7v. Carducci 1905, 212, saw that they formed a single poem.

42.7–8. *meque decent . . . quae sanguine nata* Polidori 1857] *meque docent . . . quae sanguine natam* EP 1553; *meque docent . . . de sanguine natam* Bolaffi. The relative pronoun *quae* in EP's text cannot be construed; hence, Bolaffi's conjecture *de*. However, at least as an initial response to the transmitted text, it seems preferable to preserve the parallelism of the three relative clauses (*quae . . . quae . . . quae*), each of which identifies a particular aspect of the goddess and explains the appropriateness of her bearing arms. Since the epigram turns on the seeming paradox of the goddess of love armed for combat, like the virgin warrior Minerva, the reading *decent . . . nata*, printed by Polidori and adopted by Segre and Santoro, gives the epigram a clever conclusion by asserting the appropriateness of *arma* in terms of Venus's violent birth, her affair with Mars the god of war, and her being a Lacedaemonian.

45, 46. Transmitted in EP 1553 and F (11v). In F the name of the deceased is *Philippa* (45.1, 46.1); in EP 1553 the name has been changed in both places to *Camilla*.

47. Transmitted in F only (11v); first edited by Barotti 1766.

48. Barotti 1766 is the only source for this poem.

49. Transmitted in F only (8r); first edited by Barotti 1766. There is a diagonal cancellation stroke through the whole poem.

49.1. *Manfredinus* F] *Manfredius* Barotti 1766. The *i* in the Latin suffix *-inus* is long and therefore unmetrical here. It is quite possible that Ariosto allowed himself the metrical license of treating the *i* as short. It does little honor to a dead man, even for the sake of correct meter, to commemorate him with the wrong form of his name. For a different view, see Bolaffi 1938, xxvii.

49.5. *praemia?* F, Barotti 1766] *praemia!* Bolaffi 1938. Ariosto clearly wrote a question mark after *praemia*; it is identical to the question marks after *tumulo* and *causa*.

50. Transmitted in F only (7v); first edited by Barotti 1766.

51. Transmitted in F only (11r); first edited by Carducci 1905, 233–34.

52. Transmitted in F only (3v–4r); first edited by Barotti 1741.

52.2. In F *leges* is deleted, and *mores* added suprascript.

52.4. In F the original text *intorquens . . . verbera* was changed to *intorcto* [sic] *. . . verbere*.

52.7. In F *asper* is deleted, and *durus* added suprascript.

52.9–10. There is a horizontal cancellation stroke through each line.

53. In EP 1553 the poem is printed as a continuous block of text without division into choruses. Fatini (1924) appears to be the first editor who divided the poem into choruses and inserted the headings *Ferrarienses* and *Romani*.

54.29–30. *"Ecce iterum male sana,"* inquit, *"quid . . . manent."* ITRL editors] *Ecce iterum. -Male sana, inquit, quid . . . manent.* Bolaffi. Bolaffi's text does not indicate where the speech of the poet's *mens* ends; Segre rightly prints a dash after *manent*. The lively conversational tone of *ecce iterum* suggests that it is part of what the *mens* is saying; and at this point in the poem it clearly emphasizes its recognition of its own unstable behavior.

54.33. *illam* EP 1553] *illa* Bolaffi 1938, editors. *Illum*, referring to *mens*, is the object of the impersonal verb *pertaesum est*. Editors mistakenly punctuate with a comma after *principis*. *Illa* is printed in Polidori 1857 and may have crept into the print tradition earlier.

55a. Transmitted in F only (7v); first edited by Carducci 1905, 205.

56. Transmitted in Codex Estensis S. I. 36 only (73r and 86v), with attribution to *Ludovici. Areosti*; first edited by Carducci 1905, 205.

57. Transmitted in F only (10r); first edited by Barotti 1766.

58a. Transmitted in F only (8r); first published by Carducci 1905, 205–6.

61. Transmitted in EP 1553 and in F (12r), where the top right corner of the sheet is torn away, resulting in the loss of the word *meretur* at the end of line 1.

64–67. In F (5r–v) these four poems are written in a calligraphic hand, distinct from the workday hand on the other sheets; the letters are clear and uniform in shape, with flourishes of ascenders and descenders, and the end of each poem is marked by a sign (÷). There are no revisions or crossings out. In the bottom right corner of 5r are the initials *L. A.*, for *Ludovici Areosti*.

64. Transmitted in EP and in F (5r).

65. Transmitted in EP and in F (5r).

66. Transmitted in EP and in F (5r).

67. Transmitted in F only (5v); first edited by Barotti 1766.

CARMINA INCERTA, CARMINA APOCRYPHA

All of the poems in these two sections, with one exception, do not appear in EP 1553. The one exception is poem 2 of the *Incerta* (Quis iacet hoc gelido sub marmore . . . ; EP 1553, p. 298). For arguments against their authenticity, see Pesenti, "Storia del testo," 125–34, and Bolaffi 1938, xxxiv–xxxvii.

Notes to the Translation

꙰§?꙰

Line numbers are keyed to the Latin text. We acknowledge our dependence on the indispensable commentaries of Bolaffi, Santoro, and Segre.

POEMS OF LUDOVICO ARIOSTO

I. To Philiroe

Meter: alcaic

Ariosto probably composed this poem in the summer of 1494 just before Charles VIII of France invaded the north of Italy in September. The narrator, whose tranquil life is interrupted by politics and war, invokes the Horatian topos of *recusatio*, hoping to exchange the anxieties of war for the pleasures of love (Hor. *Carm.* 1.1.21–25, 2.5.12, and 2.11). This is one of the four poems that Ariosto rewrote in two distinct versions in the autograph manuscript (see also 16, 55, and 58). In this polished version we have a glimpse of Ariosto at work on the poem, which was first written as a much longer composition (see 1a below). His main objective in revising 1a is to remove the more overt political commentary in the earlier draft. The extensive corrections visible on the autograph of 1a mark this as a poem that Ariosto strove to perfect, suggesting that anxiety about the French invasion required his utmost attention.

1–2. Compare Hor. *Carm.* 2.11.1–4.

1. *Galliarum*: In reference to France, Ariosto uses the classicizing "of the lands of the Gauls" (1). The plural *Galliae* represents the Roman division of modern France and Belgium into the *Tres Galliae* (*Lugdunensis*, *Belgica*, and *Aquitania*). The word may also be a tacit reminder that the kingdom of Charles VIII was once conquered, annexed, and administered by the *Imperium Romanum*.

Ships and horses: An allusion to Hor. *Carm.* 1.6.3, *navibus et equis*, despite the fact that Charles descended into Italy by land.

159

2. Charles: Charles VIII, king of France (1470–98), invaded the Italian peninsula in 1494 to claim the crown of Naples. The invasion and lingering presence of the French destabilized Italian politics for decades. He is referred to in 14.100 as "noble scion of Charles the Great."

3. The key Ariostan term *furor* (madness) that lies behind the title of his narrative poem, *Orlando Furioso*, is used again in *Ad Pandulphum* (2.40) to describe the invasion of Charles VIII.

4. Ausonia: A Latinized form of a Greek term for southern Italy, frequently used by extension to mean the entire peninsula. *Ausoniis ruinam*: Hor. *Carm.* 3.5.40.

5. What steps: The swift descent of the French army caught the inhabitants of city after city off guard as 25,000 soldiers moved unopposed from Pavia to Pisa to Florence to Naples. Underlying Ariosto's comment is the irony that Italians did nothing to stop Charles.

6. Strawberry tree: An allusion to Hor. *Carm.* 1.1.21–22, the ode that inspires Ariosto's invocation of the theme of *recusatio* in this poem.

8. Corydon: Name for a shepherd in pastoral poetry, e.g., Verg. *Ecl.* 2.1.

9. Philiroe: In the Ferrarese poetic tradition, Philiroe harkens back to the lady in the poetry of Tito Vespasiano Strozzi. The name appears with different spellings in Strozzi's Latin verse (*Philliroe, Philiroe, Phyliroe, Phillyroe*), and there is a more significant alternation between these various spellings and *Philoroe*. See Caterino, "Filliroe e i suoi poeti," 184 n. 15. On the tradition of Latin poetry in the Ferrarese Quattrocento, see Pasquazi, "La poesia in latino." In addition to Ariosto, other writers in the Ferrarese circle who invoke her include Gaspare Tribraco, Battista Guarini, Matteo Maria Boiardo, Ludovico Lazzarelli, Girolamo Balbi, as well as some unidentified authors. See Caterino, "Filliroe e i suoi poeti"; R. Bacchelli, *La congiura di don Giulio d'Este*, 159–70. The name *Philiroe* is not found in classical Latin poetry. The following women's names in Ariosto's poems were also used by Roman poets, on which see the respective notes: *Glycere*, poem 2.10; *Lycoris*, poem 32.1; *Lyda*, poem 54.2; *Lydia*, poem 23.3; *Megilla*, poem 17 (title); *Phyllis*, poem 54.2; *Telesilla*, poem 24.2 (revised to *Lydia*).

10–11. Compare Catull. 45.20.

12. *purpureo . . . flore:* Hor. *Carm.* 2.5.12.

13. *udum . . . caput:* Hor. *Carm.* 1.7.22–23.

14. Compare Catull. 63.8, and Hor. *Carm.* 2.5.18.

Ia. Ode on the Tranquil Life to Philiroe

Meter: alcaic

Rough draft of poem 1, from which the poet cut the charged passage in which he speaks out against political tyranny (9–29). The excised passage may criticize specific leaders of Italian states at the time of the invasion, possibly even Ercole I d'Este, ruler of Ferrara at the time. The chronological evidence suggests that this is one of Ariosto's earliest Latin compositions, which is why Bolaffi opens his text of the *Carmina* with the revised version.

1–9. See notes on 1.1–9

9. *miseri quibus:* Hor. *Carm.* 1.5.12.

14–15. Compare Hor. *Carm.* 2.18.4–8.

14. Parian: From the island of Paros, one of the Cyclades in the Aegean, famed in antiquity for its white marble.

15. Laconian: Spartan. *Lapis lacedaemonius*, Spartan porphyry, is a green volcanic stone that can be polished to a high gloss, especially prized by the Romans for mosaics. See Plin. *HN* 36.11.

African: Egyptian. Granite, porphyry, and other colored forms of marble were quarried in northern Africa.

17–20. Compare Hor. *Carm.* 2.14.21–28.

20. Greedy tyrant: In the passage later removed, the narrator implies that tyrannical princes throughout the Italian peninsula should have done more to counter the invasion of the French. The leaders of Italy are too greedy for their own good.

24. *male gratus:* Compare poem 54.33.

29. Philiroe: Ariosto canceled *Philiroe*, the original reading in F, and then wrote *Passiphile* above the line. If it is accepted that poem 1 is the revised version of poem Ia, then the name *Philiroe* in line 9 of poem 1 indicates that that name was his final thought on the matter. The shift in address

from Philiroe (named in the title in the autograph manuscript) to Passiphile has caused concern. Carducci 1905, 153–56, notes that Ercole Strozzi describes Ariosto as a lover who has lost his girl, Passiphile, and is going to write elegies about her (*Venatio*, 505–8). This reference to Passiphile in 1a would refer to her, even if she is just a supralinear variant.

33. *mero . . . vinciat*: Hor. *Carm.* 1.7.22–23.

36. Compare Theoc. 16.45 (*multichordem* = πολύχορδον). The adjective *multichordis* is not recorded in classical Latin. It is possible that the Latin epithet was coined by Marullus (*Hymni* 4.1.4, *barbiton in breve multichordem*) and then borrowed by Ariosto.

II. To Pandolfo

Meter: fourth asclepiadean

A poem to his cousin and best friend, Pandolfo, about foregoing the anxieties of courtly life for one of song and love. Catalano speculates that this composition has to be dated before the period when Pandolfo served as Cardinal Ippolito d'Este's private secretary, that is, sometime before the years 1498 to 1505 (*Vita*, 1:147). In "More Light on Pandolfo" and "A Further Note on Pandolfo," Clough argues that the poem was composed in 1494. In sonnet 37.9, Ariosto calls Pandolfo "nostro secretario antico" (our secretary of old), and he refers to his cousin's career at *Sat.* 6.220–25. The terminology for the identification of the asclepiadean meters is based on R. G. M. Nisbet and M. Hubbard, *A Commentary on Horace: Odes Book 1* (Oxford, 1970), xxxviii–xl.

2. Your prince: Pandolfo served in the court of Ercole I in the mid-1490s before serving Ippolito, Ercole's son. Clough speculates that Ariosto's link to the court of Ippolito is through Pandolfo ("More Light," 195).

4. Golden locks of mistress Fortune: In *Sat.* 6.181–83, addressed to Pietro Bembo, Ariosto uses a similar image — seizing the forelock of Occasion — to recount how he mastered Latin but failed to learn Greek as a student of Gregorio da Spoleto.

10. Glycere: Girls (*puellae*) in the Latin lyric and elegiac poetry Ariosto imitates, whether modern or ancient, usually have Greek names; compare "Phyllis" and "Philliroe" below (22). The name here is a form of the Greek adjective for "sweet." Horace uses it in his *Carm.* (e.g., 1.19.5,

1.30.3); at *Carm.* 1.33.2 Glycere is the mistress of an elegist named Albius, presumably Tibullus. Ariosto consistently uses the Greek, rather than the Latin, terminations for her name (32.1, 54.1, 69, where the Greek accusative form is required by the meter).

12. *Panum . . . capripedum*: Prop. 3.17.34.

14–16. Compare Hor. *Carm.* 1.26.5–6.

15. Mother of Memnon: Aurora, the dawn; Verg. *Aen.* 7.26; Ov. *Am.* 1.8.3–4 and *Fast.* 4.714.

17. *certantia purpurae*: Hor. *Epod.* 2.20.

18. *tenero gramine*: Hor. *Carm.* 4.12.9.

19. *tempora pampino*: Hor. *Carm.* 3.25.20.

27. *fictilia*: compare Tib. 1.1.37–40.

30–35. Sicilian King: Dionysius II, Greek tyrant of Syracuse in the fourth century BCE. Ariosto has in mind Hor. *Carm.* 3.1.16–24, where the poet juxtaposes the burden of political power with the pleasures of pastoral escape by referring to the story of Damocles. Dionysius suspended a sword over the head of Damocles to teach him about the burden of authority. See also Cic. *Tusc.* 5.61.

34. Massic: Wine from the fertile mountainous area separating Latium from Campania. *pocula Massici*: Hor. *Carm.* 1.1.19.

35–36. *docilis . . . lympha*: Prop. 1.2.12.

40–42. *Furor*: These verses allude again (compare the openings of poems 1 and 1a) to the descent into Italy of the French king, Charles VIII, here described as Celtic.

42. Ausonians: Inhabitants of the Italian peninsula.

44. Sword: Ariosto returns to the key image from the "sword of Damocles" story.

III. Epitaph of Folco Ariosto

Meter: elegiac

This is the first of twenty-four epitaphs in the collection; six of these twenty-four are three pairs of draft and revision (16 and 16a, 55 and 55a, 58 and 58a; these last two are the poet's own epitaph). Eighteen epitaphs are in the elegiac meter — the traditional meter for the sepulchral epitaph — and range in length from a single couplet to fourteen lines (3, 5, 8, 10, 11, 41, 45, 46, 47, 48, 49, 50, 51, 55, 55a, 59, 61, 62); five are in the Phalaecean hendecasyllable (16, 16a, 58, 58a, 63); and one is in iambic trimeter (13). Overall, Ariosto follows the conventional themes and formulas of the Latin inscriptional epitaph and usually includes several of the following items, though there are variations: name of the deceased, location of burial (e.g., "here lies . . ."; "under this marble . . ."), biographical information, status, personal qualities, age at death, cause of death, surviving family members and/or heirs, and a concluding formula (e.g., "may the earth be light upon you"; "do not weep"). In some cases the epitaph ends with a moralizing sentiment (46, 49, 61, 63). The poet often employs the device of the speaking stone, that is, the epitaph that addresses the reader as a stranger (*hospes*) or traveler (*viator*) with a request for attention and then speaks on behalf of the deceased (16, 16a, 47, 49, 55, 55a, 61, 63); in two instances (3, 46) it is the deceased who speaks. Ariosto's primary models for these poems are the epitaphs in Martial's epigrams, on which see Henriksén, "Martial's Modes of Mourning." See also Lattimore, *Themes in Greek and Latin Epitaphs*.

Ariosto's relative, Folco Ariosto, was killed in battle in the south of Italy in 1495, fighting — the poet is careful to observe — against Ferdinand II of Aragon. Carducci 1905, 156–58, believes that Folco was the brother of Pandolfo (see poem 2), and therefore a first cousin to Ludovico, but Catalano argues convincingly that he came from a different branch of the family (*Vita*, 1:145).

3. *a moenibus arcens*: Sil. *Pun.* 1.639–40.

4. Orsini: Folco fought against the powerful Orsini family, originally based in Rome but with branches throughout southern Italy, who were allies to the French.

trieterida: the Latinized form of a Greek word meaning "a period of three years." Martial uses it in an epitaph for a child (7.96.3); see also Stat. *Silv.* 2.6.72.

IV. [IN PRAISE OF WISDOM: TO ERCOLE D'ESTE, SECOND
DUKE OF FERRARA]

Meter: dactylic hexameter

Ariosto delivered this prolusion in 1495 to inaugurate the academic year
for his peers in jurisprudence at the Ferrarese *Studium*, when he was not
yet twenty-one (Catalano, *Vita* 1:102). His use of a mythological frame-
work to praise the pursuit of learning is typical of humanist rhetoric.
References to Hermes Trismegistos (32) and the assimilation of different
cultural traditions, including classical (1–18), Egyptian (19–31), and Judeo-
Christian (33), are common features of Quattrocento Neoplatonism.
What distinguishes this otherwise ordinary poem is its celebration of
Ercole d'Este, the "most just of men" (45), who has created a state in
which learning is respected. The poem honors Ercole for brokering the
Peace of Vercelli in 1495 between the French and the Milanese, thus sav-
ing Ferrara and Italy from an extended, hostile French occupation. Peace
enables the intellectual projects tied to the university, hence its connec-
tion with knowledge. Pigna opens the *editio princeps* with this poem
(270). The status of the text and the overall shape of this composition are
not clear, prompting Paoletti to describe the poem as "that strange *mon-
strum*" (273). In its evocation of a time when gods consorted with hu-
mans, the poem echoes Catull. 64.31–46 and 384–408.

What appears at first sight to be the title of this poem in EP 1553, the
first poem in Book 1, is in fact a dedication: *Ad Alphonsum Ferrariae Du-
cem III* (i.e., Alfonso I d'Este); the same dedication is found at the begin-
ning of Book 2 of Ariosto's poems. Pigna took full advantage of the op-
portunity of publishing a collection of three Ferrarese poets by offering
three different dedications to the Este family. Each of Pigna's four books
of poems, and his satires, begins with the dedication *Ad Alphonsum Fer-
rariae Principem* (i.e., Alfonso II d'Este); that same dedication follows
Pigna's name and his *Carminum Libri Quatuor* on the title page of EP.
Each of the three books of Calcagnini's poems, which come next in the
collection, is preceded by the dedication *Ad Herculem II Ferrariae Ducem
IIII* (i.e., Ercole II d'Este, father of Alfonso II, and the reigning duke in
1553, when the *editio princeps* was published). The two books of Ariosto's

poems, the last in the collection, are dedicated to Alfonso I d'Este, father of Ercole II. Thus each poet, arranged from youngest to oldest (Pigna, Calcagnini, Ariosto), is paired with a member of the ruling house, also arranged from youngest to oldest, with the prince heir-apparent placed first (Alfonso II); followed by his father, the reigning duke (Ercole II); followed by his grandfather (Alfonso I), Ariosto's patron.

The title given in this edition is that of Bolaffi 1938, xli; it identifies Ercole I d'Este, second Duke of Ferrara, as the leader addressed in line 45 and uses the poem's own language to summarize its theme (*Sophia*, 50, and *laudes*, 58).

1–2. *dicta Iovis*: Ov. *Met.* 1.244–45. *Murmure . . . tacito*: *Met.* 6.203. The council of the gods in Ovid's *Metamorphoses* (1.163–252) may have served as a structural model for the beginning of the poem. For the lacuna at the beginning of the poem, see Notes to the Text.

2. Jupiter: Ruler of the Roman gods.

3. *terrigenas*: Lucr. 5.1411.

5. Nile: This description of geography draws heavily on Plato's *Timaeus*, a text that Ariosto mentions in his letter to Aldus Manutius of January 5, 1498.

7. Pelusium: Port on the eastern edge of the Nile Delta.

Canopus: Port on the western edge of the Nile Delta.

13. Ariosto employs the adjective *unigena* in the sense "born of one parent only," a reference to the birth of Athena/Minerva from Zeus's head (Hes. *Theog.* 924–26); compare *nata Iove* (36), and Ov. *Fast.* 3.841–42. On the celebration of Minerva's birthday in the Roman calendar, see Ov. *Fast.* 3.809–48.

16. Mercury: Messenger god.

Pharos: Island off the western side of the Nile Delta, famous later for its lighthouse.

17. *pater omnipotens*: standard epithet in epic for Jupiter (e.g., Lucr. 5.399; Verg. *Aen.* 1.60).

20. *sancta cohors*: Juv. 8.127.

21. Busiris: Legendary Egyptian king, who sacrificed foreigners at the altar of Zeus. When he tried to sacrifice Hercules, he got his comeuppance. Ariosto may have known this story from Boiardo's translation of Herodotus, 2.45. The eponymous town of Busiris is mentioned at 2.59 and 2.61 in Herodotus. *Busiridis ara*: Verg. G. 3.5.

22. Typhaon: Evil brother of Osiris, who tried to kill him. *fraterna caede*: Catull. 64.181 and Verg. *Aen.* 4.21.

23. Osiris: In some versions of the myth a god of regeneration and rebirth, in others an ancient Egyptian king, restored to life by his wife, Isis.

23. *quaesitus, Osiri*: Ov. *Met.* 9.693.

24. *vaga . . . urbes*: Ov. *Met.* 8.267, and Verg. *Aen.* 7.104.

26. *ducere . . . convivia*: Tib. 1.9.61.

29. Vulcan: The god of fire, traditionally the son of Jupiter and Juno, but here (30) the son of the river Nile. On that genealogy see Cic. *Nat. D.* 3.55 (*Nilo natus*), where Vulcan is identified with the Egyptian god Ptah and is said to be the guardian of Egypt.

29–30. *septemflue . . . Nile*: Ov. *Met.* 1.422.

31–34. Bolaffi 1938, xxxix–xl, notes that Augustine (*De civ. D.* 18.39) mentions Atlas, Mercury Trismegistos, and Moses in the context of his assertion that the wisdom of the patriarchs and the prophets is older than the wisdom of the Greek philosophers. Augustine observes that Moses was born in the time of Atlas and therefore antedates even Mercury Trismegistos.

31. Atlas: Titan who holds up the heavens. *Sidera . . . torquet*: Verg. *Aen.* 9.93 and Ov. *Met.* 2.71. According to tradition, Atlas was credited with teaching mankind about the celestial sphere and the movements of the stars and planets (German. *Arat.* fr. v.1–3; Vitr. *De arch.* 6.7.6; Plin. *HN* 2.31. In Herodotus 4.184 Atlas is identified with the mountain chain in Africa.

Born of Libya: Mariotti ("Cronologia di congetture e congetture superflue," 364 = *Scritti*, 307) cites Plin. *HN* 7.203, as a source for this allusion to Atlas as the son of Libya, "astrologiam Atlans Libyae filius."

Pliny's text was a focal point in a debate among humanists in the 1490s over what constituted reliable medical knowledge. The Ferrarese professor of medicine Nicolò da Lunigo, or Leoniceno, argued against Poliziano and Pandolfo Collenuccio that the corrupt text of *HN* would lead doctors astray. To allude to Pliny before an erudite audience at the inauguration of the academic year was to make a statement. Approximately thirty-five years later, around 1530, Ariosto returned to *HN* 7.1 in his prose piece, *Erbolato* (at 1.35), to satirize academic humanists of the sort he had wanted to become early on.

32. Hermes Trismegistos: Hellenistic Hermes, an important figure in the popular Neoplatonic culture of Ariosto's day. The city here referred to is Hermopolis, of which Hermes Trismegistos was said to be the founder, as noted by Mariotti (above on 31, 365 = *Scritti*, 307–8), citing Lactant. *Div. inst.* 1.6, and the *argumentum* to Ficino's *Pimander* (Ferrara, 1472), his widely influential Latin translation of the *Corpus Hermeticum*.

33. Moses the lawgiver: Moses represents the Judeo-Christian tradition, which Neoplatonism tried to blend with the classical tradition. Since Ariosto is addressing specifically the students of law, he refers to him as *legifer* (lawgiver). *legifer . . . Moses*: Paulinus of Nola, *Carm.* 22.39.

34. *incluta virtus*: Stat. *Theb.* 11.412.

36. Daughter of Jupiter: Athena in her capacity as the goddess of wisdom. *Iove nata*: Ov. *Met.* 5.297.

38–39. In referring to early humans as "the ancient race made from stone," which then throws off its sluggishness and uncivilized ways, Ariosto seems to have in mind both the mythological account of the rebirth of the human race from stones after the great deluge and the ancient scientific account of the development of human culture from the harsh conditions of primitive existence. Humans are literally a *durum genus* (hard race), because they were reborn from stone (Verg. *G.* 1.60–63; Ov. *Met.* 1.395–415), and figuratively, because their early existence was difficult (Lucr. 5.925–1027). The uncommon detail of the sluggishness that ails primitive humans (*aegram segnitiem*) appears to be based on Vergil's account of the necessity of human labor under the reign of Jupiter, after the golden age of Saturn—with its agricultural abundance that required no effort—had come to an end (G. 1.121–46, especially 124, *nec [Juppiter] torpere gravi passus sua regna veterno;* nor [Jupiter] letting his kingdom slumber in heavy lethargy). *Silex* (flint stone), in a figurative sense, is proverbial, for lack of emotion, hard-heartedness (Cic. *Tusc.* 3.12; Tib. 1.1.64); Plautus uses it for stupidity (*Poen.* 291). This is the sort of humanistic rhetoric that Ariosto parodies in his late work, *Erbolato*, which opens with the topic of human progress at the beginning of civilization. It is intriguing to imagine the older author using the vernacular to critique his younger Latin self.

38–44. Bolaffi 1938, xli–xlii and 58–59, detects in these lines an echo of Poliziano, *Silvae*, "Nutricia," 67–74.

38. *antiquum genus:* Lucr. 2.1170.

38–39. *aegram segnitiem:* Val. Flac. *Arg.* 3.395–96.

40. *ignipedum . . . equorum:* Stat. *Theb.* 1.27; see also Ov. *Met.* 2.392.

41. *mundi . . . origo:* Lucr. 5.1212.

43. *Anance:* Latinized form of the Greek word for necessity, ἀνάγκη. It does not occur in classical Latin but is used by Marullus, *Hymns* 1.3.25.

44. For the lacuna here, see Notes to the Text.

45. Most just of men: Duke Ercole.

47. Insubres: Used here in reference to the people of Lombardy in Ariosto's day; originally a pre-Celtic people who lived north of the Po River.

49. Mars: God of war. *populos . . . furentes:* Luc. 2.249.

50. *Sophia:* the Greek word for wisdom; its Latin equivalent, *sapientia*, is here represented by the adverb *sapientius* in 54.

51. Hercules: The classical referent for Ercole's name.

53. Trophies of victory: The poem exaggerates greatly, as it assumes the characteristics of a panegyric in praise of the dedicatee. In truth, Ercole's most important conflict, the war with Venice in 1482 to 1484, had ended in defeat. That loss conditioned him to prefer neutrality, at least publicly, when the French descended in 1494. *Parta . . . tropaea:* Ov. *Her.* 17.244.

54. Peace: Ercole maintained a difficult position of neutrality in the wake of the French invasion of Italy in 1494, and in 1495 he brokered an agreement between the French and the Milanese, the Peace of Vercelli.

55. City in the middle of Italy: Ferrara. Through careful diplomacy and strategic marriages, Ercole was able to preserve Ferrara's independence among all the larger states that surrounded it — Florence, Milan, Naples, Venice, and the Church — each of which aggressively contended for the domination of the Italian peninsula.

The use of *Latium*, the region of central Italy in which Rome is located, to mean Italy is rare in Latin poetry; see Sil. *Pun.* 13.741. Other examples cited in the *Oxford Latin Dictionary* are questionable. It occurs again in poem 15.26.

58. Tritonian goddess: Pallas Athena/Minerva in her capacity as goddess of wisdom, appropriate conclusion to a prolusion delivered at the *Studium*. The goddess's epithet *Tritonia*, common in epic poetry (e.g., Verg. *Aen.* 2.171; Ov. *Met.* 2.783) is derived from *Tritonis*, the name of a lake in north Africa. There is considerable variation in the mythological traditions explaining the connection between Athena/Minerva and the lake. Herodotus (*Hist.* 4.180) records the tradition that Athena/Minerva was the daughter of Poseidon and Lake Tritonis. Compare Sil. *Pun.* 3.322–24 and 9.297. The epithet further enhances the mystique of the ancient origins of wisdom in Egypt and Libya.

V. Epitaph of King Ferdinand

Meter: elegiac

Epitaph composed at the death of the king of Naples, Ferdinand II of Aragon, in September 1496. His artillery killed Ariosto's lamented cousin, Folco (poem 4). He was preceded in death by his sister, Leonora, the wife of Ercole d'Este, who died on October 11, 1493.

1. Italian Valor: In keeping with the convention of using prosopopeia in Roman funerary inscriptions (see note to poem 3), this epitaph gives voice to Italian Valor. In *Canzoniere* 128, "Italia mia," Petrarch wonders if "ancient courage is not yet dead in Italian hearts" (128.95–96), a passage

that Machiavelli famously repurposes at the end of *The Prince*. Ariosto enlivens the topos. *Itala virtus*: Stat. *Achil*. 1.14; Sil. *Pun*. 6.14.

5. Mother: Naples.

6. Foreign enemy: The French. *hostis barbarus*: Ov. *Tr*. 3.10.54.

VI. To Pandolfo [Ariosto]

Meter: elegiac

Another poem to his cousin on the subject of love (see poem 2). In one of the earliest biographies of Ariosto, Girolamo Garofolo credits Pandolfo with inspiring and challenging Ariosto to perfect his studies (*Vita di Ludovico Ariosto*, 173). Whereas in poem 2 the narrator chides Pandolfo for spending too much time away from the life of love, in poem 6 the speaker encourages him to wander off into that idyllic world on his own. Ariosto's speaker, for his part, is trapped in the city but not for the typical reason of being tethered to the patron's court: "Unhappy am I because I can't go and visit the delightful meadows of my companion (it is my mistress's total control, not the city walls, that confines me)" (23–24).

1. Copparo: Important agricultural center near Ferrara under Este control.

3. *sub denso . . . tegmine*: Verg. *Ecl*. 1.1–2.

4. Aeolian plectrum refers to the lyric poetry of the great Aeolian poets Sappho and Alcaeus; see note on 18.9. Compare Prop. 2.3.19, *Aeolio cum temptat carmine plectro*.

5–8. Compare Stat. *Silv*. 1.3.99–104.

5. Fauns: Deities of the Italian countryside and also of poets, whose instrument is the reed pipe.

6. Deeds of heroes: Epic poetry.

7. Lovers' trysts: Lyric poetry.

9. Dryad: A tree nymph in Greek mythology.

10. *melos*: the Greek word for song, appropriate in the context of *Aeolio pectine* and *chelys*.

17. The flirt: In addition to the many classical sources (identified by Santoro) and the precedent in Boiardo (identified by Ponte), the poet invokes the familiar Petrarchan code in the description of the body, both hers and his. But this is a pastoral setting where love is not to be frustrated, unlike that in, say, Petrarch's *Canzoniere* 126, where the poet remembers his lady now dead and fantasizes that if he were buried in the place in the woods where they used to visit, she might come back, see his tomb, and weep.

22. Free from the city: The poet invokes the bucolic commonplace of the shepherd, whose life in the country is free from the fast pace of the urban center.

23. Not the city walls: Having called to mind the commonplace of city versus country, urban versus rural, fast versus slow, in the previous verse, the poet immediately undermines the expectation that the city constrains him. It is his lady and not the city's walls that holds him in. *imperium dominae*: Tib. 2.3.79.

25–26. *Vincior . . . Amor*: Tib. 1.1.55.

28. Silent door: Commonplace in Roman Augustan love elegy of the poet separated from his beloved by a door, often referred to by the descriptive Greek term *paraclausithyron* (lament beside the door). Compare poem 17.5–6.

30. Nemesis: Goddess in classical mythology of divine retribution, here with a play on the name Nemesis, the name of Tibullus's *domina* in Book 2, poems 3, 4, and 6. The poet may be hinting that Pandolfo, when he does feel love's bitter mystery, will become an elegiac poet.

31–36. The experienced lover's warning to another who has not yet been caught in the toils of Venus is a common theme in Latin love elegy, e.g., Tib. 1.2.87–94.

33. Venus and . . . her son: The goddess of love and her son, Cupid.

34. *libera colla*: Prop. 2.30a.8.

37. The sparrow was sacred to Venus; see Catull. 3. *aligerum . . . Amorum*: Verg. *Aen*. 1.663 and Val. Flac. *Arg*. 7.171.

38. The Paphian goddess: Venus, from the island of Paphos. *Paphies:* Ariosto uses the Greek genitive ending.

39. Naiads: Nymphs, most often associated with water, such as rivers, springs, or, as here, the sea, balancing the tree nymph at the beginning of the poem.

42. The poet leaves Pandolfo with a two-edged valediction: on the one hand, he wants Pandolfo to be happy and to think of his good friend; on the other hand, there is a more troubling suggestion in the poet's words: he tells Pandolfo to be happy because the days of his happiness are numbered, as Venus works her wiles. His request that Pandolfo think of him is a way of reminding him that eventually he will find himself in the same lovesick condition as the poet.

VII. To Pietro Bembo

Meter: elegiac
To the great arbiter of literary taste in Ariosto's generation (and for several hundred years later), Ariosto addresses this poem about being in love. Bolaffi dates it to just before the turn of the century when Bembo was in Ferrara for his first extended visit (1498–99) (69). Bárberi Squarotti suggests that it is in response to Bembo's elegiac poem "Ad Melinum," which airs similar themes. The poem plays with the notion of signs the speaker cannot make sense of—*notae non intellectae*—which, it turns out, are passion marks on his girlfriend's neck. Santoro 1989 (88) identifies Prop. 2.34 as a source. It bears recalling that none less than Bembo (according to Pigna) supposedly encouraged Ariosto to compose in Latin.

1. *Mea puella* is the signature phrase of Catullus's Lesbia poems and the absorbing poetic subject that variously inspires, frustrates, and torments the Latin elegists, Propertius, Tibullus, and Ovid. The *puella,* as a literary construction, here continues her life as the inexhaustible source of desire, erotic fantasy, and amatory tribulation.

5–6. *oculosque meos . . . potest:* Catull. 82.

12–13. *livida colla . . . vestigia:* Ov. Am. 1.8.97–98.

18. Jupiter: Not merely the ruler of the Roman gods, but infamous for indulging in infidelity. *cupiat Iuppiter:* Prop. 2.34.18; Catull. 70.2.

19–20. *Tecum . . . toro:* Prop. 2.34.

24. *ah pereat . . . potest:* Prop. 1.6.12.

VIII: Epitaph of Francesco Ariosto
Meter: elegiac
A poem on the death of his paternal uncle in 1499, who died in Modena, where he was serving as an Este official. Francesco, married to Francesca (who is celebrated in verses by Carbone [Catalano, *Vita*, 1:154]), was the father of Rinaldo, one of Ariosto's favorite cousins (*Vita*, 1:13). He was buried in the church of San Francesco in Ferrara alongside his mother-in-law, as per his wishes, "esempio forse più unico che raro" (an absolutely unique example [of son-in-law piety], *Vita*, 1:156).

3. *quantivis . . . pretii:* A phrase found in Plaut. *Epid.* 410 and Ter. *An.* 856.

4. *emensum . . . pedibus:* Tac. *Ann.* 11.32.13.

IX. To Alberto Pio
Meter: alcaic
An ode to Ariosto's friend in letters, Alberto Pio da Carpi, in which the poet celebrates the return of their teacher, the Augustinian monk and humanist Gregorio da Spoleto, from Lyon, the Italian cultural center in France. Segre 1954 notes that Gregorio died in France, probably in 1499 (25). The poem also celebrates the new humanistic education. If Gregorio taught Alberto Greek, he taught Ariosto every single thing he knows! The ongoing political tension between the Este and Alberto's aristocratic family of the Carpi, as the Este looked to expand their territory by swallowing up the smaller principalities around Ferrara, strained the close friendship between the two men such that they eventually broke off relations around 1510. Virginio Ariosto's *Memorie* refers to a poem that his father wrote about his friendship with Alberto, which begins *Iam* (Barotti, *Memorie istoriche*, 1:223). Barotti points out that we do not have a poem that begins thus in Ariosto's collection (1:373–74).

2. Both sides of the family: Alberto was descended from the Carpi on his father's side and the Mirandola on his mother's, both noble families in Ariosto's Italy.

7. *frontem severam*: Plaut. *Mil.* 201.

8. Falernian wine: Wine from the northern section of Campania.

15–16. Realm of France/princes of Italy: France was recognized for being a nation, whereas Italy was known to be a loose conglomeration of principalities, including the one ruled by the Carpi.

16. The adjective *Latinus* is used here in the extended sense of "Italian" or "of Italy." See also poem 15.29.

17. Lyon: An important center of Italian culture in France. The form *Lugdunii* is metrically and morphologically problematic. The *u* in the second syllable is treated as short; it is long. The form should be *Lugduni*, the locative of *Lugdunum*; the poet has added an extra syllable at the end. Since ancient metrical practice allows for some flexibility in the treatment of vowel quantities in proper names, the lengthening of the *u* is not without precedent. As for the addition of an extra syllable, it is possible that Ariosto came across the form *Lugdun(i)um* in a printed source or that he simply made it up.

18. My Gregorio: Mine, Ariosto says here, but he means "ours," as the poem makes clear.

Apolline studies: The study of poetry under the watch of Apollo, god of poetry.

21. The phrase "Echionian letters" is a metonymic expression for Greek language and literature. Echion was one of the heroes who sprang from the teeth of the dragon killed by Cadmus, founder of the city of Thebes in Boeotia; Echion was cofounder of the city (Ov. *Met.* 3.95–130). According to Herodotus (5.58), Cadmus, a Phoenician, and his followers brought the alphabet with them when they settled in Greece; it was then adopted by the Ionians. Herodotus refers to the alphabet as "Cadmean letters" (5.59). Thus Ariosto the student pays a compliment to his teacher's knowledge of "Echionian letters" but also to his role as a founder-figure in the poet's life.

23. *plus debeo:* See Sen. *Ben.* 6.16 on what is owed to a teacher.

28. *ad gelidas . . . Alpes:* [Tib.], Panegyricus Messallae 3.7.109.

29–30. *rude . . . dolavit:* Priapeia 10.4.

38–40. *beatius . . . beasti:* Catull. 9.10–11.

X. [Epitaph of Nicolò Ariosto]

Meter: elegiac

An epitaph for Ariosto's father, who died in February 1500, leaving Ariosto, the oldest child of ten, with the responsibility of helping his numerous siblings make their way in the world.

1. *molliter:* common in a funerary context, e.g., Verg. *Ecl.* 10.33; Ov. *Her.* 7.162.

2. *caris . . . pignoribus:* Ov. *Met.* 3.134 and *Fast.* 3.218.

Daria: Ariosto's mother, Daria Malaguzzi.

5. *decurso spatio:* a phrase found in Roman comedy, e.g., Plaut. *Merc.* 547; Ter. *Ad.* 860.

ossibus ossa: Prop. 4.7.94; *Epicedion Drusi,* 163.

XI. On the Wife of Quinzio Valerio

Meter: elegiac

No commentator has identified the husband or the wife in this epitaph. It has many points in common with poem 10, in remembrance of Ariosto's father. See the notes on previous poem.

XII. On Nicolò Ariosto

Meter: second asclepiadean

A much longer lament on the death of Ariosto's father. Santoro 1989 notes its "studied literariness" in imitation of Stat. *Silv.* 5.3, with Ovidian and Tibullan overtones as well (95). The dramatic situation of the poem is strongly reminiscent of Catull. 101.

7. *puertia:* A syncopated form for *pueritia* found in Hor. *Carm.* 1.36.8.

9–17. Compare Stat. *Silv.* 2.7.107–15 and 5.3.19–28.

13. Groves of Elysium: Classical equivalent of Paradise, situated at the ends of the earth, but here clearly less good than the "clear ether" (9), heaven, which is the first option. For the unusual detail of *lucos steriles* in Elysium, see Stat. *Silv.* 2.1.204.

17–18. *ultimum munus:* Catull. 101.3.

18. Stygian pools: A fixture of the underworld; e.g., Verg. *Aen.* 6.134, Stat. *Theb.* 4.568, and Mart. 1.78.4.

20–21. Compare Stat. *Silv.* 3.3.34–35 and 5.1.210–16.

21. Perfumes from Arabia or Cilicia: Areas famous for their perfumes. Cilicia in Asia Minor was well known for its saffron-based products.

24. *molliter:* See note on 10.1.

XIII. Epitaph of Nicolò Ariosto
Meter: iambic trimeter

1. count: Frederick III, Holy Roman Emperor, made Nicolò a count on a visit to Ferrara in January–February 1469.

XIV. To Alberto Pio
Meter: dactylic hexameter
A second poem to his good friend from their early days as young students (see 9), this one on the death of Alberto's mother, Caterina Pico, whose name Ariosto Latinizes as Pica. The wise and virtuous Caterina was the older sister of the humanist Giovanni Pico della Mirandola and a cousin of Matteo Maria Boiardo, reminding us how close the ties could be among the elite families of Emilia in Ariosto's time. Since Ariosto's own family did not share the same status as Alberto's, the poet points instead to their communal humanistic training. He also notes that they share the fate of having to assume the responsibility of siblings at the death of a parent (109–11). It may be that Caterina's maid, Diambra, strangled her to death or poisoned her (R. Bacchelli, *La congiura di don Giulio d'Este*, 307–9), but either Ariosto does not mention this in the poem or the version of the text that we have lacks a concluding section. The consolation poems in Statius's *Silvae* are a general model for this poem.

1. *crudeli funere*: A Vergilian phrase, e.g., *Ecl.* 5.20, G. 3.263, *Aen.* 4.308.

3–13. The simile has a Vergilian model, *Aen.* 2.304–8, where Aeneas wakes up to discover that the Greeks are sacking Troy; see also G. 2.203–11. A version of the simile reappears famously in *Orlando Furioso* 1.65.

5–6. *frigore membra . . . torpuerim*: Verg. *Aen.* 12.867–68.

6. *gelido . . . ore*: Ov. *Am.* 3.5.45.

12. *occupat artus*: A common hexameter line-ending for a feeling or condition that overtakes the body, e.g., Verg. *Aen.* 7.446 and Ov. *Met.* 1.548.

15. *ardenti . . . dolore*: Lucr. 3.663.

17–19. The blood: see Verg. *Aen.* 10.452 on the physiological effects of fear. Ariosto's detailed description of the heart as a pump for blood reminds us that the *Studium* in Ferrara was an important center for medical education under the direction of Nicolò Leoniceno (see Carrara).

20. *intempesta*: Stat. *Silv.* 2.1.8.

23. *tuis lacrimis . . . lacrimas*: Ov. *Her.* 2.95; Sen. *Agam.* 664.

33–34. *tumultus . . . animi*: Luc. 7.779.

34. Treacherous fortune: Alberto's family's property was illegally seized by the Este.

35. *limina supplex*: Epic phrase for the suppliant's approach, e.g., Verg. *Aen.* 6.115.

38. Philosophy: Alberto had the reputation of a keen mind and possessed a great library to which, we assume, Ariosto had at least occasional access.

40–43. On the virtues of the deceased, see Stat. *Silv.* 2.1.39–40; in this instance a young boy.

44. *morum exemplar . . . bonorum*: Hor. *Ars P.* 44; Ov. *Tr.* 2.1.233–34, *Medic.*, 43.

46–47. *qui te . . . auctor*: Verg. *Aen.* 7.47–49.

46. Laurentum: Coastal area south of Rome's port, Ostia.

Saturn: Ancient Italo-Etruscan god associated with primeval Rome. If the Picus clan could call him father, it was indeed venerable.

51. *decor ille:* [Ov.], *Epicedion Drusi,* 259.

59. *sedula nutrix:* Hor. *Ars P.* 116; Ov. *Met.* 10.438.

72. Bianor: Legendary figure associated with the founding of Mantua; see Verg. *Ecl.* 9.60.

   distissmius agri: Verg. *Aen.* 10.563.

73. Rodolfo Gonzaga: Son of Ludovico Gonzaga, who lived from 1452 to 1495.

76. *geniali foedere:* Stat. *Theb.* 3.300.

85. *viduo . . . lecto:* Ov. *Her.* 1.81.

86–87. *provida . . . mens:* Hor. *Carm.* 3.5.13; Ov. *Met.* 7.712.

88. *thalami consors:* Ov. *Met.* 10.246.

   virago: Vergil uses this word of the nymph Juturna, sister of Turnus (*Aen.* 12.468), Ovid of the goddess Minerva (*Met.* 2.765, 6.130).

92. *propositique tenax:* Hor. *Carm.* 3.3.1.

97. *multa . . . caede cruentus:* Verg. *Aen.* 1.471.

99. Taro: River in the westernmost section of Emilia, which flows into the Po near Parma.

   spumantia sanguine: Verg. *Aen.* 6.87 and 9.456.

101. King Charles: Charles VIII. Compare poem 1.

   Charles the Great: Charlemagne.

   generosa propago: *Ilias Latina,* 625.

102. Seine: The river that runs through Paris.

103. *matribus . . . puellis:* Hor. *Carm.* 1.1.24–25.

107. *melioris . . . sexus:* Stat. *Theb.* 1.393.

115. *rudibus . . . colonis:* Man. *Astr.* 1.74.

116–17. *limpidus . . . ripas:* Verg. *G.* 3.14–15.

116. Mincius: River in Lombardy in northern Italy that flows from Garda Lake to the Po, passing through Mantua.

Fields of Ocnus: The territory of Mantua. Ocnus was the legendary founder of Mantua, which he named after his mother, the prophetess Manto (Verg. *Aen.* 10.198–201).

117. *harundineas . . . ripas*: Stat. *Theb.* 6.274.

118–19. *sinus . . . undis*: Verg. G. 2.159–60.

118. Benacus: Garda Lake in northern Italy.

119. *spumantibus . . . undis*: Catull. 64.155; Verg. *Aen.* 3.268.

120. The Po glides by Venetian territory, an interesting geographical boundary marker reminding us that the political state of Venice is never far away.

121–22. *multa mole . . . parcere ruri*: Hor. *Epist.* 1.14.30. Perhaps Ariosto was responding to the alliterative challenge of this line of Enn. *Ann.* 620: *machina multa minax minitatur maxima muris.*

125–26. *aut virtus . . . actu*: Hor. *Epist.* 1.17.

127. *cum medio . . . aestu*: Hor. *Epist.* 1.2.22.

128. *sceleri . . . nefando*: Catull. 64.397; Luc. 1.667.

129. *virtutum . . . praemia*: Tac. *Hist.* 1.72.4.

130. *renovabit . . . dolores*: Verg. *Aen.* 2.3.

131. *lacrimas . . . inanes*: Verg. *Aen.* 4.449 and 10.465.

132. *medicae . . . nescius artis*: Tib. 2.3.14; Ov. *Tr.* 5.6.12; Luc. 4.744.

The healer's art: Another reference to the art of medicine. Compare lines 17–19.

134. *crudelia fata*: Verg. G. 2.495–96 and *Aen.* 1.221–22.

141. Anytus: One of the Athenians who officially accused Socrates at his trial.

Virbius: Associated with Hippolytus, son of Theseus, who died when a bull from the sea attacked his chariot. Ovid tells the story of Hippolytus/Virbius in *Met.* 15.497–546.

147. *dum vita manebat*: Verg. *Aen.* 5.724.

151–54. *ut facto . . . pudicam:* Hor. *Sat.* 1.6.82–84. Pica takes on the role of one of the most famous parents in Latin literature, Horace's father.

156–57. *muliebris . . . iram . . . ingenii:* Sen. *Dial.* 3.20.3–4; Catull. 68b.139.

158. *malesuada:* A rare adjective in classical Latin; see Verg. *Aen.* 6.276 and Stat. *Theb.* 11.656.

XV. To Ercole Strozzi

Meter: elegiac

A poem written on the occasion of the death of Michael Marullus Tarchaniota on April 11, 1500, whom Ariosto and Strozzi became acquainted with a year or so before his death. Marullus, a Greek born in Constantinople in 1453 just before the city fell to the Turks, grew up in Naples, where he studied with Pontano and Sannazaro, among others. He married Alessandra Scala, daughter of Lorenzo de' Medici's secretary, Bartolomeo Scala. Ariosto calls him a bard (*vatem*, 9), and learned (*doctum*, 35). Ariosto clearly seems to have looked up to him as a father figure in letters, and his demise so soon after Ariosto's biological father's death (41–42) weighs on the poet greatly. Fantazzi refers to this composition as "the most beautiful and heart-felt" of the many poems lamenting Marullus's death (Marullus, *Poems*, x). Ciceri speculates that Ariosto may have studied Greek briefly with Marullus in 1499. Strozzi, Ariosto's close friend and perhaps the best Neo-Latin poet of the day, is lamented in poem 59.

1–2. *nuntia fama . . . pervolat:* Verg. *Aen.* 9.474 and 3.121.

3. *scin tu:* A common expression in Roman comedy, e.g., Plaut. *Mil.* 339.

 age, fare: a lively colloquialism, e.g., Verg. *Aen.* 3.362, 6.389, and 6.531.

5. River: Marullus drowned trying to cross the swollen Cecina in Tuscany.

10. *flasse . . . animam:* Plaut. *Per.* 638.

16. *pro superi:* Ov. *Met.* 6.472.

18. Phoebus and the Pierian Muses: Ariosto defines the community he and Strozzi share as one made up of poets who are watched over by the god of poetry, Phoebus Apollo, and the Muses, associated with Pieria in

Macedonia, famous for its spring of inspiration. *sumus . . . in fide:* Catull. 34.1. *Phoebi Pieridumque:* [Tib.] 3.4.44; *App. Verg.* Elegiae in Maecenatem 1.35.

19. *si vera est fama:* Verg. G. 4.42.

20. *murmura vana:* Sil. *Pun.* 12.629.

24. Sacred Phocis: The name of the region around Delphi in north-central Greece near the mountains of Parnassus and Helicon, both sacred to the Muses.

26. Latium: Italy, which was ravaged by the French under Charles VIII.

27. Western peoples: The French army of Charles VIII.

29. Latin [king]: R. Bacchelli proposes that Cesare Borgia is the Latin king (*La congiura di don Giulio d'Este,* 298–99).

34. Land of Saturn: The Italian peninsula. *tellus Saturni:* Verg. *Aen.* 8.329.

Savage Gauls: The French army of Charles VIII. *Gallos . . . truces:* Luc. 7.231.

37. *dulci eloquio:* Sen. *Q Nat.* 6.13.1.

38. Stream of the Muses: Either the Pierian or the Castalian spring from which Marullus as poet has drunk.

plurimo ab amne: Verg. *Aen.* 6.659.

39. *liberam et immunem:* In origin a legal phrase applied to states and peoples "independent and free from taxation": Cuic. *Verr.* 2.3.13.

41. Father who was taken from me: Ariosto's father died in February 1500. Compare poems 10, 12, and 13.

43. *aura aetheria vescatur:* An allusion to Verg. *Aen.*1.546, where it is unknown whether Aeneas has drowned in the great storm.

48. *laeta fronte:* Verg. *Aen.* 11.238.

XVI. Epitaph of Niccolò Cosmico
Meter: Phalaecean hendecasyllable
On the death of Niccolò Lelio Cosmico in June 1500, a Petrarchan poet of some status in the court of Ercole I, who died at the venerable age of eighty. His *Cancion,* one of the earliest volumes of poetry in Italian to be

printed, was published in 1478 and reprinted three times in the following fourteen years (1481, 1485, 1492). Pietro Bembo praises Cosmico in *Prose della volgar lingua*, 1.15. Ariosto's respectful and grave epitaph is balanced by some of his other writings about Cosmico. In sonnet 39, dedicated to Alfonso Trotto, Ariosto comments that from Cosmico, Alfonso learned how to take his pleasure with nuns, to question his belief in God, and to practice incest and sodomy, not exactly a roster of the most worthy character traits. These sorts of scandalous claims about Cosmico are reviewed in more detail in a series of twenty-three sonnets in Italian falsely attributed to Ariosto, *In Cosmicum patavinum carmina maledica* (Fatini 1924, 243–57).

1–2. *munus habe:* Verg. *Ecl.* 8.60.

2–3. *repende damna:* Ov. *Her.* 15.32.

6. *Pieridum choro:* Ov. *Tr.* 5.3.10; see also line 14.

9. *comi et lepido:* Ter. *Hec.* 837; see also line 12.

XVIa. Epitaph
Meter: Phalaecean hendecasyllable
Rough draft of Cosmico's epitaph, which is crossed out with a large X on f. 10r in Ariosto's manuscript. See notes on previous poem.

XVII. Megilla
Meter: third asclepiadean
In this poem Ariosto brilliantly revives the Greco-Roman tradition of the *paraclausithyron* (the lover's complaint before the locked doors of his mistress's house), a popular form with the Roman elegists (Tib. 1.2, Prop. 1.16, and Ov. *Am.* 1.6) but also found in lyric (Hor. *Carm.* 3.10). For Greek antecedents, see Theoc. 3 and Callim. *Epigr.* 63. Ariosto's poem differs significantly from these models, because it combines the lover's complaint of the formal *paraclausithyron* (1–28), in which he finds himself interminably shut out by his mistress, with his unexpected expression of joyful exuberance (29–48) at being held in his mistress's embrace. The excluded lover is not, in this instance, trapped in the constraints of the genre. Lines 1–28 contain the traditional elements of the excluded

lover's complaint: the mistress's *superbia* (2), the insensitive doors (5–6), exposure to inclement weather (6–8), the rival who enters as he pleases (9–11), the assorted humiliations that attend rejection (12–14), intervention by Venus (15–20), and mythological *exempla* (21–24). Note the careful structuring of 1–28 with the emphatic placement of a form of the demonstrative pronoun *ille* (*illius*, 1; *illum*, 15; and *illi*, 25) at the beginning of each sentence. The use of the demonstrative creates the initial impression that the poet is merely offering general advice to the excluded lover to persevere in his devotion to his mistress. That impression changes completely when the poet dramatically presents himself (*en me*, 29) and his own experience as a lover as proof that perseverance in the face of amatory tribulation will pay off in the end; hope (*spes*, 1) has become reality (*mellita oscula*, 47; *bona*, 48). On the *paraclausithyron*, see F. O. Copley, *Exclusus Amator*.

Title. *Megilla*: Hor. *Carm.* 1.27.11. In the better manuscripts of Horace's *Carm.*, the name is spelled *Megylla*.

2. *superbia*: Hor. *Carm.* 3.10.2; compare Ovid's neat formulation (*Fast.* 1.419), *fastus inest pulchris sequiturque superbia formam*.

5–6. Doors deaf: The commonplace of the lover lamenting outside the door of the beloved (*paraclausithyron*). Compare poem 6.28. *surdos . . . postes*: Ov. *Am.* 1.6.54.

Boreas: The cold North Wind, which classical sources depict as falling in love with the Athenian princess Oreithyia. *trux Boreas*: Verg. *G.* 1.370. *nives*: Hor. *Carm.* 3.10.7–8.

8. Fires of passion: Petrarchan conceit of the icy fire (see Forster, *The Icy Fire*).

15–16. Mother of the Amores and Cupids: Venus. Compare Hor. *Carm.* 1.19.1 and 4.1.5; Ov. *Fast.* 4.1. *Amor* (Love) and *Cupido* (Desire) are the Latin names of the Greek god *Eros* (Love), the son of Aphrodite/Venus. In Latin poetry this plurality of *Amores* (Loves) and *Cupidines* (Desires) follows the same use of *Erotes* in Greek poetry.

17. *precibus victa*: Ov. *Met.* 1.377–78.

20. *divino . . . pede:* Like a conqueror, Venus treads down the proud. Compare Prop. 1.1.4, where it is *Amor* that forces the lover to bow in submission with his feet.

21. Son of Cinyras: Adonis, youthful lover of Venus.

21–22. *Cinyreius . . . iuvenis:* Ov. *Met.* 10.712.

22. Phrygian shepherd: Anchises, the father of Aeneas.

23. River Simois on Mount Ida: Mount Ida in Phrygia was the scene of Venus's seduction of Anchises and also of the judgment of the Trojan Paris; the Simois flowed from Mount Ida into the plain of the Troad. *Idaeum Simoenta:* Prop. 3.1.27.

24. Mars: Another of Venus's many lovers. Angelo Poliziano describes the encounter between Mars and Venus in some detail in *Stanze per la giostra,* 1.122–23.

   Mars bellipotens pater: This phrase combines an ancient prayer formula of invocation, *Mars pater,* and an epithet of the god in epic, *bellipotens* (e.g., Verg. *Aen.* 11.8).

25. Cyprian Amathus: A reference to Venus, who was associated with shrines on the island of Cyprus in the vicinity of the city of Amathus. The correct form of the adjective is *Amathusia.* The incorrect spelling *Amathuntia,* used by Ariosto and other Renaissance Latin poets, is found in late manuscripts and early printed editions of Catullus, Propertius, and Ovid. We retain the incorrect spelling for its historical value.

29. *miseris modis:* A phrase from Roman comedy, e.g., Plaut. *Aul.* 630 and *Epid.* 667.

31. *spretor divum:* Ov. *Met.* 8.613.

33–34. Ancient Cydonean custom: The poet refers to the custom of marking a day of good fortune with white chalk; as we would say, "a red-letter day." Cydonea, a city on the north coast of Crete, is used metonymically for the island of Crete, regarded as the source of the chalk. Compare Hor. *Carm.* 1.36.10.

35–36. *celebranda:* Compare Tib. 1.7.63.

40. *solacia suavia:* Lucr. 5.21 and 6.4.

41–45. *Fallorne? . . . fallimur*: Compare the disappointed lover in Ov. *Am.* 1.6.49–51 (*fallimur . . . fallimur*), who at first thinks his mistress's door is opening, only to realize that it was the sound of the door being struck by a strong wind.

XVIII. Julia

Meter: alcaic

This new Sappho—perhaps she is even a Calliope—has conquered the poet through her "Tuscan," i.e. Italian, song. The Neo-Latin poet sings of his lady in Latin while she sings to him in the vernacular.

1–36. This syntactically ambitious sentence, with its double comparison (*qualem scientem . . .* and *qualemve doctam . . .*), is modeled on the opening period of Hor. *Carm.* 4.4.1–28 (*qualem ministrum . . .* and *qualemve laetis . . .*).

1. *scientem carminis*: compare Hor. *Carm.* 3.9.10.

2. Sappho: Lyric poet from the island of Lesbos in the second half of the seventh century BCE.

5. *altis e penetralibus*: Verg. *Aen.* 7.59.

8. Favonius: Roman wind god, often equated with Zephyrus, the west wind, whose gentle breezes are a sign of spring. *flatibus . . . Favoni*: Catull. 26.2.

9. Dithyrambs: Hymns, technically in honor of Dionysus, to be sung and danced by choruses.

9–10. Aeolian lyre: Aeolian is the ethnic name for the Greeks who inhabited Boeotia and Thessaly and for the dialect of Greek that they spoke. Because immigrants from this region settled the northern coastal area of Asia Minor, including the island of Lesbos, Sappho's home, the region they settled was known as Aeolis. Since Sappho and her compatriot Alcaeus were regarded as the outstanding composers of lyric song, the use of the adjective "Aeolian" in Latin poetry evokes the emotional power and metrical discipline of their lyric expression. Horace calls Sappho the "Aeolian darling" (*Aeoliae puellae, Carm.* 4.9.12); compare his famous boast at *Carm.* 3.30.12–14.

13. Calliope: Muse of epic verse.

doctam modos: Compare Hor. *Carm.* 3.9.10.

14–15. *tinnula . . . voce*: Catull. 61.13.

18. Giants: Mythological beings who rebelled against the gods but were defeated in a cataclysmic battle.

21–22. *eburno police . . . chordas*: Stat. *Silv.* 5.5.31; and compare Prop. 2.1.9.

22. Thracian lyre: Area to the north and east of Greece, roughly following the boundaries of modern Bulgaria. Ovid describes Orpheus as the Thracian bard (*Met.* 11.1–2).

Threiciae fidis: Verg. *Aen.* 6.120.

23. *arte . . . magistra*: Verg. *Aen.* 8.442 and 12.427.

25. *vernis . . . floribus*: Hor. *Carm.* 2.11.9–10.

26. *acutis vocibus*: App. *Verg.* Ciris 107; Hor. *Carm.* 3.4.3.

27. *nervosque vocales*: Tib. 2.5.3.

28. Tuscan: Ariosto means in the vernacular, i.e., Tuscan, or what we would now call "Italian."

29–33. *cantus . . . refractulos*: A challenging passage that describes the movements of the singing voice and the quality of the sounds it creates. In lines 29–30 the poet gives a general characterization of her singing (*cantus mobiles*, 29), which is then developed in three stages signaled by the adverbs *prius* (30) . . . *nunc* (32) . . . *nunc* (33); the singing moves from quick changes in pitch (*flexosque concisosque*, 31) to a quiet, fluid movement (*murmure tacito volutos*, 32); in the last stage the voice becomes louder (*plena voce*, 33). The precise meaning of *refractulus*, the perfect passive participle of the verb *refringere* (to break), to which the suffix *-ulus* is added, is unclear; it appears to be Ariosto's coinage. Bolaffi 1938, x, following Cosattini, "A proposito," notes the similarity of these lines to a passage in Plin. *HN* 10.81–82, which describes in detail the song of the nightingale. See also Ov. *Am.* 2.4.25 and Lucr. 5.1406.

29. *presso gutture*: Verg. *G.* 1.410.

32. *murmure . . . tacito*: Ov. *Met.* 6.203.

36. *vere . . . tepente*: [Ov.], *Epicedion Drusi* 109.

37. *canoros . . . modos:* Verg. *Aen.* 7.700–701.

38. *melos:* See note on 6.10.

39–40. *hiulco . . . labello:* Catull. 61.213.

42. *grata . . . compede:* Hor. *Carm.* 1.33.14 and 4.11.23–24.

44. Elysian Lethe: Lethe is a river in the classical underworld; to drink its waters brings forgetfulness of the past. Dante transposes it to the top of Mount Purgatory, where the purged souls forget all their previous sins.

45–49. The Siren: In Homer's *Odyssey* (12.39–54, 158–200) the Sirens are enchantresses who lived at the Straits of Messina and whose song lured the curious to the point of no return, where the monster Scylla and the whirlpool Charybdis would cause their ship to wreck. Circe tells Odysseus/Ulysses to stop up his men's ears with wax and to have them bind him to the mast of his ship so that he can hear the song of the Sirens.

45. Achelous: A river in Greece, here personified as a deity, father of the Sirens; see Ov. *Met.* 5.552.

48. *cavas . . . rupes:* Verg. *G.* 3.253.

49. *Vlysseu:* The standard Latin form of the name is *Vlixes* (e.g., *sic notus Vlixes,* Verg. *Aen.* 2.44). Ariosto employs a hybrid form of the name that combines the Greek vocative Ὀδυσσεῦ with the *ul-* of the Latin spelling. Ultimately, the spelling *Vlysseus* may derive from a corrupted form found in early printed Latin texts.

49–50. *illitis . . . auribus:* Ov. *Am.* 3.314; and compare Prop. 3.12.34, and Juv. 9.148–50.

50. Pelasgian: Greek, from the name for the mythical inhabitants of prehistoric Greece.

XIX. The Golden Fleece

Meter: third asclepiadean

This is one of the few poems on an overtly classical theme in Ariosto's Neo-Latin work. Of the various interpretations proposed, the most convincing remains Mariotti's allegorical reading of the poem ("Per il riesame" = *Scritti*, 295–300) as a call to the Estense leaders of Ferrara to take back the border territory known as the Polesine from the Venetians. Horace, *Carm.* 1.14, itself a political allegory, is the crucial intertext in Mariotti's reading and, as the critic reminds us, readers have been attuned to the allegorical reach of the Horatian ode since Quintilian (*Institutio* 8.6.44). This allegory would date the poem to the fall of 1509, when hostilities between Venice and Ferrara culminate with the Ferrarese rout of the Venetian flotilla at the battle of Polesella on December 22. Ariosto reports from Rome to his Este patrons on the glee with which that news was received in the papal court in letter 5 (December 25, 1509).

1. *pubis . . . Thessalae:* Catull. 64.4.

Thessaly: Region of northern Greece.

2. *pelagi minis:* Verg. *Aen.* 6.113.

3–4. Golden fleece: Object of the quest of Jason and the Argonauts, whose ship, the Argo, was said to be the first ship ever made. *pellem . . . auratam:* Catull. 64.5.

3. Colchis: Coastal area at the eastern end of the Black Sea, destination of Jason and his men.

5. Pallas: Athena. *innuba Pallas:* Val. Flac. *Arg.* 1.87.

6–7. *velivolam . . . pinum:* Lucr. 5.1442.

8. Mount Pelion: Mountain in Thessaly. *vertice Pelei:* Catull. 64.1, 278.

9–10. *fortiter . . . portum:* Hor. *Carm.* 1.14.2–3.

9. *lecta manus:* Verg. *Aen.* 10.294.

10. Phasis: An ancient river in Colchis that flows into the Black Sea at a seaport also called Phasis.

Boreas: The north wind. *Boreae . . . spiritus:* Verg. *Aen.* 12.365.

13–15. *spolium . . . dracones:* Ov. *Her.* 6.13.

16. Mars: In Ov. *Met.* 7.101, Jason confronts the fire-breathing bulls on the field of Mars (*sacrum Mavortis in arvum;* Ap. Rhod. *Argon.* 3.409), presumably so named because the dragon's teeth sown in its soil sprouted into warriors.

ignivomi: compare Ovid's description of the bulls at *Met.* 7.104–6. The epithet *ignivomus* is not found in classical Latin; the poets instead use a noun–participle construction, e.g., *ignem vomentes*, Ov. *Met.* 2.119. The first recorded occurrence of the epithet is in the mythographer Fulgentius (*Myth.* 1 *praef.*). It is common in Renaissance Latin poets, e.g., *ignivomos apices montis* (the fire-spewing peaks of the mountain), Pol. *Silv.* 1.87.

17–18. *vigil serpens*: Ov. *Met.* 7.36 and 9.190.

19–24. In the description of the wild creature that attacks the serpent, there are echoes of the eagle simile at the beginning of Hor. *Carm.* 4.4.1–12 (note the sequence *olim* 5 . . . *nunc* 11).

22. *sanguineis . . . unguibus*: Stat. *Theb.* 1.82–83.

XX. His Girlfriend's Puppy

Meter: Phalaecean hendecasyllable

Inspired by Catullus 2, on Lesbia's pet sparrow; Catullus 3, on the death of the sparrow; and Catullus 12, on Asinius, the infamous napkin thief. The theft of the poet's pet robs him not only of a delightful companion but also of a keepsake from his beloved that provides comfort and consolation for his passionate desire. His verbal assault on the thief in the language of Roman comedy is in a sense a profession of his devotion to his mistress, his *era*, since his violent reaction to the theft gives strong evidence of the emotional upset caused by the loss of this particular bond between them. The poem is a lively blend of Catullan amatory longing and Plautine comic abuse. Ferrara was an important site for the recuperation of Catullus, including the emendation and explication of his text. The humanist teacher Guarino refers to Catullus regularly; his son Battista Guarino was involved in emending the poet's text in the 1480s and 1490s; and in the next generation Alessandro Guarino published much of his father's work in *Expositiones* (1521). It is Alessandro, perhaps channeling Battista, who argues that the sparrow of Catullus is a metaphor for the poem itself, among other things; see Gaisser, *Catullus and His Renaissance Readers*, 240–41. In the genre of puppy poems, Mart. 1.109 is an outstanding example.

1. *solaciolum*: Catull. 2.7.

2. *catellam:* The insistent repetition of this word (six times), together with the repetition of the interrogative *quis* (six times), mimics the outcry of the angry and frustrated victim of the robbery as he demands the re‑ turn of his pet.

3. *mnemosynon:* Catull. 12.13.

4. *misero mihi:* A common expression in Roman comedy; see also Catull. 68.20.

    involavit: Catull. 25.6 (here in reference to a clothes thief).

5. *malus, improbus, scelestus:* Terms of abuse from Roman comedy.

6. *tam bellum:* Catull. 3.15.

7. *molliculam:* Plautus uses this adjective in a memorable expression of endearment, *meus molliculus caseus* (my silky-soft cheese), *Poen.* 367. See also Catull. 16.4 and 8.

9. *candidulam:* This diminutive form of the adjective *candidus* is rare in classical Latin (Cic. *Tusc.* 5.46; Juv. 10.355); it occurs more frequently in Renaissance Latin poetry.

11. *delicias:* Catull. 2.1 and 3.4.

12. *levamen:* Catull. 68.61, but used in a very different context; Verg. *Aen.* 3.709.

13. *dolose:* Plaut. *Pseud.* 959, an uncommon adverb.

14. *manu . . . sinistra:* Catull. 12.1. Compare Plaut. *Per.* 26, *furtifica laeva* (thieving left hand), and Ov. *Met.* 13.111, *natae ad furta sinistrae* (the left hand born for thieving).

    Tunic: Not the typical garb of the Ferrarese literary elite.

15–16. *di . . . dent:* Catull. 28.14–15.

18. See note on line 3.

    remittis: Catull. 12.11, 25.6 and 9, for the return of stolen property.

XXI. [AGAINST THE PROCURESS]

Meter: iambic trimeter

The poem has no title in the manuscript; Pigna mistakenly titled it "In meretricem," whereas Polidori, perhaps following Ariosto's comedy of the same name, dubs it "In lenam" in his edition of 1857. Ariosto participates in a familiar Roman poetic tradition of the poet-lover who positions himself in opposition to the procuress (Tib. 1.5, 2.6; Prop. 4.5; Ov. *Am.* 1.8). As in the Roman sources, Ariosto's *lena* is a scary hag who dabbles in the black arts. For an excellent study of the *lena* in elegy, see Myers, "The Poet and the Procuress." Ariosto may have been influenced by Poliziano's poem "In Anum," also written in the iambic trimeter, a poem that sets its own standard for verbal abuse.

1–2. *blandulis . . . susurris*: Prop. 1.11.13. The adjective *blandulus*, the diminutive of *blandus*, is rare in classical Latin; it occurs most famously in the emperor Hadrian's poem addressed to his soul, *Animula vagula blandula*. Renaissance Latin poets use the adjective with greater frequency.

1. *vorax anus*: The adjective *vorax* combines the sting of personal invective (Catull. 29.2, 10; 33.4; 57.8) with an implied comparison to the insatiable gullet of the mythological monsters Scylla and Charybdis (Cic. *Phil.* 2.67; Ov. *Ib.* 385).

2–3. *satis superque*: a standard phrase in Latin prose and poetry.

12. *adulterarum . . . foedissimos*: Ov. *Met.* 8.155–56. *Coitus* is an uncommon word in Latin poetry but compare Ov. *Met.* 7.709 and Sen. *Ph.* 160.

18–24. These acts of violence, mostly threatened rather than carried out, are familiar from Roman comedy and elegy: scratching the face (Hor. *Epod.* 5.93; Prop. 3.8.6 and 3.15.14; Ov. *Am.* 1.7.50); tearing the hair (Ter. *Eun.* 646; Prop. 3.15.13; Ov. *Am.* 1.7.11, 49); gouging out the eyes (Plaut. *Rud.* 759; Ter. *Eun.* 648); and cutting out the tongue (Plaut. *Amph.* 557). Although the contexts are very different, the spirit of Prop. 4.8.51–66, a riotous brawl on the battlefield of Eros, lives on in Ariosto's lines.

19. *impetus ferox*: Sen. *Tro.* 495; *Agam.* 127.

21. *venefica*: Common term of abuse in Roman comedy, e.g., Plaut. *Epid.* 211; see also Hor. *Epod.* 5.71.

23. *primulum*: An adverb found in Roman comedy, e.g., Plaut. *Men.* 916.

31–32. *inexpiabile scelus*: Cic. *Phil.* 11.29; Petron. *Sat.* 17.7.

33–36. The elegists attributed to the *lena* the traditional powers of the witch: Tib. 1.2.41–52, 1.8.7–22; Prop. 1.1.19–24, 4.5.5–20; Ov. *Am.* 1.8.5–18.

35. *diroque carmine*: Ov. *Ib.* 85.

35–36. *pallidas . . . umbras*: Verg. *Aen.* 4.25–26.

36. Orcus: Italic and Roman divinity associated with death and the underworld.

   tristibus silentiis: Stat. *Theb.* 10.382; Livy 1.29.3.

37. *tenellos*: Stat. *Silv.* 5.5.86. Catullus has the double diminutive form *tenellulo*, 17.15.

39. *preces iustae*: Ov. *Met.* 3.406.

40. *in pessimam crucem*: *in malam crucem* ("go to hell" or "to hell with you") is a common imprecation in Roman comedy. Ariosto intensifies the phrase by substituting the superlative *pessimam* for the positive *malam*, which is then repeated in *pessima*. For added emphasis Plautus uses the superlatives *summam* (*Stich.* 625) or *maximam* (*Men.* 328) with *crucem*.

XXII. NO TITLE

Meter: Phalaecean hendecasyllable

The ostensible model for this poem is Catullus 8, the famous soliloquy that begins, *Miser Catulle, desinas ineptire*. But there are major differences that make *Infelix anime* a very different poem. Most notable in Ariosto's poem is the dramatic recognition of the deceptiveness of the *puella*'s physical attractions; the *animus* dotes on her beauty (1–9) but the speaker effectively destroys that illusion with a blunt statement of her venality (15, 18, 27), the disgusting aftereffects of her relationships with other men (22–24), and her drinking (25). By comparison the *puella* of Catullus 8 is a real charmer.

1. *infelix anime*; Catull. 63.61.

6. *nitidos . . . ocellos*: Juv. 6.8.

7. Crimson mouth, soft cheeks, snow-white neck, etc.: A typical description of the beloved in the Petrarchan lyric tradition.

   os . . . purpureum: Catull. 45.12.

   genasque molles: Ov. *Her.* 10.44; Tib. 1.4.14.

9–10. These two lines, with the all-important change of *integram* to *inte-*

grae and the addition of the negative, tersely express the contrast between attractive appearance and unsightly reality.

10. *integrae puellae:* Catull. 34.2 and 78.7.

13. *perfida et improba* [also line 28] *et scelesta:* Terms of abuse used in Roman comedy and elegy; likewise *impudica* (17, 20).

14. *delicias . . . lusus:* Mart. 10.35.9.

15. *auro vendere:* Plaut. *Mil.* 1076; Verg. *Aen.* 1.484.

16. *deum . . . fallere:* Ov. *Her.* 20.196 and *Fast.* 2.262.

18. Courtesan: Compare poem 21.

   meretrix avara: Ter. *Eun.* 927; Catull. 110.7.

19. *respira:* Ter. *Haut.* 241.

21. *moechis . . . suis:* see note on 29.

22. *spurca . . . saliva:* Catull. 78.8 and 99.10.

23. *memori nota:* Hor. *Carm.* 1.13.12.

25. *ebrioli . . . ocelli:* Catull. 45.11; for the diminutive form *ebriolus,* Plaut. *Curc.* 192.

27. *dedecorum emptorem:* Hor. *Carm.* 3.6.32.

28. *obdura:* Catull. 8.11, 19.

29. *cum moechis . . . suis:* Catull. 11.17.

XXIII. Lydia

Meter: elegiac

The poem takes up the elegiac theme of the rusticating *puella* and the lover's response to the separation: see Tib. 2.3 and Prop. 2.19. At *Ars am.* 2.229–32 Ovid gives the lover tips on how to respond to his mistress's summons to join her in the country. Probably composed before the poet left Reggio Emilia definitively in 1502.

1. Reggio: The Latin name is *Regium Lepidi* or *Regium Lepidum.* The town was established by the Romans as a station on the Via Aemilia from Rimini to Piacenza.

   Lepidus: Marcus Aemilius Lepidus (ca. 230–152 BCE, consul in 187 and 175), founder of Reggio, Modena (*Mutina*), and Parma in Emilia, which were established in connection with the construction of the Via Aemilia.

3. *Lydia*: A name used with some frequency by Horace (e.g., *Carm.* 1.13.1, 1.28.8).

patrios . . . penates: Tib. 1.3.33; Prop. 4.1.91.

5–6. *quid . . . illius*: Hor. *Carm.* 4.13.18–19.

7. My home: Reggio was the hometown of Ariosto's mother, Daria Malaguzzi, and where he was born September 8, 1474.

11. *dura*: The *dura* puella was a common complaint of the elegists; Tib. 2.6.28; Prop. 2.1.78; Ov. *Ars am.* 2.527.

17–18. Compare Ovid's advice to the lover when summoned by his mistress to the country (*Ars am.* 2.230): if you don't have wheels, then take to your heels (*si rota defuerit, tu pede carpe viam*).

21. *corruptum . . . iter*: Hor. *Sat.* 1.5.95. *pluvialibus Austris*: Verg. G. 3.429.

24. *venire iube*: Ov. *Her.* 20.80; see also line 27.

25. *gelidi . . . montes*: Tib. 2.4.8. *inhospita tesqua*: Hor. *Epist.* 1.14.19.

26. *devia rura*: Prop. 2.19.2.

27. *lustra ferarum*: Verg. G. 2.471.

29. *tum . . . silvae*: [Tib.] 3.9.15.

30. *duxque comesque*: Ov. *Tr.* 1.10.10.

31–34. On these hunting activities in winter, see Hor. *Epod.* 2.31–36 and *Carm.* 1.1.25–28; Verg. G. 1.305–10; compare also Prop. 2.19.17–26,

31. Spartan dog: Valued by the Greeks and the Romans as a hunting dog; highly praised by Xenophon in his treatise on hunting, *Cyn.* 3.1–4. Ariosto's source is mostly likely Hor. *Epod.*6.5. The adjective *Lacon* can also be used as a dog's name (*praevalidus Lacon*, Ov. *Met.* 3.219).

32. *nocturnis . . . lupis*: Prop. 4.5.14.

33. *turdum . . . edacem*: Hor. *Epod.* 2.34.

35. *mala . . . vulgi*: Ov. *Her.* 17.149.

Poems XXIV–LII

Bolaffi proposes that Ariosto composed this cluster of short poems before 1503. All are in elegiac couplets except 28 and 44. In the endnotes to his edition, Fatini 1924 refers to them as "playful poetic exercises bubbling up out of Ariosto's imagination" (350).

XXIV. no title

Meter: elegiac
Another poem for Lydia; compare 23.

1. On the power of the eyes to captivate the lover, see Prop. 1.1. It is also a common theme in the poetry of the Sweet New Style, Dolce Stil Nuovo, of Dante and his contemporaries in the late thirteenth century.

2. Ariosto originally wrote the name *Telesilla* (Mart. 6.7.4), then canceled it and wrote *Lydia* in the lefthand margin.

3. *Lydia:* See note on poem 23.3.

XXV. Statue of Bacchus

Meter: elegiac
Bolaffi, picking up on the comment at line 12, proposes that the statue of Bacchus could have been in the villa of the Boiardo family in Reggio (85). For an epigram with a similar structure, a conversation between a statue and its viewer, see Mart. 5.55. Compare poem 42.

1. *aeterna . . . iuventa:* Tib. 1.4.37.

Bacchus: Classical god (Dionysus in Greek) associated with fertility and wine.

2. Pylos: Nestor, king of Pylos, an old man by the time of the Trojan War. For Homer he is a wise elder statesman, as, for example, when he tries to reconcile Achilles and Agamemnon in *Iliad* 1.254ff.

sene . . . Pylio: App. Verg. Catalepton 9.16; Ov. *Pont.* 1.4.10.

6. *puer . . . cursitet:* Hor. *Carm.* 4.11.10.

8. Tormenting . . .: Bacchus gives his own version of *in vino veritas.* Pliny, commenting on the dangers of drinking too much wine (*HN* 14.142),

observes that under the influence people will say things that bring about their own death.

multo . . . Mero: Ov. *Rem. am.* 806; see 27.2 below.

9. *aspera . . . cornibus*: Ov. *Met.* 10.222–23 and *Ars am.* 3.348.

Spiky horns on your forehead: One of the god's attributes, either in association with goats or bulls.

10. Drinking cup: Just like at a classical symposium or drinking party.
siccato . . . scypho: Petron. *Sat.* 92.5.

11. Nysa: Mythological mountainous location, either in Africa (Ethiopia, Libya) or Asia, where nymphs raised Bacchus.

Thebes: Greek city whose king, Pentheus, resisted the arrival of Bacchus and was dismembered for it.

Dia: Island in the Aegean where Bacchus found Ariadne after she had been abandoned by Theseus.

Cithaeron: Mountain in the region of Boeotia in central Greece, associated with Bacchus. Ariosto uses the form *Citheron*, with short penult, found in Ausonius, Book 16 (*Griphus Ternarii Numeri*) 32, instead of the classical form *Cithaeron*, with long penult.

12. Boiardo: Aristocratic family from Scandiano near Reggio Emilia, whose scion Matteo Maria Boiardo (1444–94) was the primary humanistic poet and functionary in the court of Ercole I d'Este in the generation prior to Ariosto.

14. Massic: Wine from the region of Campania in southern Italy.

15. Satyr: Fertility and nature deity, companion to Bacchus, human figure with a horse's tail and ears and, often, a gigantic penis.

Lynx: Animal sacred to Bacchus; see Verg. *G.* 3.264.

16. Thyrsus: Wand symbolizing the phallus, made of a fennel staff topped with a pine cone, wrapped in vines, used at Bacchic rites.

concitus . . . thyrso: Ov. *Ars am.* 3.710.

XXVI. To Bacchus

Meter: elegiac
In praise of the fruit of the vine and the good life.

1. *vino . . . benignus:* Hor. *Sat.* 2.3.3.

4. Old age: In ancient art Bacchus is usually presented as youthful, often androgynous.

   exarat . . . senecta: Hor. *Epod.* 8.4.

6. *in multa . . . rosa:* Hor. *Carm.* 1.5.1.

XXVII. On Bacchus

Meter: elegiac
Drink and love, love and drink.

2. *multo . . . mero:* A common phrase in Roman elegy; see, e.g., Prop. 2.15.42 and Tib. 1.7.50. *rite mero:* Verg. *Aen.* 5.77; see 25.8 above.

XXVIII. no title

Meter: second pythiambic
The second pythiambic, not a common meter, consists of a dactylic hexameter followed by a "pure" iambic trimeter, i.e., a form of the verse that does not allow the substitution of a long syllable for a short. Hor. *Epod.* 16, would have been Arisoto's model for this meter. Ariosto's trimeters, lines 2 and 4, are not "pure" but allow substitution. It is possible that the edition of Horace that he read contained variant readings in *Epod.* 16, e.g., *videri* for *videre* in 14, which suggested that the substitution of long for short in the trimeter was permissible.

The poem urges: enjoy life while you can! Bolaffi comments on the elaborate metrical experimentation on the part of the poet (86). Carducci 1905, 244, notes that this epigram is copied in *ms. Estense B 29* and proposes that it is in the hand of Giovambattista Giraldi along with poem 56.

3. *dum . . . sinunt:* Prop. 2.15.23.

XXIX. Eulalia

Meter: elegiac

Eulalia has not fallen far from Pasiphile's tree. When time catches up with her in the later years of her life as a courtesan, she will earn a good living as a madam! Paoletti calls this poem "a little jewel" ("Cronica," 269) for its deft mix of Plautine, Catullan, and Horatian imagery and expressions, sealed with its unexpected climax.

1. *venustula*: Plaut. *Asin.* 223 (the sole occurrence of this diminutive of *venustus* in classical Latin).

2. Here the names *Eulalia* (sweet-talker) and *Pasiphile* (dear-to-all) seem to function in their etymological sense.

3. *parvula*: Plaut. *Poen.* 1346.

6. *de tenero . . . ungue*: Hor. *Carm.* 3.6.24.

7. *sectatrix*: Not recorded in classical Latin. Cicero uses the compound *consectatrix* (*Off.* 3.117).

9. *inertior aetas*: Ov. *Tr.* 4.8.3.

XXX. Julia

Meter: elegiac

A fourth Grace, a second Venus, or a tenth Muse — however you call and count it, Julia is the best! This is Ariosto's second poem to a certain Julia; see poem 18. Segre 1954 points to possible models in the *Greek Anthology* (e.g., V 95, IX 66) in his note on this poem (64–65).

3. *Charitum quarta*: Lucretius includes the expression *Chariton mia* (one of the Graces) among the pet-names given by lovers to their beloved (4.1162).

XXXI. Veronica

Meter: elegiac

With a clever play on words — Veronica is the "truly unique" one — the poet expresses his admiration.

1. *Vera Monique:* The pun recalls Petrarch's description of the Veronica in Rome in *RVF* 16.14.

2. *me . . . surpueris:* Hor. *Carm.* 4.13.20.

3. *soli,* together with *sola* in 5 and 6, continue the wordplay.

6. The phrase *vero nomine* (true name) signals etymologizing wordplay.

XXXII. GLYCERE AND LYCORIS

Meter: elegiac

Variation on a theme: the poet is in love with two women at the same time. The poet's divided love is reflected in the syntactic division of lines 1 and 3–4, in which he considers the shared attractions of Glycere and Lycoris. Although the poet continues the first half of line 5 with the syntax of weighing alternatives (*hanc . . . illam*), he comes to the realization, signaled by *quin* in the second half of the line, that he loves them both equally. Glycere and Lycoris, it seems, come as an inseparable pair (*geminas,* 8). On the lover's predicament of being in love with two women at the same time, see Ovid, *Am.* 2.10, especially lines 5–8.

1. *Glyceren:* See note on poem 2.10.

Lycorin: The poetic alias given by the elegist Cornelius Gallus (70 BCE–26 BCE) to his mistress Cytheris. Before 1979 the name was known only through mention of Gallus and his *puella* by other poets (e.g., Verg. *Ecl.* 10.2; Prop. 2.34.91), because only a single, decidedly nonerotic, line of Gallus's poetry had survived. In that year the famous Gallus papyrus was published, in which the name *Lycori* (vocative) is preserved among fragments of his poetry. See also poem 54.1.

2. *Cerinthus:* A name that Ariosto may have taken from the pseudo-Tibullan corpus, [Tib.], the six elegiac poems attributed to the female poet, Sulpicia, [Tib.] 3.13–18; she calls her lover by this Greek pseudonym.

si . . . disperéam: Mart. 9.95b.4.

5. *depereo:* Common in Roman comedy for feeling the total distraction of love.

7–8. These lines echo Catullus's famous couplet (85), beginning *Odi et amo* (I hate and I love).

8. *ardeo, amo, pereo:* The pleonasm is suggestive of the young lover in Roman comedy.

Poems XXXIII–XXXIX

These brief epigrams in elegiac couplets sound very similar to the sorts of poems one finds in the *Greek Anthology*, including witty poems about love, some verses inspired by Aesop, and comments on other poets. There is no proof that Ariosto knew the *Anthology*, but versions of parts of it were beginning to circulate. In addition, poets inspired by the *Anthology*, such as Michael Marullus, were also beginning to be appreciated. Stefano Grosso identified the *Anthology* as a possible source in a short piece written to Carducci and published in 1876.

XXXIII. To a Girl Selling Roses

Meter: elegiac

More variations on a theme: if you sell roses and you are a rose, are you also selling yourself? *Greek Anthology* 5.142 is a possible source.

1. *te vendes:* Catull. 106.

XXXIV. The Same

Meter: elegiac

XXXV. The Wolf and the Sheep

Meter: elegiac

An Aesopian moment in Ariosto's writing. Carducci 1905, 255–57, and Segre 1954, 68) see *Anth. Pal.* 9.47 as the source and regard Ariosto's poem as almost a translation of it: "I am rearing a wolf with my own udders against my will, but the shepherd's folly forces me to do it. When the wolf has been raised by me, it will in turn be a wild animal that preys on me. Kindness cannot change nature."

XXXVI. The Poet named Bard

Meter: elegiac

On a poetaster whose work, thankfully, is only committed to memory, not written down.

1–2. *milia . . . carmina:* Ov. *Am.* 1.8.57–58.

1. Blabbard: In Latin the noun *bardus* means bard; the adjective *bardus* means slow, dull, or stupid.

3. *perdere chartam:* Mart. 6.64.23.

XXXVII. Callimachus

Meter: elegiac

In this, the first of two epigrammatic couplets on a *puer* with the face of an old man, the poet dramatizes his shock at discovering that the person he thought was a *puer* is really a *pater*. Those two words neatly frame the couplet and are introduced by interjections indicating the poet's shift in mood: *heus* for attracting the *puer/pater's* attention from behind and *o* for expressing surprise when the face becomes visible. Callimachus, the Hellenistic poet-scholar, was collected in the *Greek Anthology*, but there is nothing to prove that Ariosto is referring specifically to him here. Michael Marullus, whose death Ariosto laments in poem 15, made textual emendations of Callimachus's *Lock of Berenice*.

XXXVIII. The Same

Meter: elegiac

In this second couplet the poet delivers an epigrammatic zinger, in the spirit of Martial, by again framing the lines with *puer* and *pater*, but this time he intensifies the verbal play by transforming the incongruity of the *puer's* face and the back of his head into the relationship of child and father, nicely underscored by the juxtaposition of the technical words *occiput* and *sinciput*.

XXXIX. To Aulo

Meter: elegiac

In this epigram Ariosto imitates a scene from Horace's famous satire (1.9), in which the Roman poet finds himself trapped in conversation with an aggressive social climber who wants an introduction to Maecenas, adviser and confidante of the emperor Augustus. Ariosto focuses on the moment when Aristius Fuscus, Horace's friend, joins the pair (1.9.60–72). Despite Horace's emphatic body language, similar to what we find in the epigram, Fuscus pretends not to understand his predicament and leaves him in the clutches of the social climber. Ariosto casts himself in the role of a slightly more cooperative Fuscus.

1. *Ne distorque . . . nuta*: Hor. *Sat.* 1.9.63–65.

3. Since *Lalius* is not a Roman name, it is possible that Arisoto is punning on the Greek adjective λάλος, meaning "talkative," in which case the adjective *loquaci* would be a gloss on the Greek name.

XL. To a Boy

Meter: elegiac

Yet another love poem in the style of the *Greek Anthology*.

1. *fractus . . . arcus*: Ov. *Am.* 3.9.8.

   nisu in medio: Ov. *Her.* 4.126.

2. God of Claros: Apollo, who was worshipped in particular on the island of Claros.

   Clarii . . . dei: Val. Fl. *Arg.* 3.299; Ov. *Ars am.* 2.80.

XLI. A Dead Boy

Meter: elegiac

An epigram to memorialize a boy recently dead turns into another love poem.

1. Paphian goddess: Venus, from the island of Paphos.

2. Adonis: Allusion to the myth of Venus and Adonis, the young lover of the goddess, who died in a hunting accident according to Ov. *Met.* 10.300–559, 708–39. Compare poem 17.21–22.

XLII. Armed Venus in Sparta

Meter: elegiac

Playful classicizing piece on the battle of love divided into two parts. In the first we hear the voice of the *hospes*, who is looking at a statue of Venus in arms; in the second Venus herself responds and explains her martial origins. On the theme of Spartan Venus, see Nohrnberg, *The Analogy of the Faerie Queene*, 454–56.

1. Mars: God of war, who was one of the many lovers of Venus. Compare poem 17.

inutile pondus: Ov. *Am.* 3.7.15.

3. *nuda potentem:* The juxtaposition underscores the goddess's supremacy in amatory maneuvers and combat.

5. Sparta: Greek city whose culture emphasized military prowess.

6. *de patrio . . . more:* Ov. *Met.* 12.11.

7. Blood spilled: Reference to the myth of the birth of Venus, who was born from the severed genitals of Uranus when he was castrated by his son Cronus.

sanguine nata: Tib. 1.2.41.

XLIII. Trivulzia

Meter: elegiac
In praise of a woman who seems to have it all. On the qualities of the deceased listed here, compare Stat. *Silv.* 2.7.81–88, on Polla, wife of the poet Lucan.

3–4. *nullique . . . forma:* Ov. *Am.* 1.8.25.

7. *docta . . . sciens:* Hor. *Carm.* 3.9.10.

8. Deiphobe: The Cumaean Sibyl, a prophetess of Apollo at the oracle of Cumae, near Naples.

Lesbian lyre player: Sappho, Greek lyric poet born on the island of Lesbos in the second half of the seventh century BCE. See 18.1–12.

XLIV. Trivulzia

Meter: Phalaecean hendecasyllable
But if she doesn't share her many gifts in love, no one will care about all that she has.

XLV. Epitaph of Philippa

Meter: elegiac
A riff on the theme of the unfaithful wife. Readers of Boccaccio's *Decame-*

ron 6.7 will hear an echo of the feisty Madonna Filippa in this poem and the next.

1. *ingenti . . . pondere:* Verg. *Aen.* 9.752.

XLVI. Epitaph

Meter: elegiac

Her tomb turns into a kind of Delphic Oracle and speaks to the passerby, first advising him to embrace the maxim "know thyself," then telling him to be on his way! The epigram is noteworthy for its lively conversational tone with the deceased clearly in control of the conversation. The departed Philippa cleverly turns the opening question about her own identity into a question about the identity of her interlocutor. Her quotations of the comic poet Terence and the Delphic Oracle suggest learning and sophistication.

3. *nil . . . putavi:* Philippa sums up her character with an adapted quotation of a famous line from Ter. *Haut.* 77, *homo sum: humani nil a me alienum puto* (I am a human being: what concerns my fellow man I regard as a matter of concern to me).

5. *Quid tibi vis:* A common phrase in Roman comedy.

6. *ipsum . . . noscis:* The interrogative form of the Delphic Oracle's well-known prescription *nosce te* (know thyself); compare Cic. *Tusc.* 1.52, Sen. *Ep.* 94.28 and *Dial.* 6.11.3.

XLVII. [Epitaph of Labulla]

Meter: elegiac

His knowledge of Roman antiquities not inconsequential, here the poet shows that he can compose an epitaph in the spirit of the many inscriptions he would have seen around him on trips to Rome and elsewhere.

1. Holy Mother: A reference to the goddess who watched over ancient Rome, Bona Dea, attended by the vestal virgins. Or perhaps it is a reference to the Virgin Mary.

3. Flamen: An ancient Roman priest, here used as an honorific title.

funere acerbo: Verg. *Aen.* 6.429.

6. *dulcis . . . viri*: Catull. 67.1.

7. *caelum . . . fatiga*: Verg. *Aen.* 1.280.

XLVIII. [The Same]

Meter: elegiac

In a tone heard in many passages of the *Furioso*, the poet empowers his female character, literally giving her a voice that enables her to tell her own story and have the very last word.

2. *muta . . . cinis*: Catull. 101.4.

4. *mater . . . potest*: Suet. *Tib.* 59.1.

XLIX. [Epitaph of Manfredini]

Meter: elegiac

In memory of one of Ariosto's relatives, Rinaldo Manfredini, who was murdered by the brother of the woman he loved. What would her kinfolk have done, the poet wonders, if he had hated her? For a similar type of funerary epigram, cast in the form of question and answer, compare Marullus, *Epigrams* 1.52. See also *Incerta* poem 2. See Catalano, *Vita*, 1:13, for speculation on Rinaldo's family line.

1. Traveler: As in poem 42, in this funerary inscription, the stone engages in dialogue with the stranger who is passing by.

3. *necis . . . saevae*: Sen. *Oed.* 634.

4. *interfectoris*: A word common in Latin prose but not used in poetry.

   perdite amasse: A phrase that echoes Roman comedy (Ter. *Haut.* 97) and Catullan lyric (45.3).

5. *pro scelus*: Mart. 2.46.8.

L. [Epitaph]

Meter: elegiac

The poet invokes the topos of the man who dies from lack of love. Or is it that he dies from too much sex?

3. *durum . . . Amorem*: Verg. *Aen.* 6.442.

LI. [Epitaph of Badino]

Meter: elegiac

Epitaph for a member of Duke Ercole's entourage, written before the death of the duke in 1505.

3. *felix ter*: An expression found in a *makarismos*, the formal laudation of a person's good fortune; see Prop. 3.2.15 and Ov. *Met.* 8.346.

LII. To Timoteo Bendidei

Meter: elegiac

Bendidei, whom Ariosto praises in *Furioso* 42.92, died in 1522, which provides a *terminus ante quem* for the poem. Fatini 1924 is unimpressed with it: "The paltry poem seems like a youthful dabbling" (351). Carducci and Polidori work themselves into a fit trying to figure out just who Ariosto refers to in the poem (cited in Bolaffi, 93). For Carducci, it is Lidia in Reggio, for Polidori, Alessandra Benucci in Florence. In order to strengthen his excuse for not accompanying his friend and soften any offense, the poet presents himself as the servant, not of his mistress, but of *Amor* himself. Thus the choice the poet has to make is not between his love for his mistress and affection for his friend, but rather between the consequences of offending a divinity and a mortal; it is the mortal who is more likely to be forgiving.

4. Twirling his whip: Love does not carry a whip in the typical Petrarchan love poem.

intorto verbere: Tib. 1.9.22.

7. *durus Amor*: See poem 50.3.

LIII. Wedding Song

Meter: dactylic hexameter

Division into choruses of Ferrarese citizens and Romans not indicated in the *editio princeps* of 1553.

An epithalamium for the wedding of Lucrezia Borgia and Alfonso d'Este in February 1502, specifically celebrating Lucrezia's entry in the city of Ferrara on January 2, 1502. Sung by a double chorus comprised of happy Ferrarese citizens welcoming the bride and saddened Romans lamenting her departure, this grand poem in hexameters reflects a challenging moment in Ferrarese culture, when the aging Ercole was struggling to position his duchy favorably in the volatile politics of the early modern Italian peninsula through a strategic alliance with the Borgia papacy. We do not know exactly when the poem was performed, assuming that it was. Upon Lucrezia's arrival in Ferrara, there were five full days of entertainment in the Estense court, which included dancing during the day and a different Plautine comedy staged each evening. This poem of welcome could have been performed on one of those opening five days.

The poem is modeled on Catullus 62, a wedding poem in the form of amoebaean song, i.e., two groups alternating with each other in reciting their verses, each one picking up on the language and themes of the other and trying to outdo them; the verbal and thematic parallels are quite clear. Ariosto has cleverly orchestrated the contest heavily in favor of Ferrara: the Roman youth devote their poetic talents to lamenting the decline of their city with an impressive portrait of abandoned ruins; that portrait allows the young men of Ferrara to launch into an enthusiastic panegyric of their vibrant and growing city. At the end of the poem (150) the Ferrarese chorus graciously invites the Romans to join them in harmonious song. Perhaps we are to imagine that the two choruses join together to sing the last line (151). Ariosto's poem continues a tradition that goes back to Sappho in the seventh century BCE. In addition to Catull. 62, Catull. 61 and Stat. *Silv.* 1.2 are important models.

1. *surgite*: Catull. 62.1; *venientis nuptae*: Catull. 62.4.

2–3. *iugato . . . olore*: Hor. *Carm.* 3.28.15.

3–4. Compare Catull. 39.12–14 and Verg. *Aen.* 10.86.

3. Venus: Goddess of Love.

Memphis: Ancient capital of Egypt, located near the Delta of the Nile. Herodotus comments on the temple of the "foreign Aphrodite" in Memphis (2.112), a passage Ariosto could have known through Boiardo's translation of the Greek historian, which circulated in the Estense court. See also Hor. *Carm.* 3.26.10.

Cythera: Island off the coast of Greece said to be the birthplace of Venus.

4. Idalian grove: Area on the island of Cyprus, another island in the Aegean associated with the birth of Venus.

Amathus: Major city on Cyprus with a sanctuary to the goddess of Love. See poem 17.25.

6. *osque genasque*: Lucr. 1.920.

7. Charis: One of the Graces, female deities who embody grace, beauty, and charm.

8. *levibus pennis*: Ov. *Met.* 2.581.

9. *tenerorum lusus Amorum*: A modification of Ovid's famous self-description in his autobiographical poem, *Tr.* 4.10.1.

Amores: Deities of Love, often attending Venus.

10–14. Compare Stat. *Silv.* 1.2.17–23.

11–12. *fronti . . . niveae*: Ov. *Met.* 10.133.

12–13. *immortales amarantos . . . purpureasque rosas*: Columella *Rust.* 10.175; *Appendix Vergiliana*, "Copa" 14.

15. Of Rome: The adjective *Latinus*, "of or belonging to Latium," the region of central Italy where Rome is located, is used here in the restricted sense of "belonging to or from the city of Rome."

With downcast faces: The Romans are sad, for they will have to leave Ferrara and return to Rome on the appointed day at the end of the wedding festivities.

17. *tacita . . . voce*: Ov. *Met.* 9.300.

20. Hymen, Hymenaeus: Traditional refrain in the typical ancient Greek wedding song, which refers to the deity associated with marriage. Catullus uses the refrain in poems 61 and 62; it also appears in Plaut. *Cas.* 800, 809.

21. Hercules: Ferrarese men who represent their leader Duke Ercole, the person most responsible for orchestrating the marriage of his son with the daughter of the pope.

27. *externi . . . thalami:* Verg. *Aen.* 6.94.

28. Romans: See note on 15.

29–34. Compare Catull. 62.11–16.

29. Ausonian bards: The chorus of singers from Rome who have accompanied Lucrezia to Ferrara.

32. Amoebean singing: A form common in pastoral poetry, in which two interlocutors, or as in this case, two choral groups, sing back and forth to each other in alternation. The poem defines the form below: "we . . . sing the happy wedding song in alternating verses" (113).

35. *docto . . . cantu:* Ov. *Met.* 5.662.

37. *omnia vertuntur:* Prop. 2.8.7; Ov. *Met.* 15.165.

37–39. Compare Verg. *Ecl.* 1.23–25.

40. Albula: Ancient name of the Tiber River; it is a fixture in accounts of Rome's legendary past (Verg. *Aen.* 8.332; Livy 1.3.5). Ariosto wants to show his erudition on this august occasion.

   tenues . . . rivos: Ov. *Met.* 5.435.

41. *moenibus altis:* An echo of Vergil's proud verse, *altae moenia Romae* (*Aen.* 1.7).

43. Capitol: The Capitoline hill at Rome overlooking the Forum, together with its fortified citadel and the temple of Jupiter Capitolinus. *Capitolia celsa:* Verg. *Aen.* 8.653.

44. Curia: Senate House in the Roman Forum.

   sancto . . . senatu: Enn. *Ann.* 272; Verg. *Aen.* 1.426. *Capitolia, Curia,* and *Senatus* form a resonant triad that conjures up Rome's bygone power as the capital of a vast Mediterranean empire.

45. *flexipedes . . . hederae:* Ov. *Met.* 10.99.

46. *turpes . . . latebras:* Sen. *Tro.* 504. *serpentibus atris:* Verg. *Aen.* 4.472; Ov. *Met.* 14.410.

48. *habitare sub antris:* Ov. *Met.* 3.394.

49. Virgin: Reference to Lucrezia, definitely not a virgin. She had been married twice before her betrothal to Alfonso and was rumored to have

had an incestuous relationship with her brother, Cesare Borgia. *pulcherrima virgo*: Ov. *Met.* 9.9.

52. *viridi ripa*: Verg. *Ecl.* 7.12.

  limosa palude: Sen. *Agam.* 768.

53. Lowly Ferrara: Ferrara's economy was challenged as it vied for status with many other wealthier and more powerful states. To have a connection to the papal treasury was enviable.

57. Apenninus: Personification of the great mountain chain that runs down the center of the Italian peninsula from north to south.

  Hills of Bacchus: Mount Cithaeron in the region of Boeotia in central Greece, associated with Bacchus.

58. Eridanus: The Po River. Vergil calls it the monarch of rivers (*fluviorum rex*, G. 1.482). As with Albula for Tiber at line 40, the poet seeks to demonstrate his humanistic learning.

59. Hesperia: The ancient Greek name for Italy, the land to the west.

  Neptunus uterque: Catull. 31.3.

60. *piscoso . . . gurgite*: Verg. *Aen.* 11.457.

61. *in aprico . . . campo*: Calp. *Ecl.* 5.8.

  siccabant retia: Ov. *Met.* 11.362.

63. Herculean walls: A pun on the size of the large walls built by Ercole but also an adjective that recalls the massive urban project to develop a new portion of the city, called the Herculean Addition, under the direction of court architect Biagio Rossetti, during the 1490s and into the new century.

69. Ionian sea: The area of the Mediterranean between southern Italy and the western coast of Greece, one of the most seismically active seas in the world and, therefore, treacherous. *in Ionio magno*: Verg. *Aen.* 3.211.

70. Syria: For Ariosto and his contemporaries, the land at the eastern end of the Mediterranean between Arabia and Asia Minor.

  Bithynia: Ancient province in Asia Minor at the Hellespont and thus full of traders.

71. *scopulis . . . acutis:* Verg. *Aen.* 1.45 and 1.144–45.

72–73. Ariosto combines the image of the shipwrecked sailor (see Catull. 68.3) with Aeneas's emotional apostrophe to his helmsman Palinurus, who he assumes was drowned at sea (*Aen.* 5.871).

72. *volvitur expes:* Hor. Ars P. 20–21.

75. *informi in limo:* Verg. *Aen.* 6.416.

80. *nemus . . . querelis:* Verg. *Aen.* 8.215–16.

82. Quirites: Ancient name for citizens of Rome.

83. Vatican Hill: Hill across the Tiber that is the site of St. Peter's Church, the symbolic center of Christendom.

   flexisset lumina: Stat. *Silv.* 5.1.217.

84. Illustrious Borgia: Pope Alexander VI.

87. *novo . . . munere:* Catull. 66.38.

88. Seven Hills: The seven hills that define the topography of Rome.

   Tiber: The river that flows from the Apennines westward through Rome and into the Mediterranean at Ostia. *Tiberis pater:* Enn. *Ann.* 26; Livy 2.10.11.

89. *imperi monimenta:* Tac. *Hist.* 4.26.

90. Este brothers: Three of Alfonso's brothers, Ippolito, Sigismondo, and Ferrante, were commissioned by Ercole to lead the wedding entourage from Rome to Ferrara.

96. *mobilibus . . . rivis:* Hor. *Carm.* 1.7.14.

   per quadrua compita: App. *Verg.* De Rosis Nascentibus 5.

97. Idaean Goat: The she-goat who suckled the infant Jupiter in a cave on Mount Ida in Crete and was rewarded by being transformed into the star Capra, located in the constellation Auriga. The goat belonged to Amalthea, a Cretan Naiad who lived on Mount Ida; see Ov. *Fast.* 5.111–28. Capra rises at the end of September and is associated with cold, stormy weather: *sub sidere Caprae,* Hor. *Carm.* 3.7.6. In this list of astronomical signs of the seasons, Libra (fall), Sirius (summer), Taurus (spring), Capra is somewhat unusual as a sign of winter. However, its

association with cold (*frigidas . . . noctis*, Hor. *Carm.* 3.7.6–7) suggests that it could function as an indicator of winter's onset. It seems unlikely that Capra is to be understood as a reference to Capricorn, home of the winter solstice, a meaning not attested in Latin poetry. After all, Capra is a she-goat and Capricorn, in part, a he-goat.

98. Libra: The autumnal equinox occurs when the sun is in Libra.

Sirius: The brightest star in the night sky, commonly called the Dog Star for its position in the constellation Canis Major, associated with the dog days of summer.

99. *egelidos . . . tepores*: Catull. 46.1.

Taurus: Constellation that is a sign of spring.

100. *lento e vimine*: Verg. *Aen.* 6.137.

101. *variis . . . coloribus*: Mart. 2.46.1.

106. *studiis . . . ingenuis*: Cic. *Fin.* 5.48.

107–8. *tauro . . . annum*: Verg. *G.* 1.217–18. Ariosto has devised a clever astronomical conceit in which Lucrezia is likened to Europa, who was carried off by Jupiter disguised as a bull; the bull was then translated to the heavens as the constellation Taurus. See Ov. *Fast.* 5.603–20.

109. *summittit . . . colores*: Prop. 1.2.9; Lucr. 1.8.

vere . . . novo: Verg. *G.* 1.43.

112. *teneris . . . ab annis*: Ov. *Pont.* 2.3.73.

122. *tacitos . . . questus*: Luc. 1.247.

123. *viduo . . . lecto*: Ov. *Her.* 123.

127. Phaethon's crash: Phaethon, the son of Apollo, crashed the chariot of the Sun at the delta of the Po. Ferrarese poets turn to the myth frequently.

131. Ursa Major: The constellation of the Big Bear.

134–35. Herculean labors: Ercole worked hard to reclaim land from the marshes and make many of the low-lying areas around Ferrara suitable for agriculture.

134. *pinguia . . . culta*: Verg. *G.* 4.372.

135. *labores Herculeos*: Prop. 3.18.4.

135–36. *contudit hydram:* Hor. *Epist.* 2.1.10.

136. *ignavis . . . flexibus:* Verg. G. 3.14.

137. *exporgite frontem:* Ter. *Ad.* 839.

138–39. *opaca in nocte:* Verg. *Aen.* 4.123.

139. *picea . . . caligine:* Verg. G. 2.309; Ov. *Met.* 1.265.

144. Herculean hero: Here the adjective refers to Alfonso, son of Ercole, who was married to Anna Maria Sforza, sister of the duke of Milan, from 1491 to 1497. Alfonso was a widower from 1497 to 1502.

145. Aurora, wife of Tithonus: Dawn. *Aurora . . . exoriente:* Catull. 64.271. By adding the adjective *Latina* to identify *Aurora* as Lucretia, Ariosto has transformed a formula that indicates the arrival of dawn into a courtly compliment.

146. *visilis:* Not recorded in classical Latin; Marullus uses the adjective, probably coined by him, at *Hymni* 3.1.35.

148. Bards of Romulus: An honorific form of address to the members of the Roman chorus, which recognizes the legendary status of their city.

LIV. A Multiplicity of Loves
Meter: elegiac
In the guise of a poem imagining which one of many possible women he might love (he mentions many by name), the poet sketches out his career up to this point to raise the more important question: what is his true vocation? He abandoned legal studies for poetry, but the initial decision to write pastoral verse did not work. He then tried epic poetry. After that he focused his energies on being a courtier. That in turn was interrupted by a stint as a captain for the Este rulers. Now he is resuming his love life despite the difficulties of choosing from among the many women before him! This poem is noteworthy for the biographical allusions (Bárberi Squarotti, "Ludovico Ariosto," calls it Ariosto's most important poem in Latin, 302), and for its variation on the Neoplatonic theme of the one and the many, in this case, one lover and many beloveds, which will have many permutations in the *Furioso*.

1. *Glycere:* See note on poem 2.10.

   Lycoris: See note on poem 32.1.

2. *Lyda:* The name occurs, with Greek termination, in Hor. *Carm.* 2.11.22 and 3.9.6.

   Phyllis: A name that appears in bucolic poetry (Verg. *Ecl.* 7.63; Calp. *Ecl.* 3.9) and in elegiac poetry (Prop. 4.8.29; Ov. *Am.* 2.18.32).

3. The name *Glaura* is unattested.

   Hybla: The name of a mountain in Sicily famous for the honey produced by its bees. Its use as a personal name is unusual. Ariosto may have had in mind a line from Vergil (*Ecl.* 7.37): *Nerine Galatea, thymo mihi dulcior Hyblae* (Galatea, daughter of Nereus, sweeter to me than the thyme of Hybla). The word's close association with honey and honeybees makes it an apt name for a lover.

6. *vesano . . . amore:* Prop. 2.15.29.

9. *vitales . . . auras:* Verg. *Aen.* 1.387–88 and 10.898–99.

13. Aurora: Dawn.

    rosea . . . quadriga: Verg. *Aen.* 6.535.

17. *de more capillos:* Verg. *Aen.* 10.832.

18. *estque . . . toga:* Catull. 68.15.

    Toga pura: Also called the *toga virilis* in ancient Rome, the article of clothing that symbolized a free male citizen's arrival at the age of manhood.

19. Law courts: Ariosto's father urged him to pursue an education in jurisprudence, which he did with great reluctance. He read "De laudibus Sophiae" (poem 4) before his peers in jurisprudence at the Ferrarese *Studium* in 1495.

    me . . . leges: Ov. *Am.* 1.15.5.

20. *amplaque . . . lucra:* Plaut. *Amph.* 6.

    clamosi . . . fori: Sen. *HF* 172; Ov. *Tr.* 4.10.18.

21. *optatam . . . metam:* Hor. *Ars P.* 412.

23. Permessus and Aonian Aganippe: Streams on Mount Helicon, dear to the Muses, symbols of poetic inspiration. Aonia is the region in Boeotia where they are found.

Aoniamque Aganippen: Verg. *Ecl.* 10.12.

24. *virgineis . . . choris:* Ov. *Ars am.* 3.168.

mollia prata: Verg. *Ecl.* 10.42.

27. Mars: God of war. To position himself well at the court, Ariosto tried to write an epic in Italian *terza rima* on Obizzo d'Este, a warlord of the late Middle Ages, but only a fragment remains.

28. *bella canenda:* Tib. 2.4.16.

31. *dominam . . . potentem:* Verg. *Aen.* 3.438.

32. Fortune, that powerful lady: Ariosto served in the court of Ippolito d'Este from around 1503 till their break in 1517, when the poet refused to follow his patron to Hungary.

33. Ungrateful prince: Ippolito.

35. Soldier: While not known for his military exploits, Ariosto did indeed serve the family of his patrons as a diplomat, engaging especially in papal diplomacy (1509–16), and as a soldier (ca. 1509–13).

aeratis . . . telis: Stat. *Theb.* 2.532; Tib. 1.10.25.

36. *forti . . . equo:* Tib. 1.2.70.

37–38. *patiensque . . . corpus:* Ov. *Tr.* 1.5.71.

39. *bellator sonipes:* Ariosto combines two epic expressions for warhorse, the epithet noun phrase *bellator equus* (Verg. *Aen.* 11.89) and the adjective *sonipes* used substantively (Verg. *Aen.* 4.135).

40. *acri . . . militia:* Hor. *Carm.* 1.29.2 and 3.2.2.

41. Renowned prince: Alfonso d'Este led an army that included Ariosto to fight alongside the French against the Spanish-Papal army at the Battle of Ravenna in 1512. The poet is critical of the pyrrhic victory in *Furioso* 14.1–7.

42. *Martia . . . signa:* Stat. *Theb.* 9.827; Mart. 11.3.3.

43. *castra . . . nobis:* Hor. *Carm.* 1.1.23.

44. Getae: Thracian tribes who inhabited the land where Ovid was exiled. Synonymous with barbarians.

tela . . . cruenta: Ov. *Tr.* 5.7b. 34.

45. *humano . . . sanguine*: Ov. *Met.* 14.168.

47. *horridus . . . portitor*: Verg. *Aen.* 6.298.

Ferryman: Charon, who ferries the souls of the dead over the Styx in the pagan underworld.

47–48. *umbram . . . immitem*: Stat. *Silv.* 3.3.206.

49. *sede piorum*: Hor. *Carm.* 2.13.23.

50. Eumenides: Avenging spirits in the underworld.

verbera saeva: Verg. *Aen.* 6.557–58.

52. *munere Martis*: Sil. *Pun.* 6.477.

57. *Dryadasque puellas*: Verg. *Ecl.* 5.59.

58. *fistula . . . terat*: Verg. *Ecl.* 2.35.

59. Catos: Cato of Utica (95–46 BCE), Roman senator and statesman renowned for his stern adherence to moral law. In Dante's *Purgatory*, Cato, the guardian of the mountain of repentance, scolds the pilgrim and others for pausing to listen to a newly-arrived soul sing a version of one of Dante's lyric poems (*Purg.* 2.76–114). See also Mart. 10.20.21.

61. *limite certo*: Ov. *Fast.* 2.683.

63. *senio . . . inerti*: Stat. *Silv.* 2.4.36; Tib. 1.1.5.

LV. Epitaph of Gianfrancesco Gonzaga

Meter: elegiac

As Bolaffi points out, it is difficult to know exactly which member of the Gonzaga family this is for (99).

1. *vivente anima*: Luc. 6.529.

mortua membra: Mart. 13.34.1.

3. *novus incola*: Ov. *Met.* 13.904.

6. *vanus . . . dolor*: Sen. *Dial.* 10.3.3.

LVa. NO TITLE
Meter: elegiac
Earlier draft of the previous poem.

LVI. NO TITLE
Meter: elegiac
An example of Ariosto's capacity for schoolboy wit, which is playful but not without point: Ercole d'Este was criticized for not paying members of his court enough, while spending lavishly on public projects. Carducci 1905, 244, proposes that Giovambattista Giraldi is the copyist of this epigram along with poem 28 in *ms. Estense B 29.*

LVII. [TO IPPOLITO D'ESTE, BISHOP OF FERRARA]
Meter: elegiac
Composed to celebrate Ippolito's nomination as bishop of Ferrara in October 1503.

2. *ora verenda:* Stat. *Silv.* 2.6.79.

5. *invicto . . . Hercule: Priapeia* 20.5.

LVIII. EPITAPH OF LUDOVICO ARIOSTO
Meter: Phalaecean hendecasyllable
An ironic twist on the theme of the typical epitaph: the soul needs the inscription to guide it to the bones with which it will be united at the end of time. For an analysis of the two versions (see next poem) of this epitaph, see Mutini, "Nota sull'*Epitaphium Ludovici Areosti.*"

1. Bones: Originally buried in the Church of San Benedetto, Ariosto's bones were translated to their current resting place in the Palazzo Paradiso, now home of the Biblioteca Ariostea, with much pomp and ceremony described in the celebratory volume *Prose e rime per il trasporto del monumento e delle ceneri di Lodovico Ariosto.* Capasso reports that this epitaph was never inscribed on the poet's tomb, which had instead "l'iscrizione d'un padre gesuita" (an inscription by a Jesuit) (*Poesie latine,* 77).

1–2. *humantur . . . marmore*: Mart. 6.28.4.

5. Compare Prop. 2.11.4.

10. *inscribi . . . sepulcro*: Ov. Her. 2.145.

15. *cinerem . . . revellens*: Verg. Aen. 4.427.

LVIIIa. NO TITLE

Meter: Phalaecean hendecasyllable

This version is canceled with a diagonal stroke through all the lines in Ariosto's manuscript. One is hard pressed to understand why he didn't like it.

8. Last Day: The day of the Last Judgment at the end of time.

10. *tumulos . . . vagetur*: Luc. 6.574.

LIX. EPITAPH OF ERCOLE STROZZI

Meter: elegiac

Dedicated to the memory of Ercole Strozzi, murdered on June 6, 1508. Catalano's research into the notarial archive connected with Barbara Torelli, Strozzi's widow, convincingly establishes that this poem was written for the first anniversary of Ercole's death in 1509 (*Vita*, 1:243–61). For a more detailed discussion of Strozzi's death and how Torelli responded to it, see Catalano, *Lezioni di letteratura italiana*.

1. Country's government: Elected to be one of the state's judges, one of the so-called "XII Savi," in 1497, which he held till 1506.

moderatus habenas: Sil. Pun. 16.343.

2. But a boy: He was probably born in 1473, thus assuming the position of judge at the relatively young age of twenty-four.

3–4. The poet specifies three genres of poetry: elegy, epic (*grandia*), and lyric.

3. *molles elegi*: Ov. Pont. 3.4.85.

grandia: Ov. Am. 2.18.4.

4. *canenda lyra*: Ov. Fast. 4.81.

5. Ashes: Other than poem 48, where the author refers to Labulla's "mute ash," and poem 58, where Ariosto refers to his own ashes, this is the only other passage where he refers to "ashes" of the dead, lending it an impressively austere tone.

tegitur cinis: Juv. 1.171.

LX. To Fusco

Meter: alcaic

The poet salutes a young member of his extended family.

1. Aristio: Noble Roman family with which Ariosto fantasizes a genealogical connection. Pigna dismisses the notion, pointing out that the family's origins are Bolognese (*Romanzi*, 71).

1–2. *claraque . . . propago:* Lucr. 1.42.

6–8. *grandia . . . praemia:* Hor. *Epist.* 2.2.38.

8. *tergeminos honores:* Hor. *Carm.* 1.1.8.

9–10. *tenera . . . aetas:* Ov. *Tr.* 4.10.33.

11. Augustus: Ariosto conflates the Roman emperor of the past with the Ferrarese duke of his contemporary moment.

20. Caesar: Augustus, i.e., the leader of the state.

LXI. On Raphael from Urbino

Meter: elegiac

On the death of the painter, Raphael Sanzio, in 1520. He included Ariosto in his portrait of poets on Parnassus in the Vatican Apartments.

1. *non . . . est:* Hor. *Carm.* 1.28.35.

3. *picta manu:* Ov. *Tr.* 2.1.522.

5. Urbino: Town where Raphael was born in April 1483.

Rome: Where he lived the latter years of his life and where he died in April 1520.

7–10. Compare Stat. *Silv.* 4.6.20–30.

7–8. Gave life to marble: The statues that Raphael represented in his painting could be said to come to life.

7. *iuvenem exanimum:* Verg. *Aen.* 11.51.

8. *vivere signa:* Prop. 2.31.8.

9. *os oculosque:* Catull. 9.9.

12. Fates: Classical deities that controlled the course of one's life from birth to death, often depicted as three women.

14. *stare . . . negant:* Luc. 1.70–71.

invida Fata: Stat. *Theb.* 10.384.

LXII. To Alfonso, Third Duke of Ferrara
Meter: elegiac
Written at the death of Ippolito d'Este, Alfonso's brother, in September 1520. Despite claims to the contrary in the poem, Ippolito did not die trying to save his brother; rather, he died from food poisoning, having overindulged in too much shellfish.

3. Getae: Ippolito was cardinal in Hungary.

3–4. These lines refer to the Roman ritual devotion (*devotio*) of one's life, here represented by *caput*, as an offering to secure the safety of others. *vovet . . . caput:* Ov. *Her.* 3.94.

5. *deos faciles:* Ov. *Her.* 16.282.

Orcus: The underworld, Death.

7. Pollux and Castor: The poet illustrates the depth of the brothers' mutual love with a mythological *exemplum*, the twin brothers Castor and Pollux (Polydeuces), one of whom, Castor, according to the most popular tradition, is the mortal son of Leda and her husband Tyndareus, and the other, Pollux, is the immortal son of Leda and Zeus/Jupiter. As Castor lay dying, after being wounded in an ambush, his brother Pollux prays to Zeus to die alongside him. Zeus in response offers him a choice: Pollux can live among the gods on Olympus or spend half of his days under the earth and half in the heavens, alternating with his brother in life and death. Pollux without hesitation chooses to share his immortality with Castor. See Pind. *Nem.* 10.103–70 and Ov. *Fast.* 5.697–720. The *ex-*

emplum enhances the devotion of Ippolito; unlike Pollux, he chooses a one-way trip to the underworld.

Morte . . . Pollux: Verg. *Aen.* 6.121.

redimis . . . Castora: Ov. *Fast.* 5.719.

9–10. *inani spe:* Verg. *Aen.* 11.49.

10. *avidi . . . Ditis:* Sen. *Agam.* 752; *Tr.* 723.

LXIII. Epitaph of Zerbinato
Meter: Phalaecean hendecasyllable
In memory of Francesco Zerbinato, who fought for the Ferrarese against the Venetians in the battle of Polesella in 1509, and who was killed in 1521 in an act of betrayal in the Este court. The author of the *Furioso* raises the issue of what kind of *furor* (l. 4), "madness," could drive a friend to murder a friend.

4. *quis furor:* Tib. 1.10.33.

8. *insidiis . . . necarit:* Cic. *Att.* 13.10.3; Livy, 28.22.5.

LXIV. An Olive Tree
Meter: elegiac
Perhaps, as Bolaffi notes (104), this poem was written after Ariosto set up his new house in the development of Ferrara carried out by Biagio Rossetti. Virginio Ariosto mentions this poem in *Memorie* XIV, pairing it with another, now missing, on a marble column that broke while being transported to Ferrara (Barotti, *Memorie istoriche*, 1:225). Santoro 1989 proposes that the *Greek Anthology* 9.130 is a model (175). The olive tree takes on the virtues of its patron goddess.

1. Venus: Goddess of Love.

Priapus: Fertility god associated with the phallus. Bulbous plants, e.g., garlic, were thought to be efficacious aphrodisiacs: Mart. 3.75.3, *bulbique salaces.* See McMahon, *Paralysin Cave.*

2. Bacchus: Classical god (Dionysus in Greek) associated with fertility and wine.

Pallas Athena: Greek goddess of wisdom. *Palladis arbor:* Ov. *Ars am.* 2.518.

LXV. Poverty

Meter: Phalaecean hendecasyllable

Feigning poverty, the poet asks that his guest not disdain the new house. Barotti reports that this poem was inscribed on a wall in the courtyard's loggia, "[n]ella Loggetta" (*Memorie istoriche*, 1:225). In composing these lines Ariosto may have had in mind Horace's description of his Sabine farm (*Sat.* 2.6.1–19); see also Mart. 12.31 and 4.64.

4–5. *suspende . . . recurvis*: Hor. *Sat.* 1.6.5.

brevemque mensam: Hor. *Ars P.* 198.

4. *humilem casam*: Tib. 2.5.26; Verg. *Ecl.* 2.29.

6–9. The poet offers three mythological *exempla* of humble but generous hospitality involving gods, or, in the case of Hercules, a half-divine hero, who after death becomes a god, entertained by mortals: Jupiter and Mercury at the home of the old couple Philemon and Baucis; Hercules at the home of Molorchus; and Bacchus at the home of Icarus. Baucis, Molorchus, and Icarus are all addressed in the vocative, a rhetorical move that establishes an immediate connection with otherwise remote mythological figures and creates a certain sense of solidarity among these hosts of modest means, a solidarity which may stymie the disdain of guests. The *exempla* of Icarus and Molorchos occur together in [Tib.] 3.7.9–15, Panegyricus Messallae.

6. Baucis: With her husband Philemon, she welcomes two guests into their humble abode. The visitors are in fact Jupiter and Mercury, who reward the elderly couple for their generosity. See Ov. *Met.* 6.21–96.

Molorchus: Poor elderly man who hosted Hercules when he was sent to subdue the Nemean lion.

7. Icarus: An Athenian man who welcomed Dionysus/Bacchus with hospitality when he arrived in Attica. In return Dionysus taught him the cultivation of the vine.

pauperem tabernam: Hor. *Carm.* 1.4.13.

8. *viles . . . cibos*: Sen. *Herc. Oet.* 655.

modica . . . patella: Hor. *Epist.* 1.5.2.

9. Jupiter: Sovereign ruler of the gods.

Hercules: Hero par excellence.

Bacchus: Classical god (Dionysus in Greek) associated with fertility and wine.

Lyaeus: Cult title of Dionysus/Bacchus.

LXVI. The Poplar and the Vine

Meter: elegiac

Another poem that is perhaps tied to Ariosto's new house with its garden (Bolaffi, 105). Whether or not this is a description of actual trees in his garden, the writer finds meaning in the image of trunk and vine, from the very beginning of his career as a poet; see Looney, *Compromising,* 170–73. The poem is modeled on an epigram in the *Anth. Pal.* 9.231 (Carducci 1905, 257–58; Segre 1954, 103): "A withered plane-tree, I am covered by a climbing grape vine. Now I flourish in the full bloom of another's shade, but once I tended the grape clusters with my thriving branches, once I was as leafy as this vine. Well then, let a man care for a mistress like this, who, unique among women, repays him even when he is dead."

1. *arida . . . populus: App. Verg.* Priapea 2.2.

2. *racemiferis . . . comis:* Ov. *Fast.* 6.483.

5. *memor officii:* Sen. *Ben.* 4.20.3.

LXVII. no title

Meter: elegiac

Virginio Ariosto refers to his father's enthusiastic gardening in *Memorie* XV: "He gardened in the very same way he composed poetry, never leaving anything alone" (Barotti, *Memorie istoriche,* 1:225; Baruffaldi, *La vita,* 198–99).

POEMS OF UNCERTAIN ATTRIBUTION

See Notes to the Text.

I. Epitaph of Francesco Gerbinato

Meter: Phalaecean hendecasyllable

A version of poem 63, on which see notes, with a different spelling of the last name.

4. *caede . . . cruenta*: App. Verg. Culex 112.

7. *aevi flore*: Lucr. 1.564.

optimaeque matri: Verg. Aen. 10.557.

8. *fratrique unanimi*: Catull. 9.4.

II. Epitaph of the Marquis of Pescara

Meter: elegiac

On the death of Ferdinando d'Avalos in 1525, husband of Vittoria Colonna. For three Spanish translations of this poem, see Morby, *Latin Poem*. Although this poem is printed in EP 1553 (p. 298), its authenticity is rejected by Pesenti, "Storia del testo," 127–31, and Bolaffi 1938, xxxv–xxxvi.

2. Fisherman: The poet puns on the town attached to the marquis, Pescara, on the Adriatic coast of the Italian peninsula.

Renowned in war: In the *Furioso*, Ariosto calls him "the best knight of his time" (33.33.8).

4. *magnanimos reges*: Stat. Theb. 7.375.

7. Commander: An Italian condottiere of Spanish origins, he was an effective leader of the Habsburg army.

9. *fama superstes*: Hor. Carm 2.2.8.

III. Francesco Maria Molza from Modena

Meter: elegiac

In praise of the humanist poet Molza, one of his contemporaries whom the poet imagines welcoming him into port at the end of the long narrative of the *Furioso* (46.12.4). Of Molza, Lilio Gregorio Giraldi writes in his *Modern Poets*, "No one seemed more crazy for the love of women."

1. *blandos . . . amores*: App. *Verg.* Ciris 11.

2. Paelignian: The Paeligni were an ancient tribe from what is now the Abruzzi region of Italy, east of Rome. Ovid, the Roman poet, identified as a descendant of the Paeligni, described himself as "the glory of the Paelignian people" (*Am.* 3.15.8). For Ariosto, then, this adjective might be synonymous with Ovidian.

    ardua . . . gloria: Ov. *Tr.* 4.3.74; Stat. *Silv.* 2.3.77.

4. *signa propinqua*: Ov. *Fast.* 2.189.

5. *difficilis Venus*: Tib. 1.9.20.

    immedicabile vulnus: Ov. *Met.* 10.189.

IV. NO TITLE

Meter: elegiac

1. *nomina bina*: Ov. *Her.* 8.30.

    geminos . . . maritos: Luc. 2.339.

V. NO TITLE

Meter: elegiac

1. *gravi . . . iaceret*: Phaedrus *Fab. Aes.* 1.14.5.

3. Libitina: The Roman goddess of burials.

4. Graces: Female deities who embody grace, beauty, and charm, and who often attend Venus.

5. *fax . . . oculis*: Stat. *Theb.* 5.508.

8. *Mors saeva*: Luc. 2.100.

10. *bina . . . refert*: Ov. *Rem. am.* 158.

APOCRYPHAL POEMS

I. HIS HOUSE IN THE COUNTRY

Meter: elegiac

On the house façade, if we are to believe his son, Virginio, Ariosto placed this inscription (*Memorie XVII* in Barotti, *Memorie istoriche*, 1:225). Evidence suggests that the inscription was placed there by the previous owner, Bartolomeo Cavalieri (Chiappini). Catalano outlines how Ariosto bought several houses and various plots of land in the *Addizione nova*, the extension of Ferrara created by the urban planner and architect of Ercole I, Biagio Rossetti (*Vita*, 1:565–71). At that time the house, now in an urban setting, could be said to be "rustica," in the country.

II. VITTORIA COLONNA

Meter: elegiac

This poem is, in part, modeled on, and, in part, a response to, Mart. 1.42, also in the elegiac meter. Bolaffi attributes it to Pietro Gravina (1453–1527), a humanist in Pontano's circle in Naples (109–10).

1–2. The Porcia here referred to was the wife of Marcus Brutus, one of the assassins of Julius Caesar, and the daughter of Marcus Porcius Cato the younger. Her father, Cato, resolved not to accept pardon from Caesar after defeat in the civil war, committed suicide in 46 BCE. Her husband, Brutus, committed suicide after he was defeated by the forces of Marcus Antonius and Gaius Octavianus (later Augustus) at the battle of Philippi in 42 BCE. When Porcia learned that Brutus was dead, she killed herself by swallowing hot coals. See Val. Max. 4.6.5, and Plut. *Vit. Brut.* 53.5–6.

III. CHESTNUT TREE

Meter: dactylic hexameter

A medieval *enigma*: See Galloway, "The Rhetoric of Riddling in Late-Medieval England," 100 no. 23. (As Bolaffi says, it's an easy, misogynistic riddle to solve [110]).

Bibliography

CARMINA AND OTHER WORKS BY ARIOSTO

Ariosto, Ludovico. *Aliquot carmina autographa Ludovici Areosti ferrariensis*, ms. cart., sec. XVI. Classe I C, Biblioteca Comunale Ariostea, Ferrara.

Bolaffi, Ezio, ed. *Ludovici Areosti Carmina*. Pesaro, 1934.

———. *Ludovici Areosti Carmina*. 2nd ed. Modena, 1938.

Bonucci, Anicio. *Epitalamio*. Fano, 1838.

Capasso, Aldo, ed. *Poesie latine dell'Ariosto*. Florence, 1947.

Fatini, Giuseppe, ed. *Lirica*. Bari, 1924.

Looney, Dennis, trans. *'My Muse Will Have a Story to Paint': Selected Prose of Ludovico Ariosto*. Toronto, 2010.

Pezzana, Giuseppe, ed. *Opere di Ludovico Ariosto*. 3 vols. Paris, 1784.

Pigna, Giovanni Battista, ed. *Io. Baptistae Pignae carminum lib. quatuor, ad Alphonsum Ferrariae principem. His adiunximus Caelii Calcagnini carm. lib. III. Ludovici Areosti carm. lib. II*. Venice, 1553.

Ronchi, Gabriella, ed. *Erbolato*. In *Tutte le opere di Ludovico Ariosto*, vol. 3, edited by Cesare Segre. Milan, 1984.

Santoro, Mario, ed. *Opere*. Vol. 3, *Carmina, Rime, Satire, Erbolato, Lettere*. Turin, 1989.

Segre, Cesare, ed. *Opere minori*. Milan-Naples, 1954.

———. *Satire*. In *Tutte le opere di Ludovico Ariosto*, vol. 3, edited by Cesare Segre. Milan, 1984.

Stella, Angelo, ed. *Lettere*. In *Tutte le opere di Ludovico Ariosto*, vol. 3, edited by Cesare Segre. Milan, 1984.

Wiggins, Peter DeSa, trans. *The Satires of Ludovico Ariosto: A Renaissance Autobiography*. Athens, OH, 1976.

OTHER WORKS CITED OR CONSULTED

Agnelli, Giuseppe, and Giuseppe Ravegnani. *Annali delle edizioni ariostee*. 2 vols. Bologna, 1933.

Alberti, Giuseppe. "Un'ominosa ode latina di Ludovico Ariosto per Placido Foschi, il 'prognoste.'" *Gazzetta Internazionale di Medicina e Chirurgia* (February 15, 1941): 72.

Alighieri, Dante. *De vulgari eloquentia*. Edited and translated by Vittorio Coletti. Milan, 1991.

Anastasi, Alfio. *Catullo e l'umanesimo*. Acireale, 1919.

Ariosto, Galasso. Letter to Pietro Bembo, July 8, 1533. In *Delle lettere di diversi re et principi et cardinali et altri huomini dotti a monsignor Pietro Bembo*, 71r–72r. Venice, 1560.

Ariosto, Virginio. *Memorie della Vita dell'Ariosto*. In Barotti, *Memorie istoriche*, 1:223–227.

Bacchelli, Franco. "Appunti sulla formazione culturale e religiosa di Alberto Pio." In *Alberto III e Rodolfo Pio da Carpi. Collezionisti e mecenati*, edited by Manuela Rossi, 177–94. Tavagnacco, 2004.

Bacchelli, Riccardo. *La congiura di don Giulio d'Este*. 2nd ed. Milan, 1983.

Bárberi Squarotti, Giorgio. "Ludovico Ariosto." In *Storia di Ferrara*, vol. 7, *Il Rinascimento. La letteratura*, edited by Walter Moretti, 298–378. Ferrara, 1994.

Barotti, Giovanni Andrea. *Memorie istoriche di letterati ferraresi*. 2 vols. 2nd ed. Ferrara, 1792–93.

Baruffaldi, Girolamo. *La vita di M. Lodovico Ariosto*. Ferrara, 1807.

Bembo, Pietro. *Prose della volgar lingua*. Edited by Carlo Dionisotti. 2nd ed. Turin, 1966.

Bertoni, Giulio. "Il codice ferrarese dei *Carmina* di Ludovico Ariosto." *Archivium Romanicum* 17, no. 4 (1933): 619–58.

Bigi, Emilio. "Vita e letteratura nella poesia giovanile di Ludovico Ariosto." *Giornale Storico della Letteratura Italiana* 145 (1968): 1–37.

Binni, Walter. *Metodo e poesia di Ludovico Ariosto e altri studi ariosteschi*. Edited by Rosanna Alhaique Pettinelli. Scandicci [Florence], 1996.

Bolaffi, Ezio. "Il carme di Ludovico Ariosto: *Extolli clamor patrem*." *Il Mondo Classico* 5 (1935, suppl. settembre): 12.

——. "Ancora sulla mia edizione dei *Carmina* dell'Ariosto." *Il Mondo Classico* 6 (1936): 23.

——. "Altre note ai *Carmina* dell'Ariosto." *Il Mondo Classico* 7, nos. 3–4 (1937): 267–75.

———. "Alcune correzioni marginali ed interlineari del cod. ferrarese dei *Carmina.*" *Il Mondo Classico* 7 (1937, suppl. settembre): 111–12.

Bonazza, Mirna, ed. *ManuScripti. I codici della Biblioteca Comunale Ariostea.* Ferrara, 2002.

Calcagnini, Celio. *Equitatio.* In *Caelii Calcagnini ferrariensis, protonotarii apostolici, opera aliquot . . .* , edited by Antonio Musa Brasavola, 558–90. Basel, 1544.

———. "Inventario dei libri di Celio Calcagnini." In Archivio Calcagnini. Busta 95. Archivio di Stato, Modena.

Carducci, Giosuè. *Delle poesie latine edite ed inedite di Ludovico Ariosto. Studi e ricerche.* Bologna, 1875.

———. *Delle poesie latine edite ed inedite di Ludovico Ariosto. Studi e ricerche.* 2nd ed. Bologna, 1876.

———. *La gioventù di Ludovico Ariosto e le sue poesie latine. Studi e ricerche.* 2nd. ed. Bologna, 1881.

———. *La gioventù di Ludovico Ariosto e la poesia latina in Ferrara.* In *Opere,* vol. 15, *Studi su Ludovico Ariosto e Torquato Tassoi,* 3–260. 3rd. ed. Bologna, 1905.

Carrara, Daniela Mugnai. "Nicolò Leoniceno e Giovanni Mainardi: aspetti epistemologici dell'umanesimo medico." In *Alla corte degli Estensi. Filosofia, arte e cultura a Ferrara nei secoli XV e XVI,* edited by Marco Bertozzi, 19–40. Ferrara, 1994.

Casari, Federico. "Storia, erudizione, poesia. I primi studi ariostei di Giosuè Carducci (1872–1875)." *Giornale Storico della Letteratura Italiana* 189 (2012): 481–529.

Casini, T. "Di un'ode alcaica di Ludovico Ariosto." *Rivista Critica* n.s. 8, no. 5 (1891): 150–52.

Catalano, Michele. *Lezioni di letteratura italiana.* Vol. 1, *Questioni dantesche.* Vol. 2, *La tragica morte di Ercole Strozzi e un sonetto di Barbara Torelli.* Messina, 1951.

———. *Vita di Ludovico Ariosto.* 2 vols. Geneva, 1930–31.

Caterino, Antonello Fabio. "Filliroe e i suoi poeti: da Tito Strozzi a Ludovico Ariosto." *Annali Online di Lettere – Ferrara.* Vols. 1–2. (2011): 182–208.

Celenza, Christopher S. *The Lost Italian Renaissance: Humanists, Historians, and Latin's Legacy*. Baltimore, 2004.

Cerlini, Aldo. "Scrittura e punteggiatura negli autografi dell'Ariosto." *Cultura Neolatina* 4, no. 5 (1944–45): 37–60.

Charlet-Mesdjian, Béatrice, and Dominique Voisin. "L'épicède de Tito Strozzi par son fils Ercole." *Studi Umanistici Piceni* 31 (2011): 149–65.

Chiappini, Luciano. "The *parva domus* of Ludovico Ariosto." http:// rivista.fondazionecarife.it/en/2000/12/item/263-la-parva-domus-di-ludovico-ariosto (accessed September 18, 2012).

Chines, Loredana. *La parola degli antichi. Umanesimo emiliano tra scuola e poesia*. Rome, 1998.

Ciceri, Pier Luigi. "Michele Marullo e i suoi *Hymni naturales*." *Giornale Storico della Letteratura Italiana* 64 (1914): 289–357.

Clough, Cecil H. "More Light on Pandolfo and Ludovico Ariosto." *Italica* 39, no. 3 (1962): 195–96.

———. "A Further Note on Pandolfo and Ludovico Ariosto." *Italica* 40, no. 2 (1963): 167–69.

Copley, Frank O. *Exclusus Amator: A Study in Latin Love Poetry*. New York, 1956.

Corniani, G. B. "Lodovico Ariosto." In *I secoli della letteratura italiana dopo il suo risorgimento. Commentario ragionato*. Brescia, 1819.

Cosattini, Achille. "A proposito di un'alcaica dell'Ariosto." *Atene e Roma* 7 (1904): 359–61.

Cosmico, Niccolò Lelio. *Le cancion*. Edited by Silvia Alga. [San Mauro Torinese], 2003.

Croce, Benedetto. *Ariosto, Shakespeare e Corneille*. 3rd. ed. Bari, 1944.

Curti, Elisa. *Una cavalcata con Ariosto. L'Equitatio di Celio Calcagnini*. Ferrara, 2016.

Dalmasso, Lorenzo. Review of *Ludovici Areosti Carmina*, edited by Ezio Bolaffi. *Giornale Storico della Letteratura Italiana* 106 (1935): 147–50.

Degli Antoni, Vincenzo. "Discorso intorno alle poesie di Eustachio Manfredi." *Giornale Arcadico di Scienze, Lettere ed Arti* 12 (1821): 58ff.

Dionisotti, Carlo. *Geografia e storia della letteratura italiana*. Turin, 1967.

Durling, Robert M. *The Figure of the Poet in Renaissance Epic*. Cambridge, MA, 1965.

Fatini, Giuseppe. *Bibliografia della critica ariostea* (1510–1956). Florence, 1958.

——. "Su la fortuna e l'autenticità delle liriche di Ludovico Ariosto." *Giornale Storico della Letteratura Italiana*, suppl. 22 (1924): 142–48.

Ferroni, Giulio. *Ariosto*. Rome, 2008.

Fiorentino, Remigio. *Considerazioni civili*. Venice, 1582.

Folin, Marco. *Rinascimento estense. Politica, cultura, istituzioni di un antico stato italiano*. 2nd ed. Bari, 2004.

Forster, Leonard. *The Icy Fire: Five Studies in European Petrarchism*. Cambridge, 1979.

Frizzi, Antonio. *Memorie storiche della nobil famiglia Ariosti*. Ferrara, 1779.

Gaisser, Julia Haig. *Catullus and His Renaissance Readers*. Oxford, 1993.

Galloway, Andrew. "The Rhetoric of Riddling in Late-Medieval England: The 'Oxford' Riddles, the *Secretum philosophorum*, and the Riddles in *Piers Plowman*." *Speculum* 70 (1995): 68–105.

Gandiglio, Adolfo. "Contributo alla revisione del testo dei carmi ariostei." *Annuario Liceo–Ginnasio di Fano* (1924–25): 3–17.

——. "Intorno al testo di alcuni carmi latini dell'Ariosto." *Giornale Storico della Letteratura Italiana* 88 (1926): 194–200.

Gardner, Edmund G. *Dukes and Poets in Ferrara*. New York, 1904.

——. *The King of Court Poets: A Study of the Life, Work, and Times of Lodovico Ariosto*. New York, 1968. First published New York, 1906.

Garofolo, Girolamo. *Vita di Ludovico Ariosto*. In Barbara Mori, "Le vite ariotesche del Fornari, Pigna e Garofolo." *Schifanoia* 17/18 (1997): 135–78.

Giovio, Paolo. *Elogia veris clarorum virorum imaginibus apposita. Quae in Musaeo Joviano Comi spectantur. Addita in calce operis Adriani pont. Vita.* Venice, 1546.

Giraldi, Lilio Gregorio. *Due dialoghi sui poeti dei nostri tempi*. Edited by Claudia Pandolfi. Ferrara, 1999.

——. *Modern Poets*. Edited and translated by John N. Grant. Cambridge, MA, 2011.

Giucciardini, Francesco. *Storia d'Italia*. 3 vols. Edited by Silvana Seidel Menchi. Turin, 1971.

Grabher, Carlo. *La poesia minore dell'Ariosto. La lirica latina, la lirica volgare, le satire e una nota sul carattere dell'Ariosto.* Rome, 1947.

Grilli, A. "Carmina di Ludovico Ariosto." *Corriere Padano,* January 18, 1935.

Grosso, Stefano. "Ad Eugenio Camerini salute, Lettera." In *Carmina: Opere di F. Berni,* edited by E. Camerini, 215–19. Milan, 1874.

———. "Della grecità di alcuni epigrammi latini di Ludovico Ariosto." In Carducci, *Delle poesie latine edite ed inedite di Ludovico Ariosto,* 285–95.

Hall, Robert A. *The Italian 'questione della lingua': An Interpretive Essay.* Chapel Hill, 1942.

Henriksén, Christer. "Martial's Modes of Mourning: Sepulchral Epitaphs in the Epigrams." In *Flavian Poetry. Mnemosyne Suppl. 270,* edited by Ruurd R. Nauta, Harm-Jan van Dam, and Johannes J. L. Smolenaars, 349–67. Leiden, 2006.

James, Sharon L. "Economics of Roman Elegy: Voluntary Poverty, the *recusatio,* and the Greedy Girl." *American Journal of Philology* 122, no. 2 (2001): 223–53.

Javitch, Daniel. *Proclaiming a Classic: The Canonization of* Orlando Furioso. Princeton, 1991.

Knight, Jeffrey Todd. *Bound to Read: Compilations, Collections, and the Making of Renaissance Literature.* Philadelphia, 2013.

Lattimore, Richmond Alexander. *Themes in Greek and Latin Epitaphs.* Illinois Studies in Language and Literature 28, 1–2. Urbana-Champaign, IL, 1942.

Looney, Dennis. "Ariosto's Dialogue with Authority in the *Erbolato.*" *Modern Language Notes* 128 (2013): 20–39.

———. *Compromising the Classics: Romance Epic Narrative in the Italian Renaissance.* Detroit, 1996.

Lo Parco, F. "Un epigramma in lode di Vittoria Colonna di un accademico pontaniano erroneamente attribuito a Lodovico Ariosto, a Marcantonio Flaminio e Tommaso Musconio." *Fanfulla Domenica* 38, no. 8 (1916).

Mariotti, Scevola. "Per il riesame di un'ode latina dell'Ariosto." *Italia Medievale e Umanistica* 2 (1959): 509–12. Reprinted in Scevola Mariotti.

Scritti medievali e umanistici. 3rd ed. Edited by Silvia Rizzo, 295–300. Rome, 2010.

McMahon, John M. *Paralysin Cave: Impotence, Perception, and Text in the Satyrica of Petronius*. Leiden, 1998.

Mercati, Giovanni. "Sul carme latino di Ludovico Ariosto ad Ercole I duca di Ferrara, Ultimi contributi alla storia degli umanisti." In *Studi e Testi della Biblioteca Apostolica Vaticana* 91, fasc. 2 (1939): xii–128.

Monosini, Angelo. *Floris italicae linguae libri novem*. Venice, 1604.

Morby, E. S. "A Latin Poem of Ariosto in Spanish." *Modern Language Notes* 70 (1955): 360–62.

Mutini, Claudio. "Note sull'*Epitaphium Ludovici Areosti*." *Bibliothèque d'Humanisme et Renaissance* 25, no. 1 (1963): 198–206.

Myers, K. Sara. "The Poet and the Procuress: The *Lena* in Latin Love Elegy." *Journal of Roman Studies* 86 (1996): 1–21.

Nohrnberg, James. *The Analogy of the Faerie Queene*. Princeton, 1976.

Paoletti, Lao. "Cronaca e letteratura nei *Carmina*." In Segre, *Ludovico Ariosto: lingua, stile e tradizione*, 265–82.

——. *Retorica e politica nel Petrarca bucolico*. Bologna, 1974.

Pariset, Camillo. "Per la revisione dei carmi ariostei." *Cispadana* (num. straord.), II (1933): 3–6.

Pasquazi, Silvio. *Ariosto minore e l'Umanesimo ferrarese. Motivi e problemi danteschi*, 177–87. Rome, 1976.

——. "La poesia in latino." In *Storia di Ferrara*, vol. 7., *Il Rinascimento. La letteratura*, edited by Walter Moretti, 99–162. Ferrara, 1994.

Pavan, Alberto. "Ercole Strozzi's *Venatio*: Classical Inheritance and Contemporary Models of a Neo-Latin Hunting Poem." *Humanistica Lovaniensia* (2010): 29–54.

Pesenti, Giovanni. "La fortuna di un epigramma misogino." *Didaskaleion* 3 (1914): 321–26.

——. "Storia del testo dei carmi latini dell'Ariosto." *Rendiconti del Reale Istituto Lombardo di Scienze e Lettere* 57 (1924): 120–135.

Petrarch, Francis. *Petrarch's Lyric Poems: The Rime Sparse and Other Lyrics*. Translated by Robert M. Durling. Cambridge, MA, 1976.

Petrocchi, Giorgio. "Orazio e Ariosto." In *I fantasmi di Tancredi. Saggi sul Tasso e sul Rinascimento*, 263–65. Caltanissetta-Rome, 1972.

Pigna, Giovanni Battista. *I romanzi, divisi in tre libri, ne' quali della poesia, et della vita dell'Ariosto con nuovo modo si tratta*. Venice, 1554.

Poliziano, Angelo. *Le stanze per la giostra*. Translated by David Quint. Amherst, 1979.

Ponte, Giovanni. "Boiardo e l'Ariosto." *Rassegna della Letteratura Italiana* 79 (1975): 169–82.

Prandi, Stefano. "Premesse umanistiche del *Furioso*: Ariosto, Calcagnini e il silenzio (O.F. XIV, 78–97)." *Lettere Italiane* 58, no. 1 (2006): 1–32.

Prose e rime per il trasporto del monumento e delle ceneri di Lodovico Ariosto. Ferrara, 1802.

Salza, Abdelkader. "La cronologia dei carmi di Ludovico Ariosto al parente Pandolfo." In *Miscellanea di studi critici in onore di Ettore Stampini*, 115–23. Turin-Genoa, 1921.

Sangirardi, Giuseppe. *Ludovico Ariosto*. Florence, 2006.

Savarese, Gennaro. "Il progetto del poema tra Marsilio Ficino e 'adescatrici galliche.'" In *Il Furioso e la cultura del Rinascimento*, 15–37. Rome, 1984.

Scorrano, Luigi. *Ludovico Ariosto*. Rome, 2015.

Segre, Cesare, ed. *Ludovico Ariosto: lingua, stile e tradizione*. Milan, 1976.

Sorbelli, Tommaso. "Della fortuna del carme terzo di Catullo presso gli umanisti." *Classici e Neolatini* 8 (1912): 170–81.

Strozzi, Ercole. *Herculis Strozae Titi filii Venatio ad divam Lucretiam Borgiam Ferrariae ducem. La chasse d'Ercole Strozzi à l'intention de Lucrèce Borgia*. Edited by Béatrice Charlet-Mesdjian and Dominique Voisin. Aix-en-Provence, 2015.

———. *Venatio*. In *Strozii poetae pater et filius*, edited by Aldo Manuzio, 14–31. Paris, 1530. http://www.uni-mannheim.de/mateo/itali/autoren /strozzi_itali.html (accessed November 10, 2015).

Viviani, Francesco. "La musa latina nell'opera di Ludovico Ariosto." *Annuario del Regio Liceo-Ginnasio 'Ludovico Ariosto' di Ferrara* 6 (1932–33): 81–106.

Zingarelli, Nicola. "Il carme di Ludovico Ariosto, *Extollit clamor patrem*." *Rendiconti del Reale Istituto Lombardo di Scienze e Lettere* 67 (1934): fasc. 19–20.

Index of First Lines

𝕯𝕾?𝕽

Entries are referenced by poem number.

General Index

𝕬𝕾𝕻𝕾

Note numbering corresponds to line numbers in the Latin text.

241

Publication of this volume has been made possible by

The Myron and Sheila Gilmore Publication Fund at I Tatti
The Robert Lehman Endowment Fund
The Jean-François Malle Scholarly Programs and Publications Fund
The Andrew W. Mellon Scholarly Publications Fund
The Craig and Barbara Smyth Fund
for Scholarly Programs and Publications
The Lila Wallace–Reader's Digest Endowment Fund
The Malcolm Wiener Fund for Scholarly Programs and Publications